HENRY VII'S
RELATIONS WITH SCOTLAND
AND IRELAND

HENRY VII'S
RELATIONS WITH SCOTLAND
AND IRELAND
1485–1498

BY

AGNES CONWAY, M.A. (Lond.)

Associate of Newnham College

With a Chapter on

THE ACTS OF THE POYNINGS PARLIAMENT
1494–95

by EDMUND CURTIS, M.A.

Professor of Modern History
Trinity College
Dublin

CAMBRIDGE

AT THE UNIVERSITY PRESS

1932

CAMBRIDGE
UNIVERSITY PRESS

University Printing House, Cambridge CB2 8BS, United Kingdom

Published in the United States of America by Cambridge University Press, New York

Cambridge University Press is part of the University of Cambridge.

It furthers the University's mission by disseminating knowledge in the pursuit of education, learning and research at the highest international levels of excellence.

www.cambridge.org
Information on this title: www.cambridge.org/9781107675285

© Cambridge University Press 1932

First published 1932
First paperback edition 2013

A catalogue record for this publication is available from the British Library

ISBN 978-1-107-67528-5 Paperback

TO

THE MEMORY OF

SIR HENRY WYATT

OF ALLINGTON CASTLE

c. 1460–1537

PREFACE

This is a dry book, but to me it has been an adventure; a detective story lasting four years. The accident of a May day, with swans nesting in a moat, sent me to live in Henry Wyatt's Castle. My quarry was *his* career. I wished to know why the Wyatt family MSS stated that the Earl of Richmond owed him his crown; why Henry VII and Henry VIII paid him a pension for over thirty years towards his ransom "from the cruel hands of the Scots"; and why he was the one Englishman mentioned in the Scottish Trial in Parliament of James III's supporters. The search, lightly undertaken, led me to chase his name through the royal accounts, printed and unprinted. The clues began to appear and with them some light on obscure aspects of the reign of Henry VII.

The motor thieves, who stole my luggage with the finished manuscript inside, threw the loose leaves over the wall of a distant garden. It did not rain. Fate preserved and returned the book; and now I send it forth with thanks to all who have helped me: to Professor Curtis for encouragement and the clue to Irish words and place-names; to the members of the Staff of Professor Pollard's Seminar at the Institute of Historical Research, in particular Mr C. H. Williams; to the officials of the Public Record Office and British Museum; and to Mr Herbert Wood, late of the Dublin Record Office. Since its birth as a thesis, the book has been completely remodelled.

A. C.

ALLINGTON CASTLE
NEAR MAIDSTONE

July 1931

vij

CONTENTS

ix

Hattecliffe-Wyatt Accounts of the Poynings Administration
(APPENDICES VIII–XVII)

CONTENTS

Genealogical Table of the Houses of York and Lancaster

available for download from www.cambridge.org/9781107675285

ABBREVIATIONS

B.M.   British Museum.
D.N.B. *Dictionary of National Biography.*
E.H.R. *English Historical Review.*
G.E.C. G. E. Cokayne, *The Complete Peerage.*
N.E.D. *New English Dictionary*, edited by Murray.
P.R.O. Public Record Office.
V.C.H. *Victoria County History.*

BIBLIOGRAPHY

To compress this bibliography into a reasonable compass all works yielding negative results have been omitted, with the exception of the Account Books of the Treasurer of the King's Chamber, of which I have tried to compile a complete list. MSS and printed books, slightly used, have been dealt with in the footnotes. The bibliography is divided into four sections, England, the Border, Scotland and Ireland.

ENGLAND
OFFICIAL RECORDS

I. COLLECTIONS
A. Printed

Campbell, William. *Materials for a History of the Reign of Henry VII.* 2 vols. Rolls Series. London. 1873 and 1877.

Gairdner, James. *Letters and Papers illustrative of the Reigns of Richard III and Henry VII.* 2 vols. Rolls Series. London. 1861 and 1863.

Pollard, A. F. *The Reign of Henry VII from Contemporary Sources.* 3 vols. Longmans. 1914.

Rymer, Thomas. *Foedera.* 1475–1502. London edition. Vol. XII. 1721.

Letters and Papers, Foreign and Domestic, Henry VIII. Vol. I, parts 1, 2 and 3. Second edition. 1920. J. S. Brewer and J. H. Brodie.

B. Unprinted

Rymer, Thomas. Collectanea. A series of transcripts from miscellaneous original sources. B.M. Add MSS, 4617, 4618.

II. PARLIAMENT

Rotuli Parliamentorum. Vol. VI. 12 Edward IV–19 Henry VII (1472–1503). Record Commission.

Statutes of the Realm. Vol. II. 1377–1509. 1816.

A list of the names of members of Parliament who sat in the Parliament of 1491. B.M. Harl. MS, 2252, fols. 28–32, printed in

Bulletin of the Institute of Historical Research, III, 168–175.

BIBLIOGRAPHY

III. The King's Council

Scofield, C. L. *A Study of the Court of Star Chamber*. University of Chicago Press. 1900.
(This contains extracts from the "Liber Intrationum" of Henry VII.)

IV. Chancery
A. Printed

Calendar of Patent Rolls. Henry VII. Vol. I. 1485–1494. Vol. II. 1494–1509.
Rotuli Scotiae. 1291–1516. Vol. II. Edited by D. Macpherson. Record Commission. 1819.

B. Unprinted

P.R.O. Chancery Warrants, C.82, Series II, 1 Henry VII–13 Anne.

V. Exchequer
A. Printed

Oppenheim, M. *Naval Accounts and Inventories of the Reign of Henry VII*, 1485–8 *and* 1495–7. Navy Records Society. 1896.

B. Unprinted
Exchequer of Receipt

Tellers Rolls of the Exchequer for the reign of Henry VII. P.R.O. E 405, 75–81.

P.R.O. Exchequer, T. R. Miscellaneous Books, E.36, vol. 125.

A book of entries of receipts and payments at the Exchequer kept by Stokes, one of the Tellers, for the years 1, 2, 7 and 8 Henry VII. (The entries are sometimes fuller than the corresponding ones on the Tellers Rolls, and are often dated. Receipts and letters are bound in with it.)

P.R.O. Exchequer, T. R. Miscellaneous Books, E.36, vol. 124.

A book of entries of receipts and payments at the Exchequer. Easter Term, 5 Henry VII, to Michaelmas Term, 6 Henry VII. A few notes at the end of the volume refer to 1–4 Henry VIII. (The entries are fuller than the Tellers Rolls.)

A Register of Writs of Great and Privy Seal from 1 Henry VII to 14 Henry VIII. P.R.O. E 403, 2558.

Exchequer Plea Rolls. P.R.O. E 13, 172.

WARDROBE AND HOUSEHOLD
A. Printed

Liber Niger Domus Regis Angliae, id est Domus Regiae sive Aulae Angliae Regis Edw. IV. Printed for the Society of Antiquaries. 1790.

B. Unprinted

Accounts of the Clerk of the Marshalsea of the Household. 7–8 Henry VII. P.R.O. Exchequer, T. R. Miscellaneous Books, E 36, vol. 208.

Account Book of William Cope, Cofferer of the Household, 11 Henry VII. P.R.O. E 101, 414/3.

THE KING'S CHAMBER

Unprinted

Account Books of the Treasurer of the Chamber for the reign of Henry VII

RECEIPTS

1. P.R.O. E 101, 413/2. 3 vols. The Treasurer of the Chamber's receipts in English, each entry initialed by Henry VII. Vol. I. July 9, 1487–July 4, 1489 (Lovell). Heron's handwriting. Vol. II. September 30, 1489–Oct. 1, 1495 (Lovell). Heron's handwriting. Vol. III. October 1, 1502–October 1, 1505 (John Heron).[1]

2. P.R.O. Acc. Ex. T. R. Miscellaneous Books, E 36, vol. 123, is a version in Latin of E 101, 413/2, vol. III; more roughly done and not initialed by Henry VII.

Account Books of the Treasurer of the Chamber for the reign of Henry VII

PAYMENTS

1. Craven Ord's transcripts from the King's Book of Payments. December 24, 1491–September 27, 1505. B.M. Add. MSS 7099.

   (These extracts are incomplete, but the only source for payments before October 1, 1495.)

2. King's Book of Payments. October 1, 1495–October 1, 1497. P.R.O. E 101, 414/6.

3. King's Book of Payments. October 1, 1497–October 1, 1499. P.R.O. E 101, 414/16.

4. King's Book of Payments. October 1, 1499–October 8, 1502. P.R.O. E 101, 415/3.

   A preliminary copy, in Heron's handwriting. At the end are lists of the King's Revenues, Recognizances, Obligations, Tayles, Debts, Wards, Lyvery of lands and Memoranda.

5. An imperfect account for 20 Henry VII. P.R.O. E 101, 415/16.

---

[1] Heron succeeded Sir Thomas Lovell as Treasurer of the Chamber about 1492 (Newton, *E.H.R.* XXXII, 355).

6. King's Book of Payments. October 1, 1499–October 1, 1505. B.M. Add. MSS 21480.

   A beautifully written volume, in Heron's handwriting, initialed throughout by Henry VII, containing totals of weekly payments from October 1, 1499, to April 1, 1505. From April 1, 1505, to September 19, 1505, it contains daily payments. The lists at the end are the same as in E 101, 415/3. (Add. MSS 7099 is an incomplete copy of numbers 2, 3 and 4, and of an earlier lost book. Selections from Add. MSS 7099 are printed in Samuel Bentley's *Excerpta Historica*, 1833, pp. 85–133, and in the appendix to Robert Henry's *History of Great Britain*, 1824.)

7. King's Book of Payments. 1505–9. P.R.O. Exchequer, T. R. Miscellaneous Books, E 36, vol. 214.

8. Summary of the State of Accounts by the Treasurer of the Chamber, 17–20 Henry VII. P.R.O. Exchequer, T. R. Miscellaneous Books, E 36, vol. 213.

9. Summary of the State of Accounts by the Treasurer of the Chamber, 21 Henry VII. P.R.O. Exchequer, T. R. Miscellaneous Books, E 36, vol. 212.

10. "Obligations of Henry VII in 1500, 20 Henry VII." *Archaeologia*, xxv, 390–3. From B.M. Lansdowne MSS 160, fol. 311.

11. "Obligations of Henry VII in the custodie of Edmund Dudley." 21–23 Henry VII. B.M. Harl. MSS 1877, fol. 47.

12. Dudley's Book of Accounts. September 9, 1504–May 28, 1508. B.M. Lansdowne MSS 127.

MINT

P.R.O. Foreign Accounts, E 364, 119.

   (Used for the return of the Chamberlain of Berwick. There is no pagination and the Roll is about 8 ft. long by 3 ft. wide.)

VI. JUDICIAL PROCEEDINGS

Archbold, W. A. J. "Sir William Stanley and Perkin Warbeck." *English Historical Review*, vol. xiv.

VII. CONTEMPORARY CORRESPONDENCE—PUBLIC AND PRIVATE

Printed

Hinds, Allen B. *Calendar of State Papers, etc.*, Milanese. Vol. 1, 1385–1618. 1912.

Brown, Rawdon. *Calendar of State Papers, etc.*, Venetian. Vol. 1, 1202–1509. London. 1864.

Bergenroth, G. A. *Calendar of Letters, State Papers, etc.*, Spanish. Vol. 1, 1485–1509. London. 1862.

Madden, Sir Frederick. "Documents relating to Perkin Warbeck, with remarks on his history." *Archaeologia*, xxvii, 153–210. 1837.

Ellis, Henry. *Original Letters illustrative of English History*. First Series. Vol. I. 1824.

Gairdner, James. *The Paston Letters*. Vol. III. 1471–1509. London. 1910.

Foxwell, A. K. *The Poems of Sir Thomas Wiat*. 2 vols. University of London Press. 1913.
(Consulted for two letters from Sir Thomas Wyatt to his son, written in 1538.)

Allen, P. S. and H. M. *Letters of Richard Fox*. 1486–1527. Clarendon Press. 1929.

Unprinted

P.R.O. Ancient Correspondence, S.C.I. vols. LI, LVII, LVIII.

Henry VII's Instructions to Richmond Herald, December 30, 1494. B.M. Cotton, Caligula, D VI, fols. 20.

Henry VII's Instructions to Richmond Herald, March 5, 1494/5. B.M. Cotton, Caligula, D VI, fol. 26–26 v.

Henry VII's Instructions to Norroy King of Arms, February 1498. B.M. Cotton, Vespasian, C XVI, fol. 118.

Wyatt Manuscripts (in the possession of the Earl of Romney). See "The Wyatt Manuscripts", by Agnes Conway, in *Bulletin of the Institute of Historical Research*, I, 73.

VIII. ECCLESIASTICAL

Printed

Wilkins, D. *Concilia Magnae Britanniae et Hiberniae*. Vol. III. London. 1737.

Batten, E. C. *Register of Richard Fox*, while Bishop of Bath and Wells, 1492–1494, with a life of Bishop Fox. 1889. (Privately printed.)

Unprinted

Wills proved in the Prerogative Court of Canterbury. Somerset House.

IX. MISCELLANEA

Printed

De Walden Library. 1904. Published by Lord Howard de Walden from MS I. 2. College of Arms. (Consulted for the illustration of Sir Henry Wyatt's standard, with motto.)

Black Books of Lincolns Inn. Vol. I. 1422–1586. Lincoln's Inn. 1897.

BIBLIOGRAPHY

NARRATIVE SOURCES

WHOLLY OR ALMOST CONTEMPORARY

Printed

Leland, John. *De rebus Britannicis Collectanea*. Edited by Hearne. Second edition. 6 vols. London. 1770. (Vol. IV, 185–257) from B.M. Cotton, Julius, B XII, 4–11.

Kingsford, C. L. *Chronicles of London*. (Cotton, Vitellius, A XVI.) Oxford. 1905.

Sneyd, C. A. Translation of *A Relation of the Island of England about the year* 1500. Camden Society. 1847.

Polydore Vergil. *Historia Anglica*. Book XXVI. Leyden. 1651.

Hall, Edward. *Chronicle*. Edited by H. Ellis. London. 1809.

LATER NARRATIVE SOURCES

Bacon, Francis. *The History of the Reign of King Henry the Seventh*. In *Bacon's Works*, vol. VI, 1858, edited by Spedding, Ellis and Heath.

MODERN WORKS

I. Books of Reference

Cokayne, G. E. *The Complete Peerage*. New edition edited by Vicary Gibbs. A–G. 5 vols. 1913. G–L. 2 vols. 1926, 1929. Edited by H. A. Doubleday and Lord Howard de Walden. L–Z. Vols. V–VIII. 1892.

Dictionary of National Biography. London. 1885 ff.

II. General Works

Busch, William. *England under the Tudors*. Vol. I. Stuttgart. 1892. Translated by A. M. Todd. 1895.

Conway, Agnes. "The Maidstone Sector of Buckingham's Rebellion." *Archaeologia Cantiana*, XXXVII.

Dietz, Frederick Charles. *English Government Finance*. 1485–1558. University of Illinois Studies in the Social Sciences, vol. IX, no. 3, September, 1920.

Fisher, Herbert A. L. *The History of England from the Accession of Henry VII to the Death of Henry VIII*. 1485–1547. London. 1906.

Gairdner, James. *History of the Life and Reign of King Richard III; to which is added the Story of Perkin Warbeck from original documents*. Third edition. London. 1898.

Labaree, L. W. and Moody, R. E. "The Seal of the Privy Council." *English Historical Review*, vol. XLIII.

Newton, A. P. "The King's Chamber under the Early Tudors." *English Historical Review*, vol. XXXII, 1917.

Newton, A. P. *Tudor Reforms in the Royal Household*. Tudor Studies, edited by R. W. Seton Watson. 1924.

Roth, Cecil. "Perkin Warbeck and his Jewish Master." *Transactions of the Jewish Historical Society of England*, vol. IX, 1918–20.

Stubbs, William. *Seventeen Lectures on the Study of Medieval and Modern History*. Clarendon Press. 1900.

Verney Family, Letters and Papers of, to 1639. Camden Society, vol. LIV. 1853.
(Consulted for the Introduction.)

THE BORDER

Armstrong, Robert Bruce. *History of Liddesdale, Eskdale, Ewesdale, Wauchopedale and the Debateable Land*. Part I. From the Twelfth Century to 1530. Edinburgh. 1873.
(This contains transcripts of original documents.)

Bates, C. J. *The Border Holds of Northumberland*. Society of Antiquaries. Newcastle. 1891.

Creighton, Mandell. *Carlisle*. Historic Towns. Edited by E. A. Freeman and William Hunt. 1889.

Ferguson, R. S. *Royal Charters of the City of Carlisle*. Cumberland and Westmorland Antiquarian and Archaeological Society. 1894.

Hodgkin, Thomas. *Wardens of the Northern Marches*. Creighton Memorial Lecture, 1907. Published for the University of London by John Murray. 1908.

Pease, Howard. *The Lord Wardens of the Marches of England and Scotland*. London. 1913.

Raine, James. *Priory of Coldingham*. Surtees Society, vol. XII.

Reid, Rachel. "The Office of Warden of the Marches. Its Origin and Early History." *English Historical Review*, vol. XXXII, 1917.

Reid, Rachel. *The King's Council in the North*. Longmans. 1921.

Thomson, G. Scott. "The Bishops of Durham and the Office of Lord Lieutenant in the Seventeenth Century." *English Historical Review*, vol. XL.

Tough, D. L. W. *The Last Years of a Frontier*. Clarendon Press. 1928.

SCOTLAND

OFFICIAL RECORDS

Bain, Joseph. *Calendar of Documents relating to Scotland, preserved in H.M. Public Record Office*. Vol. IV. (1357–1509.) Edinburgh. 1888.

Teulet, J. B. A. T. *Inventaire Chronologique des Documents rélatifs à l'histoire d'Écosse conservés aux Archives du Royaume à Paris*. 1480–1600. Abbotsford Club. 1839.

Teulet, A. *Papiers d'État relatifs à l'histoire de l'Écosse au XVI siècle.* Bannatyne Club. Vol. I. Paris. 1851.

Acts of the Parliaments of Scotland, The. Vols. II and XII. (1424–1557.) London, 1814.

Acta Dominorum Auditorum. 1466–1494. Record Commission. 1839.

Acta Dominorum Concilii. 1478–1495. Record Commission. 1839.

Registrum Magni Sigilli Regum Scotorum. 1424–1513. Edited by James Balfour Paul. Edinburgh. 1882.

Rotuli Scaccarii Regum Scotorum, the Exchequer Rolls of Scotland. Edited by George Burnett. Vols. IX, X. 1878–91.

Accounts of the Lord High Treasurer of Scotland. Vol. I. 1473–1498. Edited by Thomas Dickson. Edinburgh. 1877.

Pitcairn, Robert. *Criminal Trials of Scotland.* Bannatyne Club. Vol. I. 1833.

Marwick, J. D. *Charters and Documents relating to the City of Edinburgh.* 1143–1540. Scottish Burgh Records Society. 1871.

Stuart, J. *Extracts from the Council Register of the Burgh of Aberdeen.* 1398–1570. 2 vols. Spalding Club. 1844–8.

Nisbet, Alexander. *A System of Heraldry.* Edinburgh. 2 vols. First edition. 1742.

    (Consulted for a letter from James IV to Arbuthnot of Arbuthnot, September 26, 1489.)

Fraser, Sir William. *The Lennox Book.* 2 vols. Vol. I. Memoirs. Vol. II. Muniments. Privately printed. Edinburgh. 1874.

Registrum Episcopatus Moraviensis. Edited by C. Innes. Bannatyne Club. 1838.

Forbes-Leith, William. *The Scots Men-at-Arms and Lifeguards in France.* 1418–1830. 2 vols. Edinburgh. 1882.

Unprinted

P.R.O. E. 39. Exchequer T. R. Scots Documents.

NARRATIVE SOURCES

I. WHOLLY OR ALMOST CONTEMPORARY

Rentale Dunkeldense. Being Accounts of the Bishopric (A.D. 1505–1517) with Myln's Lives of the Bishops (A.D. 1483–1517). Translated and edited by Robert Kerr Hannay. Scottish History Society. Second Series. Vol. X. 1915.

Boetii Hectoris (1465–1536). *Murthlacensium et Aberdonensium episcoporum vitae.* Edited and translated by James Moir. New Spalding Club. 1894.

    (Published in 1522 and written between 1518 and 1521, before Major's history was published. Valuable for the Life of Bishop Elphinstone, Boece's friend.)

BIBLIOGRAPHY

Major, John. 1469. *A History of Greater Britain.* Translated by A. Constable. Scottish History Society, vol. x. 1892. (Published in 1521.)

Ferrerius, J. (Giovanni Ferrerio). Continuation of Hector Boece. *Boethius Scotorum historiae...libri XIX...Accessit. continuatio per J. F.* 1575.

(Ferrerius, a native of Piedmont, first visited Scotland in 1528. While Abbot of Kinloss (1531–7) he wrote his continuation of Boece's *History of Scotland,* from 1451 to 1489. Lang has analysed his contradictory views on James III's character in his *History of Scotland,* I, 359–60.)

II. NON-CONTEMPORARY, IN THE ORDER OF THEIR APPEARANCE

Lindsay, Robert, of Pitscottie. (1532–78.) *History of Scotland.* Edited by Aeneas J. G. Mackay. 3 vols. Scottish Text Society. 1899, 1911.

Buchanan, George. *Rerum Scoticarum Historia.* Translated by James Aikman. 1827. 4 vols. Glasgow. (1506–82. The history was published in 1582.)

Balfour, Sir James. (1600–57.) *Annals of Scotland.* 1057–1603. Historical works. 4 vols. London and Edinburgh. 1825.

Drummond, William, of Hawthornden. *History of the Five James's.* 1711.

Drummond of Hawthornden (1585–1649) has never been considered an important authority for the reign of James III. But after his account of the death of the young Earl of Mar in 1479, in which he maintains that he "died unawares amongst the hands of his best friends and servants", in spite of what some writers have written to the contrary, he continues in these words: "But no such faith should be given to them as to Bishop William Elphinstone, who was living in that time, and whose records we have followed, who for his place could not but know, and for his possession would not but deliver the very Truth". William Elphinstone, Bishop of Aberdeen (1431–1514), is known to have collected materials for a history of Scotland "from the first rise of the nation till his own time" upon which his pupil, Boece, based his history which stopped in 1461. The collections themselves do not appear to have survived and the chronicle of James I in the Fairfax MSS at the Bodleian, attributed to Elphinstone, was written by Maurice de Buchanan in 1461.[1] But Crawfurd,[2] in the eighteenth century, wrote that "My learned and worthy friend, Dr George Mackenzie (1669–1725)[3] tells us that General Fairfax got his MSS from one Mr Drummond, a brother of Hawthornden, in 1650; "perhaps it was his brother's, the learned Mr Drummond our Historian, who died much about this time". If Fairfax owned

[1] W. F. Skene, *Proceedings of the Society of Antiquaries of Scotland,* March 11, 1872, vol. IX, p. 447.
[2] Crawfurd, *Officers of the Crown,* p. 52.
[3] Author of *Lives of the Scots Writers.*

xxiij

Elphinstone MSS which are not now among his papers at the Bodleian, but had been the property of Drummond of Hawthornden, Drummond's history may be a more important source for the period of James III and IV than has been recognised. The closeness with which Drummond's narrative is corroborated by record evidence is striking; in wealth of detail and a certain sense of life it resembles the chronicle of a contemporary. It is strange that it has found no editor and must still be read in an edition of 1711.

MODERN WORKS
Books of Reference

Paul, Sir James Balfour. *The Scots Peerage*. 1904–14. Founded on Wood's edition of Sir Robert Douglas's Peerage of Scotland. 9 vols.

General Works

Brown, P. Hume. *History of Scotland*. Vol. I. Cambridge University Press. 1911.

Burnett, George. *Prefaces to the Exchequer Rolls of Scotland*. Vols. IX (1480–1487) and X (1488–1496). Edinburgh. 1886, 1887.

Burton, John Hill. *History of Scotland*. Vol. III. Edinburgh. 1867.

Cowan, Henry. "Bishop William Elphinstone." *Studies in the History and Development of the University of Aberdeen*. Edited by P. J. Anderson. Pp. 1–20. Aberdeen. 1906.

Crawfurd, George. *Lives and Characters of Officers of the Crown and of the State in Scotland*. Edinburgh. 1726.
(This quotes original documents not found elsewhere.)

Dickson, Thomas. *Preface to the Accounts of the Lord High Treasurer of Scotland*. Vol. I. 1473–98. General Register House. Edinburgh. 1877.

Ferrerii Historia Abbatum de Kynlos. Edited by W. D. Wilson. Bannatyne Club. 1839.
(Consulted for the Introductory Life of Ferrerius.)

Fraser, Sir William. *The Douglas Book*. 4 vols. Edinburgh. 1885.

Herkless, J. and Hannay, R. K. *Archbishops of St Andrews*. Vol. I. Blackwood. 1907.

Lang, Andrew. *History of Scotland*. Vol. I. Blackwood. 1900.

Mackay, Aeneas J. G. *History of Fife and Kinross*. 1896. The County Histories of Scotland.

Mackenzie, George. *The Lives and Characters of the most eminent writers of the Scots Nation*. 3 vols. Edinburgh. 1708–22.

Pinkerton, John. *The History of Scotland from the Accession of the House of Stuart to that of Mary*. 2 vols. London. 1797.
(Containing appendices of original documents.)

Rait, R. S. *Outline of Relations between England and Scotland*. 1901.

Rait, R. S. *The Parliaments of Scotland.* Glasgow. 1924.

Smith, George Gregory. *Days of James IV.* London. 1900.

Terry, C. S. "The Historians." *Studies in the History and Development of the University of Aberdeen.* Edited by P. J. Anderson. Pp. 97–146. Aberdeen. 1906.

Tytler, Patrick Fraser. *History of Scotland.* 1843. Eadie's edition. Glasgow. 1873–7.

IRELAND

OFFICIAL RECORDS

Printed

Lascelles, J. *Liber Munerum publicorum Hiberniae,* or the Establishments of Ireland. 1152–1824. 2 vols. Record Commission. 1824.

Reports on the Public Records of Ireland. 3 vols. 1810–1815. Record Commission.

Reports of the Deputy Keeper of Irish Records. 44 Reports to 1913.

Gilbert, John Thomas. *Facsimiles of National Manuscripts of Ireland.* Stationery Office. London. 1878.

Gilbert, John Thomas. *Calendar of Ancient Records of Dublin.* Vol. 1. 1889.

Statutes at Large. Ireland. (20 vols.) Vol. 1. 1786.

Calendar of Patent and Close Rolls of the Irish Chancery. Vol. 1. Henry II–Henry VII. Record Commission. 1827.

(Close Rolls used as the only record of the Parliament held at Trim in September 1493.)

Graves, James and Prim, J. G. A. *History of St Canice Cathedral, Kilkenny.* 1857.

(Consulted for Ormond Correspondence temp. Henry VII.)

Smith, Charles. *State of the County and City of Waterford.* 1746.

(Consulted for correspondence with Henry VII.)

"Rental Book of the 9th Earl of Kildare. 1518." See *Journal of Kilkenny Archaeological Society,* 1858–59, p. 309; 1862–63, pp. 110–137; 1864, 501–18; and MSS of Duke of Leinster, *Historical MSS Commission,* 9th Report, Part II, 1884, pp. 274–289.

Calendar of State Papers. Henry VIII. Vols. I, II, III. 1830–34.

Unprinted

The Attainder of the 8th Earl of Kildare, chap. 41. Poynings' Parliament at Drogheda. Carew MSS, vol. 603, fol. 177. Lambeth Palace.

List of Statutes of Poynings' Parliament at Drogheda. Carew MSS, vol. 608, fols. 113 v.–116. Lambeth Palace.

Anglo-Irish Diplomatic Documents of the year 1496. P.R.O. Irish Exchequer Accounts. E 101, Bundle 248, nos. 18, 19, 20. See P.R.O. *Lists and Indexes*, vol. xxxv.

Anglo-Irish Diplomatic Documents, 1494–1496. P.R.O. Diplomatic Documents, E 30, 1542, 1548, 1562, 1563, 1565, 1667. See P.R.O. *Lists and Indexes*, vol. xlix, 1923.
    (This list has for the first time furnished references to the above documents.)

Hattecliffe, William. Accounts as Under-Treasurer of Ireland in the Poynings Administration, 1494–1496. B.M. Royal MSS, 18 C xiv.

Accounts of money received in Ireland "pro domino Cancellario termino Mich. anno xi" and "pro Barone de Delvyn term. Trin. anno xi". B.M. Royal MSS, 7 C xvi, fol. 4.

A miscellaneous collection of Irish documents from the thirteenth to the sixteenth centuries. B.M. Cotton, Titus, B xi, vol. i.

NARRATIVE SOURCES
CONTEMPORARY

Annals of Ulster. Vol. iii. 1379–1541. Edited by B. MacCarthy. Rolls Series. Dublin, 1895.

Annals of the Kingdom of Ireland by the Four Masters. Vol. iv. Edited by John O'Donovan. Rolls Series. 1851.

Annals of Loch Cé. Vol. ii. 1014–1590. Edited by William M. Hennessy, 1871. Rolls Series.

"The Register of ye Mayors of Dublin with other memorable observations." 1406–1574. B.M. Add. MSS, 4791, fols. 133–135 (modern pagination).

NON-CONTEMPORARY, IN THE ORDER OF THEIR APPEARANCE

"State of Ireland, and Plan for its Reformation. 1515." *State Papers, Henry VIII*, vol. ii, part iii.

"Book of Howth" (*circa* 1544). *Calendar of Carew MSS.* Edited by J. Brewer and W. Bullen. 1871.

Stanyhurst, Richard. *A Continuation of the Chronicles of Ireland comprising the reigne of King Henrie the eight.* In Holinshed, *Chronicles*, vol. vi, pp. 275–320, 1808. (Published 1577.)

Rothe, Robert. "A register contayning the pedigree of the right honorable Thomas, late Earl of Ormond, and a storie of his ancestres etc." 1616. B.M. Add. MSS, 4792, no. 47, fols. 241–65.

Ware, Sir James. *Antiquities and History of Ireland.* London. 1705.
    (Containing the *Annals of Ireland during the Reign of King Henry VII.* Published 1665.)

Cox, Sir Richard. *Hibernia Anglicana.* 2 vols. 1689–90.

BIBLIOGRAPHY

Modern Works

Butler, W. F. T. *Gleanings from Irish History.* Longmans. 1925.

Curtis, Edmund. *History of Medieval Ireland.* 1923.

D'Alton, John. *History of the County of Dublin.* Dublin. 1838.
(This contains extracts from unprinted records.)

Fitzgerald, Charles William, Duke of Leinster. *The Earls of Kildare and their ancestors from* 1057 *to* 1773. Second edition. Dublin. 1858–62.
(This is full of mistakes.)

Gilbert, John Thomas. *History of the Viceroys of Ireland.* London. 1865.
(This is a tiresome book owing to lack of references, but contains subject-matter extracted from unprinted records, burnt in 1922.)

Green, Alice Stopford. *The Making of Ireland and its undoing.* 1909.

Wilson, Philip. *Beginnings of Modern Ireland.* 1912.

INTRODUCTION

By 1498 Henry VII's work was done. The Yorkist pretenders were quelled, and the throne secure. Peace after long years of negotiation had been made with Scotland. Ireland, disciplined by the Poynings Administration, had entered upon a temporary period of calm. The evils of feudalism were checked, and the departments of government reorganised, working smoothly, and in the hands of well-trained officials whom the King could trust, linked to him by the bonds of early struggles in adversity. Six millions of gold in ducats (according to the Milanese envoy) was piled up in his coffers. There is little to relate of the latter years of his reign. Peace and tranquillity leave no landmarks.

This result had been achieved in thirteen years by ceaseless attention to detail. Henry knew of the movements of the Yorkist conspirators in their early stages, through the agents whom he kept on the Border, in Ireland, and at the Courts of Charles VIII, Maximilian and Margaret of Burgundy. He was never taken by surprise. Perkin Warbeck, the most formidable of his enemies, was outplayed before each of his five invasions. Only by following the King's preparations and negotiations in detail can his finger be felt continuously on the pulse of danger.

The following pages make this attempt in the case of his relations with Scotland and Ireland. Scotland had been England's enemy for 200 years. During periods of ineffective monarchy, strong Scottish barons had been accustomed to seek England's help against a weak King; and Edward IV and Richard, Duke of Gloucester, backed James III's rebels in Scotland. James retaliated in due course by supporting the Earl of Richmond's bid for the English crown.

No period in Anglo-Scottish history is more obscure than the last years of the reign of this unhappy King, murdered in 1488, while fleeing from the battlefield of Sauchieburn, defeated by a rebel faction that gathered around his son. The following pages show that Henry VII was in truth invited to invade Scotland and rid James III of his rebellious nobles, and that his best friends were justly condemned by the first Parliament of his successor for their treachery in "the inbringing of Englishmen ". The parts played in the struggle by James III's attainted favourites, John Ramsay, Lord Bothwell, and his half-uncle James, Earl of Buchan, both of whom afterwards acted as Henry VII's spies at the Court of James IV, have never been explained. Yet their doings can be followed over a period of twelve years, during which they were continuously associated with Henry Wyatt, one of Henry VII's "new men" and trusted officials, who served the Tudors in office for fifty years and was the father of Sir Thomas Wyatt, the poet.

In the first chapter the movements of Bothwell, Buchan and Wyatt form the links in a long chain of evidence proving the close relations of Henry VII with James III. Henry's policy was perfectly consistent. Rymer's chaotic misdating, in *Foedera*, of Anglo-Scottish documents from the Scots Rolls, has misled all historians of the period. The unravelling of the story involves a recapitulation of the stages of successive diplomatic negotiations and is tedious and difficult, though allowable, perhaps, if in the end light can be thrown upon a hitherto baffling episode.

Henry VII's dealings with Ireland from 1491 to 1496 have never been closely investigated. The publication in 1923 of the Public Record Office List of Diplomatic Documents has made accessible a number of previously unknown Irish indentures and oaths of allegiance, facilitating the reconstruction of the march of events in the years immediately preceding Henry VII's experiment of direct rule in Ireland through the administration of Poynings. A detailed analysis of the unpublished accounts of the two years' régime, audited by Hattecliffe and Wyatt, throws new light upon the political history of the period; and the study of some unnoticed contemporary letters has led to a somewhat new interpretation of the causes and results of the administration. The text of the unprinted and burnt Poynings statutes has been partially re-established from new sources, the acts of the Parliament as a whole being dealt with in a chapter by Professor Curtis.

In any study of Henry VII's gradual domination of the Yorkist party, his Scottish and Irish activities must be co-ordinated at every step. Their history is one and indivisible, till the capture of Perkin Warbeck in 1497 rounded off the critical period of Henry's reign. The complete collapse of his conspiracy, backed by France and the Netherlands, had so impressed the continent that Henry was freed for the future from all danger abroad.

The King's cautious and tenacious statesmanship, which from the chaos of civil war raised England to the commanding position on the continent which she henceforth maintained, can be traced almost day by day from the accounts, which form the raw material of the following pages. The figures should be multiplied by 15 to 20 to obtain the approximate equivalent in modern money. The secret of the King's success was unceasing vigilance over dangerous areas, such as the Scottish Border and the Irish Pale, where a new class of royal official, trained to efficiency under his supervision, acted as his eyes and ears. His was the master-mind throughout, originating every policy; but the loyal help afforded him by some of his "new men" is worthy of commemoration. I plead indulgence for the wearisome accumulation of detail by which alone this can be illustrated.

CHAPTER I

THE RELATIONS BETWEEN ENGLAND AND SCOTLAND, 1482–88

The traditional view of the character and capacity for kingship of James III of Scotland has best been expressed by Drummond of Hawthornden, writing 150 years after his death.

He seemeth too much to have delighted in retiredness and to have been a hater of business; and that he troubled not himself with any but for formality's sake, more desirous of quietness than honour. This was the fault of the Governours of his youth, who put him off business of State, that they might the more easily reach their own ends, and by making him their shadow govern after their pleasure. Of this delight in solitariness, his brothers took their advantage, and wan the people to their observance. He was much given to buildings and trimming up of Chappels, Halls and Gardens, as usually are the lovers of idleness; and the rarest frames of Churches and Palaces in Scotland were mostly raised about his time; An humor, which though it be allowable in men which have not much to do, yet it is harmful in princes, as to be taken with admiration of watches, clocks, dials, autometes, pictures and statues. For the art of Princes is to give Laws and govern their people with wisdom in peace and glory in war; to spare the humble and prostrate the proud.

James's laziness in the prime business of government is beyond dispute. He has been both praised, and blamed, because he dared to cultivate friendship with men of talent, irrespective of their rank. His boon companions, Robert Cochrane, the architect, and William Rogers, the musician; even Hommyll, the tailor, and Leonard, the shoemaker, were men of parts.[1] Had James been soldier and athlete as well as art patron, like the young Henry VIII, his humble friends might have been tolerated by the aristocracy. No beauty-loving, well-meaning, gentle King, deficient in all the qualities of a man of action, could escape failure and ignominy at a time when a duel between the nobles and the crown was being fought to the death in Scotland.

James III's evil genius was his brother, Alexander, Duke of Albany, who, in 1472, was painted as an innocent youth, kneeling

[1] For a commentary on these persons see Hill Burton, *History of Scotland*, III, 181–5.

behind the King on the inside of the wings of Hugo Van der Goes's altarpiece at Holyrood.[1] Heir-apparent, soldier and traitor, he soon became the natural focus of baronial discontent. The long minorities of James II and James III had increased the power of the turbulent, treacherous aristocracy of Scotland. A series of conspiracies, led by Archibald Angus, a Douglas and natural enemy of the Stewarts, marked the reign. A plot in Albany's favour made James III imprison both his brothers in 1479; the accidental death in captivity of the younger, the Earl of Mar, giving his enemies an opportunity to accuse the King of murder. At the same time the truce with England, which had lasted thirteen years, was broken owing to the intrigue of Louis XI, who hoped to keep Edward IV from invading France by encouraging Anglo-Scottish war. These two events made the year 1479 the turning-point in James III's career. Henceforth Edward IV and his brother Richard, Duke of Gloucester, consistently backed Albany's attempts to gain the Scottish crown for himself as a vassal of England.

The moves in the game are well known, but have never been considered in relation to the part subsequently played by James III in the struggle between Richard III and Henry Tudor. Early in 1480 Gloucester was appointed Edward IV's Lieutenant-General in the north to lead an army against Scotland.[2] The Pope forbade hostilities and the Scottish army turned back; the English, erastian as ever, invaded the country by land and sea, being repulsed by the great sea captain Andrew Wood.[3] In June, 1482, Albany bribed Edward IV to help him yet again by promising the cession of Berwick and the rupture of the Franco-Scottish alliance.[4] Berwick, the gate to the north, had been ceded to Scotland by Margaret of Anjou in 1461, in gratitude for help after the Second Battle of St Albans, and was the greatest prize that could be dangled before an English King. In July, the Earl of Angus, leading the disaffected Scottish Earls (amongst

---

[1] Illustrated as the frontispiece to Hume Brown's *History of Scotland*, vol. I. For a summary of the evidence as to the date, proving that the younger man represents Albany, and not James IV, then unborn, see Sir Martin Conway: *The Van Eycks and their followers*, pp. 178–9. The portrait heads were added by a Scottish artist.

[2] *Foedera*, XII, 115.   [3] *Acts Parl. Scot.* II, 138–9.

[4] *Foedera*, XII, 156.

whom were James III's half-uncles, James, Earl of Buchan, John, Earl of Atholl, and Andrew Stewart, Bishop-elect of Moray), met the King on his way south, nominally to aid him against his brother; but while Albany and Gloucester were invading Scotland, Angus "belled the cat" by arresting James III in his tent at Lauder and hanging his hated artistic favourites over the bridge. Cochrane, the architect, who had begged for a silken halter, was strangled with a rope in the presence of the King.[1] All the others save the eighteen-year-old John Ramsay and James Hommyll the tailor, perished. This mass murder of the Sovereign's intimate friends was the chief landmark of his reign. No truce could efface the memory of such a deed on either side and psychologically the tragedy of Sauchieburn was its inevitable outcome.

For a short time James III was shut up by the Angus faction in Edinburgh Castle, guarded by his uncles, Buchan and Atholl. There was no one left to impede Albany and Gloucester, and after a treaty restoring Albany to his offices in Scotland,[2] Gloucester took Berwick Castle on his way home, in fulfilment of the agreement made with Edward IV. Berwick, after its many vicissitudes, has since belonged to England.

A thread through the ensuing maze of diplomatic moves is hard to follow. Angus and Albany soon came to an understanding by which Albany in collusion with Buchan made a feint of laying siege to Edinburgh Castle, capturing it in September[3] with the King inside. Albany governed Scotland in James III's name, giving him his nominal freedom, and became his Lieutenant-General in December.[4] No monarch was ever placed in a more humiliating position. Albany dictated his instruments of government, and James III's charter to the city of Edinburgh in November, 1482,[5] signed by "our beloved uncles Andrew elect of Moray and James, Earl of Buchan", mentions "our dearest brother, Alexander, Duke of Albany" who "liberated us from imprisonment in our Castle of Edinburgh, in consequence of which attack our royal person now rejoices in liberty".

[1] Pitscottie, I, 175.   [2] Foedera, XII, 160.
[3] Great Seal Register, 1424–1513, p. 322 footnote.
[4] Acts Parl. Scot. II, 142.
[5] Scottish Burgh Records Society, Charters and Documents relating to Edinburgh, p. 157.

The liberty consisted in sealing fulsome laudations of the traitor's services.[1]

Early in the next year, Albany sent Angus into England to renew the contract with Edward IV by which he was to become King of Scotland.[2] Articles were drawn up between them in February, virtually duplicates of those of June, 1482.[3] But Albany's shiftiness antagonised even the rebel earls, and before long the nobles as a whole revolted, rallying to the side of the King. James III's first act as an independent sovereign once more seems to have been the bestowal of the barony of Bothwell on his old favourite and surviver of the Lauder murders, John Ramsay, on February 24, 1482/3.[4]

Albany, trusting to his brother's weakness, made an indenture with him in March,[5] acknowledging his own treason and renouncing his confederates, the Earls of Angus, Buchan, Atholl and Moray. Buchan was banished for three years, and the others prohibited from coming within six miles of the King. Albany had to give up his lieutenancy, but kept his estate, and Dunbar Castle. James III should have foreseen the immediate return of his brother to England to renew his intrigues for the crown. On his way there Albany purposely let Dunbar fall into English hands; but fortune turned her wheel again, for in April Edward IV died and Albany found himself deprived of his ally and labelled as a traitor in Scotland. The Scottish Parliament in July, 1483, forfeited him in his absence[6] and Gloucester, now King Richard III, finding it expedient to be outwardly on good terms with the King of Scotland, allowed his *protégé* to drop.

William Elphinstone, the founder of King's College, Aberdeen, and the most distinguished Scottish scholar and statesman of his time, received four safe-conducts as ambassador from Richard III, in November, 1483,[7] March,[8] April,[9] and

---

[1] *Great Seal Register*, 1424–1513, no. 1541.
[2] *Foedera*, XII, 172.
[3] *Ibid.* XII, 173–6.   [4] *Acts Parl. Scot.* II, 153.
[5] *Acts Parl. Scot.* II. March 16, 1482–3.
[6] *Ibid.* II, 147–51.
[7] *Rot. Scot.* II, 461. (*Foedera*, XII, 251, mistakenly dated 1484; corrected in Hardy's *Syllabus*.)
[8] *Rot. Scot.* II, 461. *Foedera*, XII, 218, 264. (264 is a copy of 218, mistakenly dated 1485.)
[9] *Rot. Scot.* II, 462.

August, 1484,[1] preliminary to the negotiation of an Anglo-Scottish peace. The defeat, at Lochmaben, of Albany, who invaded Scotland in July, 1484, with James, the ninth and last Earl of Douglas, a pensioner of Richard III,[2] must have smoothed his mission. Albany escaped to France and was killed in a tournament at Paris in the following year; while Douglas on account of his age was allowed to retire to the Abbey of Lindores as a monk.

In September, 1484, Richard III and James III concluded a three years' truce at Nottingham,[3] although there could be no peace in their hearts. In the struggle between Richard and Henry Tudor, which began at once, James would naturally incline towards the Lancastrian Earl of Richmond, who had not helped Albany to oust him from his throne; but there is little known as to the organisation of Scottish help for Henry Tudor before and at the Battle of Bosworth. Charles VIII of France, soon after his accession, had sent an embassy to Scotland under Bernard Stuart, Lord Daubigny, which renewed the ancient alliance between the two countries on March 22, 1483/4.[4] Sir James Balfour,[5] writing in the seventeenth century, said that the French ambassadors when they had concluded their business took back with them eighteen companies of Scots foot to France under the command of one Donald Robertson.[6] Balfour collected a large part of the manuscripts now in the National Library of Scotland, and if he should have alighted upon this fact in some source of information unknown to-day, the thousand Scots said by John Major and Pitscottie to have been in the Earl of Richmond's army at Bosworth would be accounted for.

No English authority even mentions a Scottish contingent at Bosworth. Charles VIII helped Henry Tudor with money and

[1] *Rot. Scot.* II, 464. *Foedera*, XII, 230.
[2] *Ibid.* XII, 213.
[3] See Gairdner, *Letters of Richard III and Henry VII*, I, 59–67, and *Bannatyne Miscellany*, II, 35 (Bannatyne Club), for the proceedings at Nottingham; *Foedera*, XII, 235–47, 250, for the treaty.
[4] The subsequent Scottish embassy to France signed the same treaty in Paris on July 9. George Crawfurd, *Officers of the Crown*, p. 45.
[5] Sir James Balfour, *Annals*, I, 209.
[6] A certain Donald Robertson is mentioned as a tenant of James III in 1480. *Exchequer Rolls*, IX, 573.

men,[1] but there were only 100 gendarmes and 124 archers in the Scots Company which had been established at the French Court by Charles VII.[2] John Major, whose history was printed in 1521, says: "Inasmuch as the Earl of Richmond had been long a dweller in France, Charles the Eighth granted him an aid of 5000 men (of whom 1000 were Scots, but John son of Robert of Haddington[3] was chief and leader of the Scots)". Pitscottie gives the numbers coming over in thirty ships with Henry Tudor from France, as 3000 English, 6000 French and 1000 men at arms, "called the Scots Company, whose captain was a noble knight, Sir Alexander Bruce of Erlshall". He adds that Bruce, Captain of the Scots horse, and Henderson of Haddington, Captain of the Scots foot, Henry's youthful companions in France, commanded the vanguard of 10,000 men at Bosworth.[4]

John, son of Robert of Haddington, and Captain Henderson of Haddington, remain unidentified, though Sir Alexander Bruce is well known. His eldest son, Sir William Bruce of Earlshall, was Pitscottie's neighbour in Fife, being quoted by him as a source for his history.[5] Sir William is certainly not likely to have been mistaken as to the part played by his own father at Bosworth. In November, 1485, Bruce was given a safe-conduct into England[6] and in the following February James III made him a grant of land for his service inside and outside the realm.[7] One month later he received from Henry VII an annuity of £20 "in consideration of good, faithful and approved services,

[1] When Lord Stanley delivered the Earl of Oxford out of prison at Hammes, Charles VIII gave the Earl of Richmond 60,000 francs and 1800 "compagnons de guerre". See *Chroniques de Jean Molinet*, ed. Buchon, II, 406. Comines says that Henry had "quelque peu d'argent du Roy et quelques trois mil hommes prins en la duché de Normandie, et des plus meschans que l'on peut trouver". Book VI, Chapter VIII.

[2] William Forbes-Leith, *The Scots Men-at-Arms and Lifeguards in France*, 1418–1830, pp. 130–1.

[3] "John of Haddington assigne to dene William Haddington", is mentioned in the *Acta Dominorum Concilii*, 1478, p. 9. The name occurs frequently in the *Acta Dominorum Auditorum*. Major's biographer, A. J. G. Mackay, suggests that John Haddington may be a mistake for John Cunningham, who was Captain of the Scots Company in 1478, Major's writing being notoriously bad.

[4] Pitscottie, I, 191, ed. Mackay. Polydore Vergil says Henry left France with 2000 men and a few ships. *Hall's Chronicle*, 410.

[5] Pitscottie, I, pp. cxviii–xxi.

[6] *Rot. Scot.* II, 469. Alexander Bruce is mentioned as "valectus Camere nostre" in 1485; P.R.O. D.L. 42, no. 21, f. 97 v.

[7] *Great Seal Register*, 1424–1513, no. 1638.

heretofore done by him with great trouble and recent personal service, by command of the King, he sustaining therein great losses, and being unceasing, according to his ability, in the performance thereof, as the King is very certainly informed ".[1] If James III had helped Henry to victory at Bosworth, there is no need to look beyond Bruce's part in the battle for the reason of the favour shown him by both Kings. Confused as is the evidence as to the composition and numbers of the Scottish contingent, it is obvious that intermediaries between the Earl of Richmond and James III must have been employed during its organisation. Bernard Stuart's embassy from France in March 1484 and the return one in July could have been utilised for this purpose; and Ramsay, Lord Bothwell, James III's favourite, whose relations with Henry VII can be followed for many years after his accession, may have helped him even at this earlier stage, working perhaps through the intermediary of Henry Wyatt, the Englishman with whom Bothwell in his later career as an English spy, was most closely associated.

An obscure youth in 1485, this Henry Wyatt became the founder of a Tudor family of distinction. He was the father of Sir Thomas Wyatt, poet and ambassador at the Court of Henry VIII, and grandfather of the leader of the unlucky Wyatt rebellion against the Spanish marriage of Queen Mary: Henry himself, the poet, his daughter Margaret Lee, and his grandson, Thomas, were all painted by Holbein. The poet wrote to his son, the rebel, in 1538,[2] that his grandfather, Sir Henry, then not cold in his grave, had once suffered "two years and more imprisonment in Scotland in irons and stocks". The poet's great-great-grandson, Thomas Scott,[3] about the year 1614, quoted from stories he had heard his grandmother (the rebel's widow) relate, that the Earl of Richmond, soon after he was crowned King, had entertained Henry Wyatt, then coming out of imprisonment and affliction in Scotland, and welcomed him at the Council, as his great benefactor. It is possible that Wyatt,

[1] Bain, IV, 1518. The corresponding entry on the Tellers Rolls describes him as "de ffrauncia." P.R.O. E 405, 75. Mich. Term, 2 Henry VII, Page mem. 2 dorso.
[2] A. K. Foxwell, *The Poems of Sir Thomas Wiat*, II, 261.
[3] The Wyatt MSS. Agnes Conway, *Bulletin of the Institute of Historical Research*, I, 73.

engaged on the Earl of Richmond's business, had fallen into the hands of some Scottish baron with Yorkist sympathies, only to be released when Henry VII was securely on the throne, after a considerable period of cruel imprisonment, and on the promise of a huge ransom. The motto on his standard was "*oublier ne puis*"[1] and the story told by Thomas Scott of his imprisonment in a cold and narrow tower "where he had starved had not God sent him a cat to feed and warm him" may refer to this unhappy episode.

Thirty years later Henry VIII renewed his father's grant of £20 a year, towards Wyatt's ransom from the cruel hands of the Scots, because he was convinced that he had not yet been able to pay off the sum.[2] From September 1485 onwards he was the recipient of grants and offices, bestowed in return for some considerable debt. Services before Bosworth, conspicuous enough to earn a pension that lasted thirty years at least, besides considerable annual fees, must have been such as could be performed by the daring, strength and courage of a youth. Liaison work on the Border was of this type; and Wyatt's capture and hardships, followed by a crippling ransom, turned out to be the making of the fortune by which his family became one of the most interesting of the Tudor "nouveaux riches".

Sympathy between James III and the Earl of Richmond did not end the usual tension between the two countries after Henry ascended the throne. Nevertheless in the bitter struggle between James III and his nobles, culminating in James's murder on the field of Sauchieburn, Henry VII was far from neutral,[3] as has been supposed. That a faction in Scotland hostile to England existed in some strength immediately after Bosworth is proved by a commission of array in September, 1485, to the northern countries, to be in readiness for an invasion of the Scots.[4] A similar commission to the officers of the Duchy of Lancaster in the following month[5] speaks of "divers the subgettes of our

[1] MS, 1, 2. College of Arms. Published in the *De Walden Library*, 1904.
[2] *L. and P. Henry VIII*, II, pt 1, 842.
[3] Rait, *Relations between England and Scotland*, p. 98, and the histories of Pinkerton, Tytler and Lang.
[4] *Cal. Pat. Rolls*, 1485–94, p. 39. Reid, *The King's Council in the North*, p. 72.
[5] Campbell, *Materials*, I, 579. *Paston Letters*, III, 887, and "Rutland Papers", *Hist. MSS Com. 12th Report*, App. IV, p. 8.

cosyne James, Kyng of Scottes,...entendying to leaye seege to our town and castel of Berwick ". This may have been no official invasion encouraged by the Scottish King. The divers subjects of the King of Scots were in all probability the Border lords; Angus Bell the Cat, the Humes, Hepburns, etc., who in 1482 had allied themselves with Albany and Richard, Duke of Gloucester, against James III and who, outwardly reconciled, remained disloyal till they caused his death at Sauchieburn. Dunbar Castle had been recaptured by the Scots in the winter of 1485–6,[1] such an attack being allowed by Richard III's treaty of 1484, and was not an act of war. By October 20 the danger was past.[2]

Meanwhile James III's favourite, Lord Bothwell, together with George Browne, Bishop of Dunkeld, and the Bishops of Aberdeen and Glasgow, were representing him at Henry VII's coronation on October 30, with safe-conducts dating from September 22.[3] The Bishop of Aberdeen was William Elphinstone, who according to Boece[4] had been nominated to the see by James in 1484 in recognition of the success of his two missions to Edward IV, resulting in the temporary reconciliation of the King with his brother. The Bishop's inclusion in all James's embassies disposes of the taunt of his enemies that only mean persons were employed as his advisers.

A few weeks after the coronation, there was a rumour in England of a new insurrection in northern parts.[5] The Earl of Northumberland, lately created Warden-General of the Scottish Marches, was made commissioner to treat for peace between England and Scotland,[6] and in February[6] safe-conducts were given to twelve unnamed ambassadors of the Scots to be chosen by James III. Lovell's Yorkist rebellion intervened and it was not till May 6 that Elphinstone, Lord Bothwell, John Ross of Montgrenan and others were named as ambassadors to conclude a truce with Henry VII, being received by him in state on June 5 after his return to Westminster from his progress in the north.[7] The peace was concluded by the King's Council in June,[8]

---

[1] *Exchequer Rolls*, IX, 433.   [2] Campbell, *Materials*, I, 93–4.
[3] *Rot. Scot.* II, 469. Rymer (*Foedera*, XII, 325) mistakenly dates this 1487.
[4] Hector Boece, *Murthlacensium et Aberdonensium episcoporum vitae*, ed. James Moir, pp. 77, 78.   [5] *Rot. Scot.* II, 471.
[6] *Ibid.* II, 471. Rymer (*Foedera*, XII, 334) mistakenly dates this 1488.
[7] Leland, *Collectanea*, IV, 203.   [8] Scofield, *Star Chamber*, p. 7.

signed as a three years' truce by both parties in London on July 3,[1] confirmed by Henry on July 26,[2] delivered to the ambassador of James in the parish church of Berwick in September,[3] and ratified by him in October.[4] On July 7[5] a fresh safe-conduct, to pass between England and Scotland at pleasure, was issued to Elphinstone, to the Archbishop of St Andrews, and to others. All stages have been recapitulated here, for Rymer's mistake in post-dating this last grant,[6] as well as the confirmation of the treaty on July 26, by two years,[6] has confused all historians of the period,[7] who invariably quote from *Foedera* in preference to the Scots Rolls.

A clause in the truce stated that commissioners should meet again in the following March to prolong it and add the tie of a three-fold marriage treaty.[8] Negotiations between Henry VII and James III were in fact almost continuous. In February, 1486/7, a commission was given by Henry to the Bishop of Carlisle and others to arrange this very meeting in March.[9] Both Kings desired the closest possible alliance. Henry feared Yorkist uprisings and James hoped to have England on his side in the event of another Border rebellion. For the same reason the discontented Scottish nobles were adverse to an English alliance, Ferrerius emphasising the unpopularity James courted with his barons by pursuing the English treaty so vigorously.[10]

Berwick, the prize yielded to England by Albany's treachery in 1482, was the insoluble factor in the situation. A preliminary treaty, with the Berwick question suspended, was nevertheless negotiated in Scotland in August, 1487, between Richard Fox and Edgecombe, on behalf of Henry; Bothwell and Elphinstone for James.[11] Fox was back in Cambridge on September 23.[12] Henry stayed at Newcastle during the negotiations,[13] keeping watch over Berwick. A surprise attack was to be feared so long

[1] *Rot. Scot.* II, 477.   [2] *Ibid.* II, 473–7.
[3] Campbell, *Materials*, I, 572.
[4] *Foedera*, XII, 316, "ex autographo".
[5] *Rot. Scot.* II, 472.   [6] *Foedera*, XII, 343, XII, 346.
[7] Lang, *History of Scotland*, I, 362.
[8] *Rot. Scot.* II, 475.
[9] Campbell, *Materials*, II, 120.
[10] Ferrerius, p. 398 b.   [11] *Rot. Scot.* II, 480.
[12] E. C. Batten, *Register of Fox*, Introduction, p. 19.
[13] *Hall's Chronicle*, p. 436.

as the question of its ownership was in dispute, and on October 15 he ordered the fortress to be provisioned.[1] No attack came. An indenture of peace was signed at Edinburgh on November 28[2] and ratified at Westminster.[3] Polydore Vergil stated that James vowed in secret life-long peace with the King of England, but did not dare to commit himself openly to more than seven years, because of the feeling in Scotland.[4] The actual treaty mentions a truce till September 1, 1489. Stipulations were made for further meetings in January, May and July, 1488, to arrange the marriage preliminaries between James III himself and the widow of Edward IV; and for both his sons with sisters of the Queen. There is no evidence that the January meeting was held. The Scots Parliament in that month considered the business for the May meeting and laid down that the Scots ambassadors should not countenance the English marriages unless Berwick were either handed over to Scotland or destroyed.[5] Both Kings were to meet in person in July and "commune for more love and tenderness between them".

It would appear that the Scots in January had planned another attack upon the fortress. The Earl of Northumberland was ordered to indent with Henry to prepare and have ready 200 men to be thrown into Berwick at once, as the Scots intended to lay siege to it within thirty days.[6] It is possible, even probable, that the raid was to be undertaken by those Border nobles who disliked the English alliance, rather than by James III himself. After his six months of negotiation to secure the preliminary treaty, ratified by England as recently as December 20, it is unlikely that he would have jeopardised his work by attacking Berwick within a month. An onslaught by the nobles, on the contrary, would have been a simultaneous blow both to England and their hated King. It did not take place, and for the moment the Berwick question lapsed owing to the grave internal condition of Scotland.

James might well have regarded the benefit to his realm from a close alliance with England, cemented by intimate marriage

[1] Bain, IV, 1528.
[2] *Rot. Scot.* II, 480–1.
[3] *Ibid.* II, 482.
[4] *Hall's Chronicle*, p. 436.
[5] *Acts Parl. Scot.* II, 181–2.
[6] Book of Entries of the Council of Henry VII. Scofield, *Star Chamber*, p. 20.

ties and the return of Berwick, as worth increasing the risk of civil war. But it was merely stupid to insult his old and powerful enemies, the Humes, by consolidating his appropriation of the revenues of the Priory of Coldingham (in which since 1461 they had usurped a family interest from the Priory of Durham)[1] in order to endow his new Chapel Royal at Stirling. At the request of the King, the Pope, in 1487, suppressed Coldingham, allocating half the revenues to this purpose.[2] The building of the Hall (the so-called Parliament House in Stirling Castle) and the Chapel, was, during the winter of 1487–8, James's main interest[3]; and the Parliament of October, 1487, passed a Statute forbidding propaganda to be undertaken contrary to the King's annexation.[4] The folly of this act, at the most critical period of James III's reign, must be held to justify to a great extent the criticism passed upon him by his nobles and reflected 150 years later in Drummond of Hawthornden's sketch.

This Hume agitation was certainly the beginning of the open confederacy of the lords against the King. When James understood that the trouble was serious he made Lord Bothwell captain of his bodyguard, giving him a warrant not to allow any man in arms to approach the Court.[5] This action naturally exasperated the rebels. Bishop Elphinstone tried to mediate between the King and his nobles,[6] but did not go to England to enlist Henry VII's sympathies, as has been suggested,[7] for his name occurs uninterruptedly as a witness to the royal charters throughout the winter of 1487–8.[8]

James III garrisoned the castles of Stirling and Edinburgh, putting his heir, the young Prince James, for safety into Stirling, trusting the Governor, James Shaw of Sauchie. He, himself, returned to Edinburgh, and the Parliament which met on January 29, 1487/8, ordered those persons unnamed, who had disobeyed the Coldingham Statute, and were doubtless the

---

[1] *Priory of Coldingham*, Letter no. CCXXXVI. Surtees Society, vol. XII.
[2] George Chalmers, *Caledonia*, III, 331, 1888.
[3] Pitscottie, I, 200.   [4] *Acts Parl. Scot.* II, 179.
[5] Ferrerius, p. 398 b.
[6] Moir, *Boece's Lives*, p. 78.
[7] George Crawfurd, *Officers of the Crown*, p. 50. He quotes Rymer's misdated safe-conduct of September 22, 1487. See Appendix II, no. 1.
[8] *Great Seal Register*, 1424–1513, nos. 1686, 1689, 1691, 1692, 1693, 1695, 1698, 1699, 1703, 1705, 1709, 1711, 1712, 1715, 1717, 1718, 1719, 1720, 1722.

Humes and their friends, to appear for trial in Parliament on May 5.[1] Fifty bishops, abbots, nobles and commissioners from towns were chosen to hear the case.[2] This summons was the height of folly, precipitating the conspiracy of the Lauder rebels, the Earls of Angus, Argyll and Lennox, and the Lords Hailes, Hume, Drummond, Lyle and Gray. The King's uncles, Buchan and Andrew Stewart, Bishop of Moray, formerly rebels at Lauder, had changed sides. According to Ferrerius the nobles were unable to choose a chief amongst themselves, compromising instead upon the leadership of the young Prince. They went in a body to Stirling, bribed Shaw of Sauchie to yield him up,[3] and won the allegiance of the boy of fifteen with threats that they would deliver Scotland to the English King if he did not join them.[4] That this was on February 2, 1487/8, is proved by a Statute made in Parliament in the following October, declaring all alienations of lands of no avail after the *second day of February* which was the day of "our soverane lord that now is cuming furth of Stirvilin".[5] With the possession of the person of the Prince, the rebel lords hoped to achieve the resignation of the King.

No less than four of the seven named conspirators (Angus, Argyll, Drummond and Lyle) were actually appointed by James III in Parliament on January 29 (only three days before they captured the Prince) to try the Coldingham case. The treachery of Sauchie, according to Pitscottie and others, did not become known to the King for some time. Exactly when the Prince's defection was discovered is still a mystery. It may have been this bad news that made James III dissolve Parliament "for certane resonable & gret cause" on February 21, the same day that he appointed the loyal Elphinstone as Chancellor in place of the rebel Argyll. Nevertheless Argyll and Angus seem to have continued to witness the King's charters at Edinburgh, under the Great Seal, till February 27 and March 7 respectively,[6] which it might be supposed they could not have done had James known that they were themselves in possession of the kidnapped

---

[1] *Acts Parl. Scot.* II, 182. [2] *Ibid.* II, 184.
[3] Ferrerius, pp. 399, 399 b. [4] Buchanan, ed. Aikman, II, 218.
[5] *Acts Parl. Scot.* II, 222–3.
[6] *Great Seal Register*, 1424–1513, nos. 1708, 1709, 1717. For a discussion as to the part played by Angus see Fraser, *The Douglas Book*, II, 82.

person of his son. Against this view may be set Buchanan's opinion[1] that James kept Angus and other suspect rebels constantly with him at Court in order to win them over by gifts and flattery. Buchanan, born in 1506, was a man of the world, moving in Court circles and should have been better informed in this matter than the monk Ferrerius, who landed in Scotland for the first time in 1528. It is known that he taught young James V about Angus Bell the Cat's rebellion of 1482 at Lauder and punished him when James said that he himself would "bell the cat in the person of Buchanan".[2] Buchanan's view gains some support from Ferrerius's[3] account of James III's effort to attach to his side as a spy the aged Earl of Douglas, the old confederate of the Lauder rebels, whose life had been spared in 1484 on condition of retirement to an abbey. Douglas succeeded in remaining neutral on the plea of old age and died in 1491.[4]

Ferrerius recounts how James, whose envoys to the nobles in Edinburgh were told that he must resign in favour of his son, decided to leave the stronghold of his enemies in the east of Scotland and join his friends in the north.[5] As no Accounts of the Lord High Treasurer are extant from 1473 to July 1488, James III's whereabouts must be inferred rather than known. A blank in the Great Seal Register from March 23 to May 18 implies a breakdown of government, and must coincide with the period of the King's wanderings.

His journey can best be followed in the narrative of Lindsay of Pitscottie. For this period Pitscottie had good sources of information, as his great-uncle David, second Lord Lindsay of the Byres, fought on the side of James III at Sauchieburn, lending the King the grey charger which bore him to his death. Patrick, afterwards fourth Lord Lindsay of the Byres, was Pitscottie's grandfather, and probably left a manuscript to which his grandson had access.[6] Pitscottie gives a vivid account of James's journey to Leith, where he boarded a ship of Andrew Wood's bound for Flanders, but landed from it in Fife. Wood received a confirmation of his grant of Largo on March 21,

---

[1] Buchanan, ed. Aikman, II, 217.
[2] George Mackenzie, *Scots Writers*, III, 179–80.
[3] Ferrerius, p. 400.   [4] *G.E.C.*
[5] Ferrerius, p. 399 b.
[6] Mackay's Introduction to Pitscottie, I, p. civ.

possibly as a reward for carrying James across the Forth.[1] The rebels, following on his heels, captured part of his baggage and money, with which they paid their men. The King went on to Aberdeen, the see of the loyal Elphinstone, and made a grant from there on April 16 to his uncle Andrew Stewart, Bishop of Moray, for his faithful service.[2] Returning from the north, he marched through Fife to the Forth, with the addition to his train of the Earls of Huntley, Erroll, Atholl, Crawford, Rothes, Sutherland, Caithness and Marischal; and of the Lords Forbes, Ogilvy, Grant and Fraser. With the lesser noblemen and their followers his force amounted to 40,000[3] men. Pitscottie adds the names of the Earl of Buchan and others, including Argyll, though Buchan was in England and Argyll soon afterwards signed a truce on behalf of the rebels. Pitscottie believed that the King was still in ignorance of the treason of his son; but it seems more reasonable to accept Ferrerius's account of James's negotiations with the Prince and the rebels before his departure from Edinburgh. Pitscottie's post-dating of the original capture of young James to the period of his father's journey in the north proves that his chronology of the period was wrong.

In the absence of the King the rebels overran the south of Scotland and captured Dunbar,[4] where Patrick Hepburn, Lord Hailes, established himself. The custody of this castle, after its recovery from the English, had been given to John Ramsay, Lord Bothwell, in June, 1486.[5] Civil war extended as far south as Jedburgh, for the abbey authorities in 1491 had to sue the Pope for pardon because they had been on the side of James III's rebels.[6] This is corroborated by Henry VII's claim of presentation to the living of Arthureth, in the diocese of Carlisle, on May 1, 1488, owing to the adherence of the Abbot and Convent of Jedworth (Jedburgh) to the "King's enemies of Scotland".[7] Civil war on the Border must have been considered by England as a threat to the safety of the north. On April 1, 1488,[8] the Earl of Northumberland was reappointed Warden-General of the

---

[1] D.N.B. "Andrew Wood", by J. K. Laughton.
[2] Registrum Episcopatus Moraviensis, 234, Bannatyne Club.
[3] Ferrerius, p. 400.
[4] Drummond of Hawthornden, p. 57.
[5] Exchequer Rolls, IX, 523.   [6] Wilkins, Concilia, III, 634.
[7] Cal. Pat. Rolls, 1485–94, p. 224.   [8] Rot. Scot. II, 484.

Scottish Marches, in the terms of a previous grant to him of January 3, 1485/6,[1] and in the Easter Term Berwick was provisioned and armed.[2] If Bothwell was defending Dunbar Castle in person, as Governor, against Scottish rebels, while James III was in the north of Scotland, he might naturally have appealed to the Earl and to Sir William Tyler, Governor of Berwick, for help.[3] He could even have issued a commission in the King's name to Northumberland and Tyler, asking them to free any Scots of his party fighting against James III's rebels who should chance to fall into the hands of the English.[4] These two charges were made against Bothwell in his trial after Sauchieburn before the Parliament of James IV.[5]

When Dunbar fell, if not before, Bothwell, who went to the Court of Henry VII as James III's ambassador, may have carried with him this forged commission from the King of Scots, asking for English help. With James III in the Highlands and civil war raging in the south, commissions could not bear his seal, and this one was said in Bothwell's trial to have been drawn up by him and Andrew, Bishop of Moray, James, Earl of Buchan, and Alexander, Lord Forbes. Henry Wyatt was first mentioned in connection with Bothwell on this mission.[6] In later years, Wyatt, as a trusted royal official, frequented the Border in times of danger and kept Henry VII informed of what was going on. He was pleading in person at the Exchequer at Westminster on February 1 and April 23, 1488;[7] but between these dates would have had time to travel to the Border and back. There is no reason whatsoever why the name of a young English official at the outset of his career should be dragged into a Scottish trial had he not been involved with Bothwell at that time, as was frequently the case in later years.

Buchan and his wife were in England in December, 1487,

---

[1] *Rot. Scot.* II, 471.   [2] Bain, IV, 1534.
[3] Pinkerton suggests that James III applied to the Earl of Northumberland at this time; *History of Scotland*, I, 329, note 3.
[4] Letters of general remission were granted by James IV to the inhabitants of Berwickshire, the Merse, and Lauderdale on October 24, 1493, "for all crimes and actions committed by them before the day of our Coronation"; Pitcairn, *Criminal Trials*, I, 14.
[5] *Acts Parl. Scot.* II, 201. See Appendix I, p. 145.
[6] See Appendix I, p. 145.
[7] Exchequer Plea Rolls, P.R.O. E 13, 172, mem. 30, 33.

receiving generous allowances from Henry VII.[1] In the spring he returned to Scotland with a harness given to "oure right well-beloved cousyn Therle Boghan" by the King, and paid for on May 6.[2] He and Lord Lyle were singled out for mention in the terms of the first Truce of Blackness between James III and the rebels, and it is easy to believe that he had a hand in the drafting of this unknown commission to which he pleaded guilty at his trial.

Towards the end of April, 1488, the King of Scots returned from the north, taking up his position at Blackness Castle, on the Forth, which belonged to his friend, Sir John Ross of Halkhede.[3] Here James was well placed for an attack upon the rebel army, whose headquarters were at Blackness, the port of Linlithgow. While both armies faced each other, Buchanan[4] recounts that "by the intervention of the Earl of Atholl, the King's Uncle, an accommodation was effected, Atholl himself being given to Adam Hepburn, as a hostage, with whome he remained till the King's death. But the concord...did not last long".

This concord was the Pacification of Blackness, quoted in full in the first recorded debate in the Scots Parliament,[5] and identical with the "promises sent and signed with James III's sign manual to our King then Prince" mentioned in the indictment of Buchan.[5] It was signed on behalf of the King by Elphinstone, the Earls of Huntley, Erroll and Marischal, Lord Glamis and Alexander Lindsay; and for the lords, by the Bishop of Glasgow, the Earls of Angus and Argyll, Lord Hailes, and Lord Lyle; all authorised to treat for the prince. By it the dissensions and discords of both parties were to be drawn to unity and concord, so that love and favour might stand between the great barons of both sides and especially between the Earl of Buchan and Lord Lyle.

[1] Buchan received two payments of £26. 13s. 4d. and £40 respectively in the Michaelmas Term of 1487-8 (Tellers Rolls, E 405, 75, Mich. Term, 3 Henry VII, Pierson mem. 2 dorso and Stokes mem. 2). In December, 1487, he was paid 20 marks (Campbell, *Materials*, II, 219). The phrase "Comes de Boughan in partibus Scocie oriundus" suggests that he may have been domiciled in England for some time.

[2] Campbell, *Materials*, II, 300.   [3] *Exchequer Rolls*, X, 33.

[4] Buchanan, ed. Aikman, II, 218.

[5] *Acts Parl. Scot.* II, 210. Paraphrased in G. G. Smith's *Days of James IV*, p. 6.

The truce was useless to the King because the lords retained the person of the Prince. Ferrerius writes that James III had sent out envoys, before his departure for the north, to Henry VII, Charles VIII of France and to the Pope,[1] begging for assistance by arms or authority. On the eve of the Feast of St George, which in 1488 was kept by Henry VII at Windsor on April 27,[2] an ambassador of the King of Scots "who is now in grete trobyll be hys son and other of the lordes of hys Londe"[3] "sat at the Borde in the medell of the Hall".[4] This ambassador was Lord Bothwell.

Wyatt, who had probably travelled from Scotland with Bothwell, was, on May 5, appointed with John Baltiswell, Clerk of the Council, as ambassador to treat with Scotland for a truce.[5] Wyatt and Bothwell were given payments of £13. 6s. 8d. and £10 respectively for expenses in the same writ of privy seal of June 25,[6] suggesting that they may have travelled back to Scotland together. Entered on the Scots Rolls of May, 1488, following next after the commission to Baltiswell and Wyatt, is a safe-conduct[7] into England for the following Scottish ambassadors: Robert, Bishop of Glasgow; George Browne, Bishop of Dunkeld; Colin, Earl of Argyll, Chancellor of Scotland; Patrick, Lord Hailes; Robert, Lord Lyle; Matthew Stuart, Master of Darnley; and Alexander, Master of Hume, with a retinue of 160 persons. These men were obviously envoys on behalf of the Prince's faction and probably the very same persons with whom Baltiswell and Wyatt were appointed to negotiate in answer to James III's request to Henry VII for help through Bothwell. As Argyll is erroneously entitled "Chancellor of Scotland", in which office he had been superseded by Elphinstone in the preceding February, the demand for the safe-conduct must have been made from Scotland before that date and before civil war had broken out. It may have been asked for at the time when James III, according to Buchanan, was flattering his rebel nobles.[8] Henry did not respond in any hurry. He

---

[1] Ferrerius, 399 b. As early as January 29, 1487/8, a papal legate was expected in Scotland. See *Acts Parl. Scot.* II, 183.
[2] Campbell, *Materials*, II, 290.
[3] *Paston Letters*, III, 904.
[4] Leland, *Collectanea*, IV, 240.
[5] *Rot. Scot.* II, 485.
[6] Campbell, *Materials*, II, p. 329.
[7] *Rot. Scot.* II, 485.
[8] Buchanan, ed. Aikman, II, 217.

waited to issue his safe-conduct till early May, during the short period after the first Truce of Blackness, when both parties were nominally at peace and James III wanted Henry's offices of mediation with his enemies.

Drummond put Henry VII's arguments into the mouth of his emissaries in a flowery speech of his own,[1] and there is no record evidence for this embassy apart from the commission and the payments to Baltiswell and Wyatt. Baltiswell had an authorisation of £50 by letters of Privy Seal,[2] in the Easter Term, as well as £20 in the Michaelmas Term, for his expenses as ambassador to Scotland[3]. No answer to James III from the French King has been preserved. The Pope's legate, Adrian de Castello, was stopped in London by the news of James's death,[4] and Drummond[1] writes that the fear of his arrival spurred the rebels on to decide their quarrel by battle, without loss of time. As in 1487, the Pope was on James III's side, for he sent letters of censure to the Abbots of the monasteries in the diocese of Glasgow and to the Chancellor of the Cathedral because they had taken part with the rebels against their King.[5]

The first Truce of Blackness, signed in late April or early May, was broken within a fortnight; for on May 18, the King was already back in Edinburgh giving rewards to the men who had helped him at the subsequent battle of Blackness.[6] This skirmish was a trifling affair, so unimportant that the chroniclers without exception have not differentiated it from the Battle of Sauchieburn of June 11. Only the trials in Parliament of Bothwell, Buchan and Ross mention the different stages and give the chronology.[7] The rebels' case was that the Truce of Blackness, secured peaceably by the mediation of Atholl, had been broken by the advice of Buchan, Bothwell and Ross; whereupon the

---

[1] Drummond of Hawthornden, pp. 58–9.
[2] P.R.O. E 403, 2558, fol. 11 v., Easter Term, 3 Henry VII.
[3] *Ibid.* fol. 13 v.
[4] Polydore Vergil. Adrian was a kinsman of Polydore and recommended him as historian to Henry VII. E. A. Whitney and P. P. Cram, "The Will of Polydore Vergil", *Royal Historical Society's Transactions*, Fourth Series, XI, 1928, p. 122.
[5] Wilkins, *Concilia*, III, 634.
[6] *Great Seal Register*, 1424–1513, no. 1725.
[7] *Acts Parl. Scot.* II, 201, 204.

Earls of Huntley, Erroll, Marischal and Glamis, who had signed the terms for James III, gave up their allegiance and went back to their homes. A second battle was fought at Blackness, after which a new pact was made. This was the skirmish before May 18, followed by the second pact, for which Buchan, William Lord Ruthven, Thomas Fotheringham and William Murray were given as hostages. According to the testimony of the trials, this truce was broken again by the advice of Bothwell and Ross, and then James III went to Edinburgh, leaving Buchan a prisoner in the hands of his enemies. By grants under the Great Seal from Edinburgh on May 18, the Earl of Crawford obtained the Dukedom of Montrose for his services at Blackness.[1] Thomas Trumbull received a grant of land for carrying the King's standard,[2] and James Dunbar and James Innes were rewarded for the defence of the royal person.[3] On May 28 Lord Kilmaurs was made Earl of Glencairn.[4]

In the judgment pronounced on Bothwell by Parliament in the following October[5] he was found guilty in all points and articles of the summons "except the tyme of the blaknes". He had been at Windsor on April 27, during the first truce; and as Carlisle was a twelve days' journey from London,[6] and the Forth another third of the way, it would have been barely possible for him to take part in the second battle at Blackness before May 18. The summons indicts him for his mission to England to invite Henry VII to invade and conquer Scotland. Buchanan wrote that ships were sent as soon as rumour reached England of the distracted affairs in Scotland,[7] though there is no evidence for this in Henry VII's Exchequer payments; they would, in any case, have been too late.

Pitscottie gives the best account of the third battle between the factions, at Sauchieburn,[8] on June 11; although the Earl of Huntley, who had changed sides after Blackness, and Atholl and

---

[1] *Great Seal Register*, 1424–1513, I, no. 1725.
[2] *Ibid.* I, no. 1723.
[3] *Ibid.* I, nos. 1727, 1730.
[4] Balfour Paul, *Scots Peerage*; from Kilkerran Papers, IV, 233.
[5] *Acts Parl. Scot.* II, 203.
[6] P.R.O. Tellers Rolls, E 405, 76, Easter Term, 3 Henry VII, mem. 4 dorso.
[7] Buchanan, ed. Aikman, II, 223.
[8] For a large scale map see Thomas Miller, *The Site of the Battle of Bannockburn*; published for the Historical Association, 1931.

Ruthven, said to have been hostages, are represented by him as fighting in the King's army. The Prince gave orders that no one should lay violent hands upon his father,[1] and burst into tears when he heard of the King's cruel murder while flying from the battlefield.[2] But there was no dislocation of the Government. Most of James III's party subscribed to the new régime, being given six weeks in which to do so. It was not till August 6 that summonses were served on the irreconcilables:[3] John Ross of Montgrenan, the first King's Advocate; Lord Bothwell, the Earl of Buchan, the Laird of Innermeath, Thomas Fotheringham, Lord Forbes, the Laird of Innes, Sir Alexander Dunbar, the Laird of Amisfield, Stephen Lockart, Cuthbert Murray, the Laird of Cockpool, John Murray and James Hommyll, the tailor who had survived the Lauder hangings. Pitscottie gives the only account of the trial of David Lindsay of the Byres, his great-uncle.[4]

The lords who attended James IV's first Parliament in October, 1488, had all been partisans of the rebels with the exception of Bishop Elphinstone. On October 9 the proceedings started with the trial of Buchan for treason. He was present, having been a hostage, pleaded guilty, and obtained a pardon for his offences, which were recited in full.[5] The summonses of Bothwell and John Ross of Montgrenan, together with the forfeitures pronounced upon them, are the only ones extant.[6] They did not appear for trial and are known to have taken refuge at the Court of Henry VII. In 1488 "the Lorde Bothvile, a Scottishman, kept his all Hallowtide" at Windsor with the King.[7] But their two summonses supplement the indictment of Buchan in several respects, giving the sequence of events after the second Pact at Blackness when Buchan ceased to be an actor. A piecing together of the three cases where they overlap gives the best consecutive account of the stages leading to the Battle of Sauchieburn.[8] The historical narratives most closely parallel

---

[1] Ferrerius, 400 b.   [2] *Ibid.* 401.
[3] *Lord High Treasurer's Accounts*, I, 92, 93. Pitscottie, I, 219, gives the number as 28 lords and 160 barons.
[4] Pitscottie, I, 219–25; see note, II, 370.
[5] *Acts Parl. Scot.* II, 201. Appendix I.
[6] *Ibid.* II, 201, 204. Appendix I.
[7] Leland, *Collectanea*, IV, 243.   [8] See Appendix I

to the trials are those of Buchanan and Drummond of Haw-thornden, who, when writing of the death of the Earl of Mar in 1479, added that he had followed the contemporary records of Bishop Elphinstone.[1]

The charge of intrigue with England brought against James III and his agents by the Parliament of James IV has been believed by one historian, Hill Burton; and even he could only cite the character of John Ramsay, Lord Bothwell, in its defence. Here his intuition served him well; but the record evidence has been universally neglected. Buchan's subsidies from Henry VII in 1487 have never been noticed; neither has Bothwell's journey to Windsor in April, 1488. No one has considered Wyatt's well-known dealings with Bothwell, when he was an English spy in 1497,[2] in relation to the coupling of their names in 1488. The cumulative evidence on this point, to which Wyatt's activities in 1489[3] form the clue, can scarcely be disregarded. By their treachery at Lauder and afterwards, the Scottish nobles drove James III to seek mediation and finally military help from the King who owed him gratitude for an army at Bosworth; the natural intermediary was his most intimate friend and survivor from the Lauder massacre, John Ramsay, Lord Bothwell.

The Scots Parliament, after debating the Terms of Blackness and the breaking of the pacts, came to the foregone conclusion that James IV and his barons were innocent of slaughter on the field of Stirling and ordered that the three estates should give their seals with the King's Great Seal to be shown to the Pope and the Kings of France, Spain, Denmark and other realms.[4] Although Elphinstone had helped James III as long as he was alive, his loyalty was to Scotland, and he agreed to represent James IV on this important mission. In December, 1489, he was rewarded on his return from France, England, Burgundy and Austria.[5]

The truce[6] between Scotland and England of July 26, 1488, widely quoted as signed for James IV by Elphinstone, *Bothwell, John Ross of Montgrenan*, and others, was never negotiated at

---

[1] Drummond of Hawthornden, p. 48. See Bibliography, p. xxiii.
[2] p. 103.   [3] Chapter II, pp. 28–9.
[4] *Acts Parl. Scot.* II, 211.
[5] *Great Seal Register*, 1424–1513, no. 1910.
[6] *Foedera*, XII, 346. See Appendix II, no. 8.

all. The unconscious invention of it is due to Rymer,[1] who post-dated in *Foedera* the truce of July 26, *1486*, copied from the Scots Rolls.[2] A situation in which Bothwell and John Ross, fugitives at the English Court, could have acted as James IV's ambassadors to Henry VII, six weeks after Sauchieburn and only eleven days before they were summoned by the King of Scots for high treason on a charge of the "inbringing of Inglishmen" into Scotland, is of course unintelligible. Such nonsense defied elucidation; and this error in the eighteenth-century publication of *one* document has clouded the whole subject of Anglo-Scottish relations in the last years of James III.

[1] *Foedera*, XII, 346. See Appendix II, no. 8.
[2] *Rot. Scot.* II, 473.

CHAPTER II

HENRY VII'S RELATIONS WITH JAMES IV
OF SCOTLAND, 1488-93

One of the most human passages of Pitscottie's history describes young King James IV at Stirling Castle, listening daily to the Chaplains of the Chapel Royal, on which James III had lavished all his love, deploring and lamenting the death of his father. His conscience moved him to consult the Dean and wear for ever after a belt of iron, adding yearly to its weight. Although only sixteen years of age at his accession, his sorrow seems to have modified the policy of Angus, Hepburn and Hume, whom Buchanan[1] mentions as the persons who "governed the young King", and who represented the strongest anti-English element in Scotland. It is difficult to imagine these hardened murderers suffering remorse for a course of action that had led to the tragedy of Sauchieburn. Yet their revolutionary government passed an act of Parliament forbidding any hurt or prejudice to the heirs of those who had fought with James III at Stirling.[2] It may be that they felt themselves none too secure in the saddle, although for the moment the majority of the late King's party seemed to have accepted the new régime with loyalty. Elphinstone was supplanted as Chancellor by Argyll, who had held the office from 1483 till the beginning of 1488; but after a short retirement to his see at Aberdeen, "he was recalled to the Court and appointed Privy Councillor to James the Fourth, being as kindly received by the King and with as much respect as he had formerly enjoyed from his royal father".[3] Andrew Wood, whose ships had been the mainstay of James III, became the equally loyal servant of his son; and in July, his lands at Largo were confirmed to him.[4] Only a handful of irreconcilables were indicted for treason in James IV's first Parliament of October 1488.

[1] Buchanan, ed. Aikman, II, 223.
[2] *Acts Parl. Scot.* II, 211.
[3] Moir, *Boece's Lives*, p. 79.
[4] *Great Seal Register*, 1424-1513, no. 1758, July 27, 1488.

In England, Henry VII was showing what sympathy he could with James III's faithful followers, "the divers Scotts that came to the King for relief".[1] He made payments to Lady Bothwell[2] in the Michaelmas Term of 1488, and Bothwell received a pension of 100 marks and acted as an English agent for the rest of his life. On January 15, 1488/9, Henry wrote to the Pope[3] that his affection for the memory of James King of Scots caused him not only to lament the shameful murder of that prince, but to commiserate his faithful attendants, who by no fault of theirs had incurred the calamity of exile, and were unjustly punished. Therefore, as Sir John Ross of Montgrenan, who had been sent as ambassador to England to perpetuate the peace between himself and James III, was doomed to exile, because, like a faithful servant, he had adhered to his sovereign—he implored him to write to the King, then reigning over the Scots, to receive Sir John Ross into his kingdom and restore him to his former estate. Ross was given a grant of £10 from Henry VII's Exchequer towards the costs of his journey to Rome,[4] and probably carried this letter with him. His mission must have met with success, for rapid reinstatement followed.[5]

Although the nobles ruling Scotland for James IV had justified their assumption of power in Parliament by pleading James III's pro-English policy, a three years' truce between England and Scotland was negotiated four months later. The preliminaries were slow, for in lieu of the treaty supposed by Rymer to have been signed on July 26, six weeks after the murder, no less than three months were allowed to elapse after Sauchieburn before Baltiswell, William Tyler and others were appointed ambassadors to treat for peace.[6] During this interval the Border fortress of Carlisle was repaired at a cost of £26. 13s. 4d.,[7] two gunners being stationed there from August 7 to October 17.[7] Berwick was provisioned on September 25,[8] and the *Mary Huberd* sent

---

[1] Leland, *Collectanea*, IV, 243.
[2] Bain, IV, 1544. This wife is not mentioned in G.E.C. In the Michaelmas Term of 1489 Thomas Turnbull was given an annuity of £40 by Henry VII. (P.R.O. E 403, 2558, fol. 19.)
[3] *Venetian Calendar*, I, 549.   [4] Campbell, *Materials*, II, 397.
[5] *Great Seal Register*, 1424–1513, nos. 1904, 1989.
[6] *Rot. Scot.* II, 487.
[7] Tellers Rolls, E 405, 76, Easter Term, 3 Henry VII, mem. 4 dorso.
[8] *Rot. Scot.* II, 487.

to guard the town during the King's pleasure.[1] The peace commissioners met at Coldstream on September 23,[2] a truce for three years being signed on October 3 and confirmed at Westminster.[3]

In spite of the generosity shown to the late King's party, James IV's Government naturally rewarded its own adherents with the offices of State and lands of the forfeited rebels. The lordships of Bothwell and Crichton were united into the earldom of Bothwell and bestowed on Patrick Hepburn, Lord Hailes.[4] Lord Lyle was made Great Justiciar, and in October, 1488, the Earl of Lennox and his son, Matthew Stuart, received the custody of the Royal Castle of Dumbarton.[5] It was inevitable that some of James IV's friends should be disappointed with their rewards, and before long these merged their grumbles with the voices of such of the late King's adherents as had accepted the new régime only to avoid trial and forfeiture. There was also in certain quarters a genuine horror that "no punishment had been imposed on the treasonable vile persons who put their hands violently on the King's most noble person".[6]

The early simmering of the new rebellion is shown in a letter to Henry VII from Alexander, Master of Huntley, son of George, Earl of Huntley, a signatory to the Blackness Truce. The letter is dated January 8, without a year;[7] but the memory of James III's death was fresh in the mind of the writer and justifies Busch's dating of 1489.[8] Young Huntley appealed to Henry for help on the ground of the tenderness of blood between James III and himself and the honour that every anointed Prince and King should keep to others, adding that the Earl of Buchan was informed at length of all their plans. During the winter of 1488-9 Alexander, Lord Forbes, a supporter of the late King, toured the north of Scotland, to incite the people to rebellion

[1] Tellers Rolls, E 405, 75, Mich. Term, 4 Henry VII, Stokes mem. 2.
[2] *Treasurer's Accounts, Scotland*, I, lxxx.
[3] *Rot. Scot.* II, 488-90.   [4] *Acts Parl. Scot.* II, 205.
[5] *Great Seal Register, 1424-1513*, no. 1794.
[6] A minute adopted by public meeting at Aberdeen on September 12, 1489. See Stuart, *The Council Register of Aberdeen, 1398-1570*, 45, and Moir, *Boece's Lives*, p. 154.
[7] Printed in Pinkerton, *History of Scotland*, under the year 1491, II, Appendix I, from B.M. Cotton, Caligula, B III, 19.
[8] Busch, *England under the Tudors*, p. 344.

by displaying the bloody shirt in which James III had been murdered.[1] By March, 1488/9, and perhaps in answer to Huntley's letter, Henry VII had decided to give some assistance, direct or indirect, to the rebels; for in spite of the truce with James IV, the Earl of Northumberland, the all-powerful Warden-General of the Marches, at the council meeting in March, "had endented with the King for the keeping out of the Scots and warring on them and was to have large money".[2]

By the beginning of April, Lord Lyle had garrisoned his Castle of Duchal in Kilmalcolm against James IV; Lennox had armed Crookston Castle, near Paisley, and was holding the royal stronghold of Dumbarton on the Clyde against the King. But the Earl of Northumberland's murder on April 28, during an insurrection in Yorkshire, and the consequent dislocation of the north, must have prevented anything effective being done by England to embarrass James IV and so help the insurgents. Every detail of the King's proceedings against Duchal and Crookston during May and June can be followed in the Lord Treasurer's Accounts.[3] On June 26, Lyle, Lennox and the other rebels were forfeited in Parliament[4] and the next day James IV granted Lyle's lands to the Earl of Buchan,[5] who was thus early completely restored to favour after his trial for treason. Buchan was a remarkably competent traitor, and remained unsuspected at James IV's Court for the rest of his life, although acting continuously as Henry VII's spy.[6]

Argyll was sent to bombard Dumbarton, while James went in person to Duchal, which capitulated before July 27.[7] Argyll was less successful, for the rebels in Dumbarton Castle made a bold sally and burnt the town.[8] The Scots King summoned the lords to come to him at Dumbarton on September 9,[9] and Henry VII issued safe-conducts for England to Lyle, Crichton and Matthew Stuart on September 6,[10] in view, perhaps, of the fall of the fortress when it should once again be invested.

---

[1] Buchanan, ed. Aikman, II, 225.   [2] *Paston Letters*, III, 908. See p. 34.
[3] *Treasurer's Accounts*, I, lxxxviii–xci.   [4] *Acts Parl. Scot.* II, 213.
[5] *Great Seal Register*, 1424–1513, 1857–8.
[6] *G.E.C.* says Buchan's death occurred between January, 1497, and January, 1499.
[7] *Treasurer's Accounts*, I, 117.   [8] *Acts Parl. Scot.* XII, 34.
[9] *Treasurer's Accounts*, I, 119.   [10] *Rot. Scot.* II, 492.

James IV received letters from the Earl of Huntley,[1] on September 19 and October 31, during the time that his son, the Master of Huntley, was a rebel in Dumbarton.[2] Meanwhile the Earl of Lennox with 2000 men had turned north from Dumbarton to collect reinforcements and was defeated near Tilly Moss in the parish of Aberfoyle by James's ally Lord Drummond.[3] His whole force was killed or captured about October 12. Articles, prepared by Lennox and endorsed as sent to the King after the "field of the mos", still exist in the Lennox Charter Chest.[4] They voice the rebels' dissatisfaction with a number of persons who were grasping the royal authority and treasure, and had tried to destroy the King, his brother, the Archbishop of St Andrews,[5] and "the whole barons and nobles of this realm".

With the rebel army defeated in the field, the King's Government made a final attack upon Dumbarton. James IV rode to besiege it in person in a black satin doublet on October 18,[6] being present from November 23 till its fall in mid-December.[7] The operations from the Scots side can be followed in the Treasurer's Accounts. Those on the English side have hitherto passed unnoticed, although they throw some light on Henry VII's methods and policy. It must be remembered that Henry was technically at peace with James. On September 5 he had appointed seven commissioners to confer with the Scots over the continual fishery disputes on the Eske;[8] and on the 10th he issued safe-conducts to the Bishop of Glasgow and six others to come to England with eighty persons, possibly on the same business.[9] Nevertheless, in the Michaelmas Term of 1489/90, he paid John Ramsay (whom, in spite of his forfeiture, he still called "Lord Bothwell"), Sir Adam Forman, John Ledell, a Scot, and Henry Wyatt, Clerk of his Jewels, to go to Dum-

---

[1] *Treasurer's Accounts*, I, 120, 123.
[2] James IV wrote to Arbuthnot of Arbuthnot on September 22 that the Earl Marischal, the Master of Huntley, Lord Forbes and others were making "certain ligs and bands at Owr Castell of Dunbertane". Printed in Nisbet's *Heraldry*, II, Appendix, p. 89.
[3] Drummond of Hawthornden, p. 64.
[4] Printed by Sir William Fraser, *The Lennox Book*, II, 128–31.
[5] William Schevez.   [6] *Treasurer's Accounts*, I, 142.
[7] *Ibid.* I, 125, 126.
[8] *Rot. Scot.* II, 491.   [9] *Ibid.* II, 492.

barton with a boatload of munitions for the reinforcement of the rebels.[1] Wyatt, who provided a cargo of bows and arrows, iron, lead and cloth, for the expedition, at a cost of £320. 1s. 0d., received £192. 8s. 0d. on account.[1] Wyatt was no novice as an agent of Henry VII in Scotland,[2] and it is not surprising to find his pre-Sauchieburn connection with Bothwell subsisting under the new conditions. These entries in the Tellers Rolls cast a strong light backwards on Henry VII's whole Scottish policy. If he was surreptitiously helping James IV's rebels with munitions in 1489, the action is likely to have been the outcome of an earlier association with these same men when they were supporting James III. The indictments of Bothwell and Ross in 1488, and Henry VII's protection of them both after their forfeiture, afford strong evidence of the side he had then taken. And when, in the following year, he subsidised Bothwell and Wyatt on a joint expedition to Dumbarton, to provision the fortress that was the backbone of the rebels' resistance to James IV, the chain of evidence seems complete.

[1] Tellers Rolls, E 405, 78, Mich. Term, 5 Henry VII, Pierson mem. 3:

"Eidem domino Bothewell misso usque Castrum de Donbreteyn in Scocia ex diversis consideracionibus Regi et concilio suo moventibus pro custis et expensis suis in hac parte per manus proprias.   xx li.

"Adam fforman militi de illis V marcas de mense in mensem solvendis per breve de privato sigillo termino michaelis Anno iiijto per manus proprias.
                                                                                        vi li xiiis iiii d.

"Eidem Adam pro custis et expensis suis misso cum prefato domino Bothewell usque castrum predictum ex consideracione predicta per manus proprias.   vi li xiiis iiii d.

"Johanni Ledell de partibus Scocie de Regardo pro custis et expensis suis misso cum prefato domino Bothewell per manus proprias.   vi li xiiis iiii d.

"henrico Wyot clerico jocalium Regis misso usque castrum predictum in comitiva predicti domini Bothewell et alibi ex diversis consideracionibus Regi et concilio suo specialiter moventibus pro custis et expensis suis per manus proprias.   xiii li vis viii d.

"Eidem henrico in partem solucionis φφφ xx li xii d sibi appunctorum per Regem super provisione frumenti brasii ferri plumbii cerisgomierum et panni lanii ac aliarum rerum necnon arcuum et sagutarum usque castrum predictum cariandorum per manus proprias.   x x
                                                                                       φiiii xii li viii s."

The word "cerisgomierum" is in no dictionary, but is probably to be translated "of measures of wax"—I owe this interpretation to Dr Charles Cotton, F.S.A.

These entries are given as they stand as a specimen of the Tellers Rolls.
[2] See pp. 7–8, 16, 18.

The royal cargo of munitions went by sea from Chester,[1] and there is no proof that it reached its destination. An English ship chased and damaged a ship of James IV's at Dumbarton,[2] during the siege, and was probably the vessel bearing Wyatt and Bothwell. Dumbarton surrendered to James IV before Christmas, and once more unusual clemency was shown by the victors. Pardons were issued by the Scots Parliament to 129 rebels by name in the following February 1489/90.[3] The forfeitures pronounced against Lennox, Matthew Stuart and Lord Lyle in the Parliament of June 26, 1489, were rescinded in the same month,[4] the King commanding the process to be erased from the Books of Parliament.

The great sea captain Andrew Wood was active against England during these same years. Pitscottie gives a circumstantial account of his capture of five English cruisers off Dunbar, with his *Flower* and *Yellow Carvel*, about the same time as Drummond's victory at Tilly Moss. Pitscottie was the friend and neighbour of Andrew Wood's son, and Hume Brown accepts his story of the battle without question.[5] A search in the Tellers Rolls of the Exchequer for the year has revealed no sign of payment by Henry VII for such an expedition to Scottish waters. In truth, the ships were neither the King's, nor in the King's service, as told by Pitscottie and Buchanan, but merchant ships, guilty of piracy.[6] The action was commemorated in a ballad:[7]

> The battle fiercely it was fought
> Near to the Craig of Bass
> When we next fight the English loons,
> May nae waur come to pass.

---

[1] Tellers Rolls, E 405, 77, Easter Term, 5 Henry VII, mem. 2: "henrico Wyott super provisione diversorum victualium ac abillimentarum guerrae et Navium apud Cestre termino Michaelis ultimo predicto ex mandato Regis et avisamenti Concilii sui pro defensione regni contra Scotos recepta denariorum de Willelmo Stanley milite Camerario Cestris Cli." (This must be the £100 from Sir William Stanley, paid into the Exchequer by the hand of Wyatt, who got it back again. Exchequer E 36, 124, fol. 9.)

[2] The repairs were paid for on February 18, 1489/90; *Treasurer's Accounts*, I, 129.   [3] *Acts Parl. Scot.* XII, 33, 34.

[4] *Ibid.* II, 217. (Beware of *Carmichaels' Tracts*, which print some of these documents under the wrong dates.)

[5] Hume Brown, *History of Scotland*, I, 241.

[6] *D.N.B.* "Andrew Wood", by J. K. Laughton.

[7] Quoted in his *History of Fife and Kinross* by A. J. G. Mackay, p. 47. I have searched in vain for the complete ballad. Tytler, *History of Scotland*, II, 109, shifted the scene to the Clyde.

Buchanan confounded this skirmish with a further exploit by Andrew Wood on August 10, 1490.[1] Stephen Bull had volunteered to Henry VII to wipe out the stain of the previous English disgrace; but after a magnificent fight, described with gusto by Pitscottie, his three ships were defeated by the *Flower* and *Yellow Carvel.* Wood sent Bull and all his men back to Henry with gifts of gold and silver. The English were naturally silent about this affair, but Henry VII repaid Bull £6 for his expenses on the sea in the Michaelmas Term of 1490–1.[2] Wood was rewarded by James IV with additional grants of land in Largo in March 1490/1,[3] and received a licence on May 18 to fortify a castle on the Forth with iron gates, on account of his great services and the cost he had been at constructing defences with English prisoners at his own expense.[4]

Many historians of Scotland ignore Anglo-Scottish relations between 1489 and the troubles of 1495, when Perkin Warbeck, the impersonator of Richard, Duke of York, the second son of Edward IV, first landed in Scotland. Only Tytler and Lang[5] trace the possible connection of James IV with the pretensions of Perkin as early as November, 1488, when he gave an audience to forty-two Englishmen at the request of Margaret, Dowager Duchess of Burgundy, the widow of Charles the Bold, the sister of Edward IV, the aunt of the Earl of Lincoln, and of Richard de la Pole, and the chief backer of the Yorkist faction in England.[6] Hall, translating Polydore Vergil, calls her "that old venomous serpent, ever being the sower of sedition and beginner of rebellion against the King of England". Her step-son-in-law, the Emperor Maximilian, is reported to have told the Milanese envoy at his Court that she was the mother of Perkin by the Bishop of Cambrai,[7] in which case he might still have been brought up by foster-parents at Tournai, the John and Katharine Osbeck known by record evidence. She had openly supported

---

[1] Used as the basis of *The Yellow Frigate* by James Grant. He quotes as an additional source, "an old MS among the records of the Scottish Court of Admiralty".

[2] P.R.O. E 403, 2558, fol. 25.

[3] *Great Seal Register*, 1424–1513, no. 2019.

[4] *Ibid.* 2040, and *Acts Parl. Scot.* II, 227, 270.

[5] Lang, *History of Scotland*, I, 367.

[6] *Great Seal Register*, 1424–1513, no. 1798.

[7] Pollard, *Henry VII*, I, p. xxii.

the risings of Lovell and of Simnel, and may perhaps have begun, as early as 1488, to prepare for the next conspiracy, which ultimately grew into that of Perkin Warbeck, although at first an impersonator of the imprisoned Earl of Warwick, son of Richard III's brother, the Duke of Clarence, was probably the claimant she had in view. The aid of James IV's anti-Tudor advisers in Scotland would naturally have been enlisted for such a project, and James received letters from the Duchess in December, 1488 and September, 1489.[1] These transactions may have been connected with a mysterious plot exposed in December, 1489, when the Abbot of Abingdon and John Maine were hanged for conspiracy to set the Earl of Warwick free.[2]

James IV can hardly have been ignorant of the help Henry VII had tried to give his rebels at Dumbarton. In May, 1490, he excused himself to the Pope from contributing to a Crusade against the Turk, on the ground that since his accession "our old enemies in England also harassed my subjects, whom I have protected against the inroads of their adversaries by my assiduous exertions".[3] Yet on December 15, 1489, two days after he had left Dumbarton on its surrender, James made a present of hawks to the English King,[4] and Henry paid £12. 12s. 1d. for a bit and harness and a purple velvet silk cloth, for his royal adversary's coucher.[5] Shortly after Christmas, and again in mid-Lent, Scottish officers of arms were present with the King at Westminster.[6] The Earl of Angus (who had a licence to come to England on pilgrimage)[7] and Lyon Herald arrived in January 1489/90;[8] Ross Herald was rewarded in the Easter Term.[9] Maybe, as a result of these visits, the Scots Parliament in February considered methods for keeping the truce with England on the borders.[10]

Henry VII had adopted Richard III's policy of dividing the Marches of Scotland from Yorkshire and governing them himself

---

[1] *Treasurer's Accounts*, I, 99, 120 and lxxxv.
[2] *Rot. Parl.* VI, 436–7. [3] *Venetian Calendar*, I, 568.
[4] *Treasurer's Accounts*, I, 126.
[5] Tellers Rolls, E 405, 78, Mich. Term, 5 Henry VII, Pierson mem. 3.
[6] Leland, *Collectanea*, IV, 256–7.
[7] *Rot. Scot.* II, 491. Sept. 6, 1489.
[8] Tellers Rolls, E 405, 78, Mich. Term, 5 Henry VII, Pierson mem. 6.
[9] *Ibid.* E 405, 77, Easter Term, 5 Henry VII, mem. 6 dorso.
[10] *Acts Parl. Scot.* II, 220.

through the King's Lieutenant in the Northern Parts.[1] The Bishop Palatine of Durham had originally been held responsible for the raising of county troops in defence of the Scottish Border. But in 1296 the office of Warden of the Marches was created for this purpose and a little later the custody of the Royal Castle of Carlisle was given to the Warden of the West March and that of Berwick to the Warden of the East and Middle Marches. Since the fourteenth century the latter office had been quasi-hereditary in the great Percy family. Richard III had established royal authority in the north and made himself very popular, so that the problem for his Lancastrian opponent and successor in those parts was peculiarly difficult. By January, 1486, Henry found it expedient to release the Yorkist Earl of Northumberland from the Tower and re-establish him as Lieutenant-General of the East and Middle Marches, the offices with which Richard III had originally rewarded his services in helping him to the throne.

This bold step is a striking illustration of the King's wisdom and courage, although he soon put limitations upon Northumberland's possible abuse of power. These checks give the first inkling of Henry's future administrative policy on the outskirts of his realm. On May 3, 1486, three months after the Earl's reappointment, Lord Dacre was made King's Deputy in the Office of Warden of Carlisle or of the West Marches,[2] while Sir Richard Salkeld, the Constable of Carlisle, continued to be paid for the safe-keeping of the Marches as well as of the castle till the Easter term of 1487.[3] The Warden of the East Marches had hitherto been *ipso facto* Governor of the Castle and City of Berwick, the Earl of Northumberland in that capacity receiving payments of £800 from the Exchequer in 1486-7.[4]

[1] Rachel Reid, *Council in the North*, p. 60. For the government of the North see also Rachel Reid, "Office of the Warden of the Marches", *E.H.R.* xxxii, and Scott Thomson, "The Bishops of Durham and the office of Lord Lieutenant in the 17th century", *E.H.R.* vol. xl.

[2] *Rot. Scot.* ii, 472. Renewed on July 18, 1486, in 1487, in 1488 and twice in 1491. *Ibid.* ii, 472, 479, 486, 498, 501.

[3] Tellers Rolls, E 405, 75, Mich. Term, 1 Henry VII, mem. 2; E 405, 75, Easter Term, 2 Henry VII, mem. 1 dorso.

[4] *Ibid.* 2 Henry VII, Pierson mems. 3 and 4; Page mem. 2; Easter Term, 2 Henry VII, Pierson mem. 2.

A letter of Richard Fox[1] to Wolsey, thirty-four years later, mentions that in the first year of Henry VII's reign, and before he, himself, became Keeper of the Privy Seal, the Earl had indented for the keeping of the East and Middle Marches and for the town of Berwick, at his whole cost and charge, and was paid 3000 marks or 3000 pounds, he did not remember which. And since the death of the Earl of Northumberland in 1489, continues Fox,[2] no man indented for the keeping of the said Borders for the time of war, for Henry VII, being wary, took Berwick into his own hands, and made Sir William Tyler captain. This was the creation of a new office, and the appointment was made before February, 1488.[3] Tyler was Master of the Jewel House, and had been employed two months earlier on the fortifications of Berwick.[4] In 1523 Wolsey was organising the Border against the Scots, and at a critical moment tapped the memory of the former Bishop of Durham, then seventy-seven years old, about a period of which, as Fox said, there were no written records.

In 1489, after the murder of the Earl of Northumberland, the problem of the government of the north was reopened. Henry took this opportunity to instal his infant son Arthur, as titular Warden-General of the Marches,[5] with the Earl of Surrey as Under Warden,[5] so that the way might be clear for the appointment of other royal officials upon his Council, in place of the local Border gentlemen, who had hitherto held the subordinate places in the gift of the Wardens of the Marches. Henry Wyatt was made Captain of the Castle and City of Carlisle, in June 1491,[5] a further step in the subdivision of the administration of the north, parallel to the appointment of Tyler at Berwick. His commission, attested by the King, is different in form from the earlier commission to a governor or warden of a castle, witnessed by the Treasurer.[6]

Such independent appointments of royal officials were paid for by Henry's assignments of the revenues of the manors which had belonged to Richard, Duke of Gloucester, when he governed

---

[1] Allen, *Letters of Richard Fox*, no. 81.
[2] See p. 27. [3] *Rot. Scot.* II, 484 a.
[4] Tellers Rolls, E 405, 75, Mich. Term, 2 Henry VII, Stokes mem. 3.
[5] *Rot. Scot.* II, 501, 500 b.
[6] See H. Hall, *Formula Book of Diplomatic Documents*, no. 56.

the north, for the maintenance of Berwick and Carlisle. Sir Richard Cholmeley had been made Receiver-General of these manors and Chamberlain of Berwick in January, 1488,[1] spending the money which came into his hands on the garrison of Berwick up to £1908. 14s. 4d. a year.[2] This arrangement was confirmed by the Parliament which met in October, 1495.[2] After 1482, when treachery betrayed it to the English, Berwick had become the all-important gate to the north. Queen Elizabeth still called the governorship "the chief jewel in her crown" and the English tenure of it was the principal bone of contention between James IV and Henry VII. Andrea Trevisano, the Venetian ambassador at Henry's Court, from April, 1497, to March, 1498, wrote in his report on England to the Senate, that all the proceeds of the wool-staple at Calais were assigned to the maintenance of the guard at Calais and Berwick[3] "a singular fortress, which the English possess, beyond the eastern arm of the sea, named the Tweed, in the Kingdom of Scotland.... And now King Henry the Seventh has built a magnificent bridge across the aforesaid arm of the sea, and as he has the command of all the eastern coast, he can throw as many troops as he pleases into the town, which is a very strong place both by nature and art".

In 1584 a German[4] described Berwick as having a long wooden bridge across the Tweed, "whilst in England they have always fine stone bridges even across small rivers". He thought the defences pretty good and called it the only fortified place in England.

Beneath the surface trouble was brewing, for another Yorkist plot was being hatched on the continent, in favour of the Earl of Warwick, the imprisoned son of Richard, Duke of Clarence. In February, 1489/90, James IV received a herald on his way from Ireland to the Court of Margaret of Burgundy,[5] and at the same time Charles VIII of France was actively backing the

---

[1] *Rot. Scot.* II, 482.
[2] *Rot. Parl.* VI, 496 b.
[3] *Italian Relation*, 50, 17.
[4] See "A Journey through England and Scotland made by Leopold von Wedel in the years 1584 and 1585", *Trans. Royal Hist. Soc.* New Series, IX, 239.
[5] *Treasurer's Accounts*, I, lxxxv, 130.

Pretender. Since 1488, Henry's relations with France had been strained owing to complications in Brittany, and on September 15, 1491, one John Taylor, a Devonshire man, then in the service of Charles VIII, wrote from France to his friend Hayes in England, about the French King's plot in favour of Warwick.[1] Perkin did not land in Ireland till November, 1491; but Henry obviously anticipated danger and the co-operation of the Scots with an expected invasion.

The Foreign Roll for 1491 contains elaborate accounts for the provision of war material for Berwick, entered in the audited return of Richard Cholmeley, Chamberlain, and treasurer of the wars in those parts.[2] Among his expenses were the annual fees of various trusted noblemen of the Marches, retained on occasion to help the King's soldiers in Berwick against the invasion of their Scottish enemies. The grand total of expenses on this Roll for the sixth year of Henry's reign was £4343. 13s. 1d., which exceeded the receipts by £478. 15s. 2½d. On May 24, 1491, Wyatt was paid 20 marks for his journey to Carlisle to take up his new work as Captain,[3] and travelled by way of Durham to hand over to the Prior the sum of £1000 in cash for the use of the King in the defence of Berwick and Carlisle against the Scots.[4] In June Henry named commissioners to treat of infractions of the truce with Scotland.[5]

Two exceedingly curious private treaties about this time show that Henry was fostering his agents in that country. In the first negotiation of April 27, 1491, his old tools, John Ramsay and James, Earl of Buchan, were once more involved. This document[6] is a promise by John (still entitled "Lord Bothwell"),

---

[1] *Rot. Parl.* VI, 454. The case of Hayes was tried after January 26, 1491/2, in the second session of the Parliament. Hayes was said to have received Taylor's letter on November 26 "last passed".

[2] P.R.O. E 364, 119, Hilary Term, 7 Henry VII. This is in the middle of a huge unwieldy roll with no pagination.

[3] Tellers Roll, E 405, 78, Easter Term, 6 Henry VII, Butler mem. 1 dorso.

[4] *Ibid.* William Thornton, the carrier, got 62s. 4d. for the expenses of carriage and his three horses.

[5] *Rot. Scot.* II, 500. *Foedera*, XII, 532, dates this wrongly as belonging to 1493. Payments of £66. 13s. 4d. to Urswick and 66s. 8d. to Northumberland Herald for Scottish expenses are made on the Tellers Rolls of Mich. Term, 7 Henry VII, E 405, 78 (Pierson mem. 1 dorso). These are followed by payments in Scotland to the same men of 150 marks and 5 marks respectively (Pierson mem. 5).

[6] *Foedera*, XII, 440.

and Sir Thomas Todd of Sereschaw[1] (moneyer of James IV), to secure the repayment of a loan of £266. 13s. 4d. made by Henry to James, Earl of Buchan, and to Todd, in consideration of their delivering into his hands the King of Scotland and his brother. The mention of this transaction has caused surprise to all commentators. Hill Burton[2] says: "The agreement stands alone among the miscellaneous records preserved in England; we know not what preceded or what followed it, or even whether there was any serious intention to give effect to it". Contemporary scholars think there is no evidence to prove that Buchan was a traitor to his country.[3] But his actions during 1488, revealed in his trial, his continuous receipt of payments from Henry VII before and after James IV's accession, the mention of his name in the Master of Huntley's letter of 1489, and his dealings with Warbeck a few years later, prove a perfectly consistent career as a spy. It was possible that the great-uncle of James IV might have succeeded in handing over the King's person or that of his brother, the Duke of Ross, to Henry VII had he been really in earnest. But Buchan preferred to retain a comfortable position in Scotland and take the King's pay. Henry knew perfectly well that only his old colleague John Ramsay, might have had the power to make him yield his unearned gold.

In the summer of 1491 the Scots sent an important embassy to France[4], including the poet William Dunbar, to renew the ancient treaty between the two countries and look for a wife for the King. It was decided that Scotland should attack England if Henry made war on Charles VIII, and the Milanese envoy in France, writing to Gian Galleazzo Sforza, said that "the chief reason of their coming was to make trouble in England by way of Scotland".[5]

The three years' truce negotiated in October, 1488, between James IV and Henry VII was due to expire on October 23, 1491. The temper of the Scots was obviously against renewal, and the

---

[1] For Todd see *Exchequer Rolls of Scotland*, x, liv footnote.
[2] Hill Burton, *History of Scotland*, III, 198.
[3] Herkless and Hannay, *Archbishops of St Andrews*, I, 177.
[4] *Rot. Scot.* II, 499 and Teulet, *Inventaire des documents relatifs à l'Histoire d'Écosse* (Abbotsford Club), p. 53.
[5] *Milanese Calendar*, nos. 440, 443, 444.

English Parliament, on October 17, passed an Act for the banishment of all Scots, not made denizens within forty days after the proclamation.[1] The preamble to the Act says that whatever agreement be concluded on the part of the King of Scots, is ever under their surest promise broken and not kept; so that it is better to be at open war with them than under a feigned peace. Nevertheless, on October 22, a safe-conduct was issued for the Scots ambassadors to come to England, with the object of renewing the truce.[2] Henry had a second string to his bow, for Angus had fallen out of favour with James IV, who, on July 29, 1491, had ordered him to be imprisoned in his own Castle of Tantallon,[3] on the Forth, where he was besieged on October 11.[4] This did not prevent the traitor of Lauder from making a secret agreement[5] with Henry VII, on November 15, in which he promised to try and persuade James IV to keep the peace with England, and in case of war to deliver his own Castle of Hermitage on the Northumbrian border, commanding the pass into Scotland through Liddesdale, to Henry, in return for compensation in England. No peace was to be concluded between England and Scotland unless Angus was a party to it. Perhaps this pact was made through the intermediary of Wyatt, who from his base at Carlisle, kept in touch with Henry VII's spies in Scotland in 1496, and may have been sent there in 1491 for the same purpose. It is difficult to understand how Angus's good services with James could have been worth anything to England at such a time; and he was actually deprived of Hermitage by exchange with Hailes, Earl Bothwell, on December 29, 1491,[6] as a result, perhaps, of his negotiations with Henry.

---

[1] *Statutes of the Realm*, II, 553.   [2] Bain, IV, 1577.
[3] *Treasurer's Accounts*, I, 180.
[4] *Ibid.* p. 181. For Angus's movements at this time see Fraser, *The Douglas Book*, II, 91–3.
[5] Gairdner, *Richard III*, p. 299. The agreement is printed in Gairdner, *Letters*, I, 385. The dating of the Angus agreement, which in the Record Office document (E 39, Box 100, no. 103) has been mistakenly said to be in a modern hand, is questioned (Fraser, *The Douglas Book*, II, 91, and Preface to *Treasurer's Accounts*, I, p. cvi). The version collated with this one by Gairdner (*Letters*, I, 385) is endorsed "1491" in contemporary writing, and a third facsimile of the endorsement, with the same full date "Nov. 15, 1491", exists in an eighteenth century hand in a bound volume which belonged to Rymer (B.M. Add. MSS 4617, art. 126). This is an exceedingly carefully made copy showing even the tags for the seals.
[6] *Great Seal Register*, 1424–1513, nos. 2072, 2073.

In Scotland the five years' truce, which had been renewed at Coldstream in December, 1491,[1] was never ratified. This must have been due to Perkin Warbeck's landing in Ireland in November, and his correspondence with James IV in March, 1492, while the negotiations were still in progress. In the same month Perkin was received as a prince by Charles VIII in France, given a guard of honour, commanded by a French Scot, the Sieur de Concressault, and collected a small court of disaffected Yorkist adherents. The peace as ratified in Scotland on March 18, 1491/2, was to last till the following November.[2] But on August 4, 1492, on the eve of Henry's sham war with France, a safe-conduct was issued to Scottish envoys,[3] and on the 22nd a commission for the extension of the truce was given to four English ambassadors.[4] On October 17 while Henry was at Calais, in state, with his best jewels,[5] James IV nominated a more impressive body of ambassadors, including Elphinstone,[6] and on November 3, the very day of the signature of the Peace of Étaples with Charles VIII, the truce was prolonged again at Coldstream till April 30, 1494.[7] A clause in the treaty provided for commissioners to meet once more on August 1, 1493, as no certain conclusions had been reached.[8]

The Treaty of Étaples insisted on the banishment of Warbeck from France, whence he removed to Flanders, where, under the aegis of Margaret of Burgundy, Maximilian, King of the Romans, her step-son-in-law, and the Archduke Philip, plans

---

[1] *Rot. Scot.* II, 503–5.   [2] *Foedera*, XII, 473.
[3] *Rot. Scot.* II, 505–6.   [4] *Ibid.* II, 507.
[5] Dietz, p. 78 n. 2. In connection with this journey Henry Wyatt as Clerk of the Jewels was paid £30 out of the Exchequer to have some of them repaired for the King to take with him. All stages of this payment can be traced in the records. The Auditors Privy Seal Book for Easter Term, 7 Henry VII (P.R.O. E 403, 2558, fol. 33), notes the warrant by Privy Seal to the Tellers of the Exchequer authorising the payment of £30 to Henry Wyatt "super provisionem opportunorum per le Juellhouse". The Tellers entered the payment of £30 "super reparationem certarum jocalium pro domino Regis versus viagium suum ad partes Franciae per ipsum factum", on the Tellers Roll for the Easter Term (Tellers Roll, E 405, 78, Stokes mem. 1 dorso) and made the same entry in a paper receipt book, kept at the Exchequer in the Lord Treasurer's Remembrancers Department for audit purposes, and signed by Wyatt with his own hand (P.R.O. E 36, 125, f. 106).
[6] *Foedera*, XII, 489; Bain, IV, 1585.
[7] *Foedera*, XII, 494–7; Bain, IV, 1586.
[8] *Foedera*, XII, 497.

for his invasion grew apace. An English force had been sent to Ireland, and this too must have made Henry more than ever anxious to secure a peace rather than a truce with Scotland. On May 28 commissioners were appointed to treat for a fresh peace.[1] The treaty was signed for seven years at Edinburgh on June 25, by Elphinstone, and ratified in July.[2] But the infractions of the previous truce, which seem by mutual consent to have been made by England,[3] had still to be paid for. On June 25, a promissory note was given at Edinburgh by Sir William Tyler to Henry, Abbot of Cambuskenneth, for the payment of £50 in English money at Wedderburn[4] and on July 31 the receipt for this £50 and 1000 marks was received by the English, the negotiations being at last at an end.[5]

The payment by Henry VII of £134. 6s. 8d. and a gilt cup to Angus, £20 to Lord Sempill, and £20 to Sir Robert Carre, ambassadors from the King of Scots, conducted from Berwick to Sheen and back by Sir William Tyler, in the Michaelmas Term of 1492–3,[6] is not accounted for by the personnel of any of these embassies. The sum paid to Angus is unusually generous for an ambassador, and must have been earned by some considerable service to the King. The Master of the Rolls travelled with him and was paid £40.[7]

If Henry was willing to pay 1000 marks to consummate what Busch has called the useless treaties with Scotland, it only proves his great anxiety at this time. He would have been more anxious still had he known that, in March, 1493, the rich Sir William Stanley, his mother's brother-in-law, who had crowned him at Bosworth, and secured the spoil, had already sent an agent to join Perkin in Flanders and organise his conspiracy.[8] Poynings and Warham were despatched in July to remonstrate with the Archduke Philip against his step-grandmother's encouragement of the Pretender and were very coolly received. Invasion was

---

[1] *Rot. Scot.* II, 508.   [2] *Ibid.* II, 509–12.
[3] These may have included the English raid of 1493, stopped by great floods, mentioned only by Pitscottie, I, 235–7, and II, 373.
[4] P.R.O. Ancient Deeds AS 242. Seal extant.
[5] For all the stages see *Rot. Scot.* II, 512; Bain, IV, 1591, 1592, 1595–7.
[6] Tellers Rolls, E 405, 78, Mich. Term, 8 Henry VII. Bain, IV, 1584.
[7] Tellers Rolls, E 405, 78, Mich. Term, 8 Henry VII, Stokes mem. 4 dorso.
[8] W. A. J. Archbold, "Sir William Stanley and Perkin Warbeck", *E.H.R.* XIV, 529.

thought to be imminent. The King's letter of July 20 from Kenilworth to Sir Gilbert Talbot,[1] requiring him to be ready and fully equipped at a day's warning in case of Perkin's landing, has been proved by Gairdner to belong to the year 1493.[2] An undated and unnoticed letter sent out by Henry from Kenilworth, on July 22, to Dynham, Bray and Robert Lytton,[3] was probably written at the same time, and gives the complementary story of his naval preparations. The addressees were to have the ships of war under Stephen Bull, John Clerk and William Wasshe victualled and "new coppered" at Orwell and waged for six weeks. An inventory was to be made of all ships in the Thames, at Sandwich and at Ipswich. Dynham, Bray and Lytton were to confer as to whether any of the great ships should be sent to sea. Orwell is mentioned because it lay conveniently between Flanders and Scotland to encounter "our rebels and their accomplices in their sailings to and fro". Nothing could more clearly imply the association of Scotland with Perkin's expected invasion from Flanders. Nevertheless, Henry's preparations were doubtless well-known on the continent and two years elapsed before Perkin dared to leave the shelter of the Courts of Margaret of Burgundy and the Emperor Maximilian.

A vital aspect of the defence against the White Rose was the strengthening of the royal power in Ireland, a country still openly Yorkist and eager to welcome Pretenders to the Tudor throne. Henry's policy in that turbulent island forms a separate story.

[1] Gairdner, *Richard III*, p. 275.　　[2] *Ibid.* p. 277.
[3] P.R.O. Ancient Correspondence, LI, no. 110, Appendix IV. Gairdner's reasons for dating Sir Gilbert Talbot's letter apply to this.

CHAPTER III

ANGLO-IRISH RELATIONS, 1485–94

Henry's victory at Bosworth made him "Lord of Ireland", the title by which all English Kings had ruled that ancient realm, since Pope Alexander III gave the island as a present to Henry II. Its partial military conquest at that time had been followed up by John, the real founder of Anglo-Ireland, who established a centralised government from Dublin with English legislative and judicial machinery. Although Ulster and Connaught were never completely conquered from the Irish there was in theory no geographic limit to the English colony in the thirteenth century. But the long absentee reign of Henry III allowed the Anglo-Norman barons to secure their position as overgrown feudal magnates, from which even Edward I was powerless to dislodge them, although under his Justiciar the King's lordship in Ireland reached its culminating point. Neglect of the country by the Anglo-Normans, and their failure to implant English culture had gradually allowed Irish culture to revive and penetrate the English. At the end of the fourteenth century black-rents began to be paid to the Irish chiefs, such as Macmurrough, the descendant of the native King of Leinster. The representatives of the royal families of O'Neill in Ulster, and O'Brien in North Munster reconquered much of their land in the fifteenth century, till by 1500 the Pale had dwindled to a coastal strip fifty miles long by twenty wide.[1] Outside this area, the English colonists, with the exception of the burgesses of a few walled towns, such as Galway, were the subjects of one or other of the three Anglo-Norman earldoms of Kildare, Desmond and Ormond. By the fifteenth century even these three Earls were Kings of provinces after the Gaelic fashion and in varying degrees beyond the control of the English Government.

[1] For a series of maps showing the limits of English rule in Ireland see Philip Wilson, *Beginnings of Modern Ireland*. The boundaries of the four obedient shires constituting the Pale were described in an Act of Parliament passed at Drogheda in 1488, which is quoted in D'Alton's *History of the County of Dublin*, from the "Liber Niger". This Parliament does not figure in the Irish *Statutes at Large*, but a charter of exemplification of one of its Acts is given in Gilbert, *Calendar of Ancient Records of Dublin*, I, 33.

The family of Butler, descending from Hubert Walter's brother Theobald Walter, who held the office of "botelier" in John's household, and had been brought to Ireland on that King's first visit, was the leading Anglo-Irish family during the fourteenth century and the first half of the fifteenth. The Butler lordship was centred in Tipperary and Ossory, but when the O'Briens reconquered northern Tipperary, compensation was found for the Butlers in Kilkenny, which from 1391 till to-day has been the chief seat of the Ormond line. Edmund Butler, Earl of Carrick, whose ruined castle still stands at Carrick-on-Suir, married a cousin of Edward III, and his descendants, as Earls of Ormond, were closely connected with the English Government. From 1328 to 1621 the earls had Palatine jurisdiction in Tipperary[1] and the "White Earl" of Ormond was recorded in the Irish "Annals" as "the best captain of the English nation that ever was in Ireland". The next earl, a Lancastrian, was taken prisoner by Sir Richard Salkeld at the Battle of Towton and beheaded. His successors were absentees, and the leadership of the Anglo-Irish passed first to the Earl of Desmond and then to the Earl of Kildare.

The Earls of Desmond and Kildare were Geraldines, of the family of Maurice Fitzgerald, Strongbow's colleague. Two Fitzgerald brothers in the thirteenth century had founded the dual branches of the house. By the fifteenth century the Earl of Desmond was almost an independent sovereign, wearing Irish dress, administering English law through sheriffs of his own appointment, and claiming to rule over the whole of Kerry, most of Cork, the greater part of Limerick, the west half of Waterford, and portions of Tipperary.[2] The seventh Earl ruled a small kingdom in which he had fused his Irish and English subjects, occupying the positions of Gaelic "Ri" and Palatine Earl. When he was suddenly and mysteriously executed, in 1468, by the Lord Lieutenant, Tiptoft, Earl of Worcester, who feared his native Irish leanings, the Desmonds were alienated at

---

[1] See *Fifth Report of the Deputy Keeper of Irish Records*, Appendix III, pp. 33–8.

[2] For a map of the Irish Lordship of MacCarthy Mor in Kerry and Cork in the sixteenth century see W. F. T. Butler, *Gleanings from Irish History*. See *ibid*. pp. 198–208 for an account of the distribution of land ownership in Ireland.

one blow from the English crown. No Earl of Desmond in future attended the Irish Parliament or Council or entered any walled city.[1]

The Earls of Kildare were feudal lords of more than half the Pale and had jurisdiction over the Irish chiefs in the southern and western marches. The entire county of Kildare and parts of counties Meath, Dublin and Carlow were under their sway, their castles stretching from Strangford on the coast of Down to Adare near Limerick.[2] The handsome and gruffly humorous Gerald Fitzgerald, eighth Earl of Kildare, was Deputy Governor of Ireland in the reigns of Edward IV, Richard III and Henry VI. The family had intermarried with the native Irish, regardless of Edward III's Statute of Kilkenny, as had the Desmonds and to a lesser degree even the Butlers. Alice, Kildare's daughter, was the wife of her first cousin Conn O'Neill of Tyrone; another daughter, Eleanor, married successively MacCarthy Reagh of Carbery in County Cork and Manus O'Donnell, grandson of the great Hugh O'Donnell of Tyrconnell. Eustacia was wedded to a Burke of Connaught, Irish as the native Irish, in spite of his De Burgo ancestry. It has been said that Anglo-Irish culture culminated in the family of the Kildare Fitzgeralds,[3] although the eighth Earl appended his signature to official documents in cramped initials, unaccustomed to the pen. His son owned a considerable library and masses of plate, including a gold strainer for oranges, costing £22. 10s.[4] Their geographical proximity to Dublin had kept them more English than the Desmond branch of the Geraldines.

When Henry VI sent Richard, Duke of York, as Lord Lieutenant to Ireland in 1449, to free himself from his most dangerous opponent at home, he could never have anticipated

<hr>

[1] For the view that Desmond was executed on a warrant forged by Elizabeth Woodville see his grandson's account in the introduction to the *Carew Papers*, 1575–88, cv. Orpen in the *English Historical Review*, xxx, 342, disposes of the story. See also Richard III's messages to Desmond; Gairdner, *Letters and Papers*, I, 68, 73.

[2] See "Rental Book of the ninth Earl of Kildare, 1518", *Kilkenny Archaeological Societies Journal*, 1858–9, 309; 1862–3, 110–37; 1864, 501–18, and note 4.

[3] A. S. Green, *The Making of Ireland and its Undoing*, p. 335.

[4] "Kildare Rental, 1518, MSS of Duke of Leinster", *Hist. MSS Com. 9th Report*, Part II, p. 278.

that Richard's great popularity would make Ireland a centre of Yorkist sedition for the next fifty years. The Anglo-Irish nobility fought in large numbers in the Wars of the Roses on the Yorkist side, leaving Ulster unprotected for reconquest by the O'Neills. The absence of the Lord Lieutenant himself at the wars allowed Ireland to attain to practical Home Rule. After 1460 the Irish Parliament claimed the right to refuse ratification of English laws. In 1471 a Parliament elected the seventh Earl of Kildare as Justiciar and he and the eighth Earl after him practically ruled the country.

Thus the lordship of Ireland to which Henry VII succeeded was a lordship only in name. The native Irish were to him "savage Irish", at least five centuries behind the times. The Anglo-Irish were Yorkist and nationalist; hostile to his Lancastrian title, wearing Irish dress and anxious to have a king of their own. The only loyal Irish were the burgesses of the Anglo-Irish towns, such as Waterford, Dublin and Kilkenny. Without this element, Anglo-Ireland, by 1485, would have reverted entirely to Irish speech and tradition. Natural enemies of feudalism as were all townsmen and traders, they were potential allies of the crown against "English rebels", the Yorkists, and "Irish enemies", the Celts.

Among the Anglo-Irish, the Butlers alone were Lancastrians and to them Henry VII turned for help from the first. James Butler, fifth Earl of Ormond, had been created Earl of Wiltshire, in the English peerage, and on his accession Henry VII restored the Earldom of Ormond, which had been forfeited after his execution in 1461, to his younger brother Thomas, the seventh Earl. Thomas, when he came into Ireland, is said to have brought with him £40,000 sterling besides his plate. James, the sixth Earl, had died on pilgrimage to the Holy Land, leaving a base son James Ormond, known as "Black" James, in the tuition and charge of his brother, Thomas; who kept and maintained him in good sort at the Court of England, where in a short time he grew to be expert in all feats of arms.[1]

---

[1] Paraphrased from "A register contayning the pedigree of the right honorable Thomas, late Earl of Ormond and a storie of his ancestres etc. by Robert Rothe Esq. (one of the said late Earles Counsell) 1616". B.M. Add. MSS 4792, no. 47, fol. 255 v.

Thomas, Earl of Ormond, owned about seventy manors,[1] and was Chamberlain to the Queen.[2] In 1487 on the death of Sir James Butler, his cousin, who had acted for him in Ireland, he appointed this James Ormond, his illegitimate nephew, as his Irish representative.[3] But Sir James Butler had given and granted by will to his son, Piers Butler, "the custody and defence of the lands of my lord the Earle of Ormonde, as it was given and possessed by me ".[4] A feud between Piers Butler and James Ormond was inevitable, ending only with the murder of James by Piers ten years later.

The Butlers had for some time been hemmed in by the Kildare earldom in the north and the Desmond principality in the west, and continual disputes between all three earls over borderlands in Leinster and Munster had taken place. Their discord was intensified by the Wars of the Roses, and, in the reign of Henry VII, the Geraldine-Butler feud waxed strong, while the Yorkist Kildare, the ancient enemy of the Butlers, was Deputy for a Lancastrian King.

On Henry VII's accession Gerald, eighth Earl of Kildare, took the precaution of allying himself with the Lancastrian Butlers by marrying his daughter, Margaret Fitzgerald, to Piers in 1485. For the next few years Henry was but a shadowy far-off figure as Lord of Ireland and the island became a happy hunting-ground for Yorkist pretenders. Even after Kildare had crowned Lambert Simnel King of Ireland, as Edward VI, and despatched the army of German mercenaries to England on his behalf, which was routed at the Battle of Stoke in 1487, Henry did not dare to supplant him as Deputy. A letter from the King to the Earl of Ormond, written from Kenilworth when he first heard of the landing of Martin Schwartz in Ireland, called upon him to come at once to give his advice and counsel in the subduing of the rebels

---

[1] Ormonde muniments, *Hist. MSS Comm. 2nd Report*, Appendix, p. 210.

[2] *Cal. Pat. Rolls*, 1485–94, p. 122.

[3] The deputation occurs in full on the Patent Roll of 19 Henry VIII and is printed from a transcript by Lynch in Graves and Prim, *History of St Canice Cathedral*, p. 193 note *a*.

[4] Quoted from a notarial instrument preserved in the Evidence Chamber, Kilkenny Castle, and printed by Graves and Prim, *History of St Canice Cathedral*, p. 187.

THE ORMOND GENEALOGY Based upon *G.E.C.*

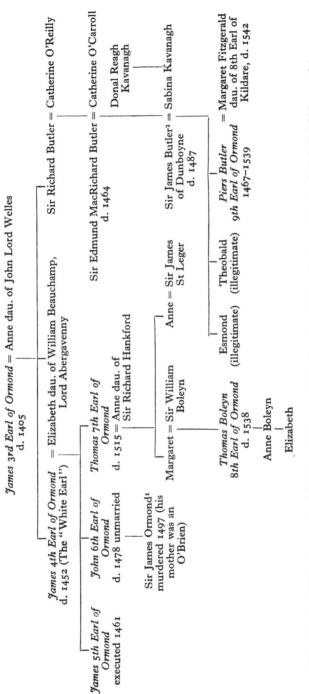

[1] The *Annals of Ulster* (III, 419) call Sir James "the son of John", as does Robert Rothe, writing in 1616, Add. MSS 4792, fol. 255 v.

[2] See *Nat. MSS of Ireland*, Part III, xlix.

and to bring with him "our derrest wife and lady moder".[1] In July, 1490, Henry pardoned Kildare and most of the other rebels who had taken Simnel's part, on condition that the Deputy should come to England the following summer to consult with him as to the state of Ireland. Kildare sent no answer for ten months and then excused himself on the plea of dissensions at home.[2]

During the following year another Yorkist plot was being organised by Charles VIII,[3] and in November 1491 Perkin Warbeck landed at Cork, within the domain of the Earl of Desmond. The presence of a known Yorkist conspirator, John Taylor,[3] with Perkin on his first appearance on Irish soil, discredits the Pretender's story of the accidental character of that landing.[4] There was nothing unpremeditated about it, since in 1499 the Milanese ambassador mentioned the surrender by the King of France of the person of this same John Taylor "who devised Perkin's expedition to Ireland when the latter first declared himself the son of King Edward".[5] Whether Margaret, Dowager Duchess of Burgundy, Edward IV's second sister and the mainstay of the Yorkist party in England, was also backing Perkin on this, his first appearance, is still disputed. She had openly identified herself with the risings of Lovell in 1486 and of Simnel in 1487. Polydore Vergil writes[6] that she instructed Perkin in the details of the Court life of Edward IV, his supposed father, but does not commit himself to the period at which this was done. Bacon, in enlarging Vergil's statement, makes the plot begin with Margaret, who "cast with herself from what coast this blazing star should first appear", and naturally enough chose Ireland. The payment of £18 by James IV, in February 1490, to a herald that came from Ireland and passed on to the

[1] *Ellis's Original Letters*, 1st series, I, x.
[2] Gairdner, *Letters*, I, 380. For a discussion as to the date, see *ibid.* I, p. xxxii and Busch, p. 325. See also the letter from the lords of Ireland to Henry VII (Gairdner, I, 377) and from Desmond to Henry VII (*ibid.* I, 381). Pollard is inclined to date them all 1492 (*Henry VII*, III, 92), but the letter from Desmond must belong to 1491, as it bears the date, July 10, and Kildare had been superseded as Deputy on June 11, 1492.
[3] *Rot. Parl.* VI, 454. Pollard, *Henry VII*, I, no. 57.
[4] *Hall's Chronicle*, p. 489.
[5] *Venetian Calendar*, I, 799
[6] Polydore Vergil, *Historia Anglica*, p. 589.

Duchess, should confirm her agency.[1] Ware,[2] who may have copied Bacon, states unequivocably that Margaret sent Perkin to Ireland with Sir Edward Brampton. Since Gairdner analysed the evidence,[3] more has been discovered about Brampton. He was Perkin's master and a converted Jew, who trained him for his part while he was in his service[4] and may well have done so at the instigation of Margaret. Knowing the Duchess's previous history, her ignorance of a prepared Yorkist landing in Ireland needs more explanation than her part as an accomplice. Maurice, Earl of Desmond, probably invited him to land in Cork, where he was received by the citizens, "particularly by John Water, the merchant",[5] who remained loyal to Perkin till both suffered on the same scaffold in 1499.

Henry VII dealt with the menace of this landing by despatching an army to Kilkenny and Tipperary in December, 1491, under the leadership of Lord Ormond's deputy, James Ormond, and Captain Thomas Garth; at the same time he absolved all persons from obedience to the Deputy Kildare, who was naturally suspected of acting in co-operation with Desmond.[6] James Ormond and Garth were in fact jointly to supersede the functions of the Deputy during a period of martial law and rebellion; for, in addition to commanding the army, they were to make statutes and issue proclamations and arrest and commit to prison all delinquents. Their patent in a measure forestalls that of Poynings as Deputy and the comparison is an interesting one. A Deputy in succession to Kildare was not appointed for six months.

James Ormond[7] was granted lands in the Butler counties of Meath, Kilkenny and Tipperary,[8] and it seems probable that this was his first journey to Ireland as the official Butler repre-

---

[1] *Treasurer's Accounts, Scotland*, I, 130.
[2] Ware, *Annals, Henry VII*, p. 17.
[3] Gairdner, *Richard III*, pp. 269–72.
[4] Cecil Roth, "Perkin Warbeck and his Jewish Master", *Transactions of the Jewish Historical Society of England*, IX.
[5] Ware, *Annals, Henry VII*, p. 22.
[6] *Cal. Pat. Rolls*, 1485–94, p. 367.
[7] James Ormond was still "armiger" on November 26, 1492 (Exchequer T.R. Misc. Books, E 36, 125, fol. 200). The *D.N.B.* mistakenly says he was knighted for his services against Lambert Simnel.
[8] *Cal. Pat. Rolls*, 1485–94, p. 368.

sentative. He had been one of the five Irish benchers elected to Lincoln's Inn between 1437 and 1513,[1] notwithstanding the theoretic exclusion of all Irishmen, and was entered on June 24, 1486. There is no evidence of his presence in Ireland till the winter of 1491–2, when an Irish chronicler mentions his return after being a long time in England.[2] His character, as drawn by his Fitzgerald enemies, was that of a turbulent, quarrelsome fellow who richly deserved to meet his end by murder. A long letter to his patron, the Earl of Ormond,[3] reveals him clearly as a man of spirit, self-seeking, mincing no words and writing with originality and force. His hand is unusual, although clear and regular and better than that of Sir Reginald Bray or Sir Thomas Lovell, the King's chief advisers. After many years of service in Ireland under Henry VII, he supported Perkin Warbeck's last adventure through jealousy of the Fitzgeralds, and died under a cloud.

Thomas Garth had already had a long and complicated career. A "king's servant" of this name was rewarded by Edward IV in 1477 for good services at Barnet and Tewkesbury.[4] Three years later Thomas Garth was named executor to Anne, Duchess of Buckingham, in company with Morton, Bishop of Ely,[5] and was probably identical with the Thomas Garth mentioned in connection with Wales[6] and Brecknock[7] in 1488 and 1491. A man of the same name was executor of the will of Thomas Bourchier, Archbishop of Canterbury,[8] Controller of the Customs at Sandwich,[9] and Justice in Kent for the supervision of the River Medway[10] under Richard III. In 1484–5 he had a special admission to the Society of Lincoln's Inn and was pardoned all vacations.[11] He was elected M.P. for Blechingley in the Parliament of 1491,[12] probably as a nominee of the Duke of Buckingham, who was Lord of the Manor,[13] but could only have attended

[1] Black Books of Lincoln's Inn, II, fol. 61. In the printed Black Books of Lincoln's Inn, I, 83, the name is incorrectly given as John Ormond of Ireland.
[2] Annals of the Four Masters, IV, 1197. Pollard, Henry VII, III, no. 95.
[3] Appendix v.　　　　　　　[4] Cal. Pat. Rolls, 1476–85, p. 60.
[5] Will. P.C.C. 2 Logge.　　　[6] Cal. Pat. Rolls, 1485–94, p. 216.
[7] Ibid. p. 354.　　　　　　　[8] Ibid. p. 153.
[9] Pipe Roll, 2 Richard III.　　[10] Cal. Pat. Rolls, 1476–85, p. 344.
[11] Black Books of Lincoln's Inn, I, 81.
[12] Bulletin of Institute of Historical Research, III, 172.
[13] Uvedale Lambert, Blechingley, I, 199–206.

the first session. As the Thomas Garth employed in Ireland had died before July, 1505, when his son, William Garth, was named his father's successor in the office of Marshal of the Town of Berwick,[1] he was the right age to be the subject of all these entries. His association with Brecknock, the Buckingham family, and Bishop Morton, implies his probable conversion to the Lancastrian cause at the time of Buckingham's rebellion, and he may have been one of the inner Lancastrian ring that organised it.[2]

Some information about the Irish expedition under the leadership of Ormond and Garth can be gleaned from the Tellers Rolls of the Exchequer. At first the King and Council despatched 200 soldiers and 30 sailors to Ireland for a month.[3] They stayed from December 1, 1491, onwards, for at least three months, "to suppress the rebellion against the King".[4] Ormond took 90 yards of "skarlet" with him to distribute according to the King's orders,[5] and he and Garth were paid £66. 13s. 4d. each for their services.[3] The sum total for the payment of their army made from the Exchequer was £805. 11s. 8d.[6]

Nothing is known of Perkin Warbeck's doings in the rebellion of 1491–2. A letter from him in Ireland written by the hand of Stephen Frion, ex-French Secretary to Henry VII, who had deserted him and taken service with the French King, was received by James IV of Scotland in March, 1491/2.[7] His medievally armed adherents were naturally helpless against the professional Ormond-Garth army and in the spring Perkin

---

[1] Cal. Pat. Rolls, 1494–1509, p. 403.
[2] Agnes Conway, "The Maidstone Sector of Buckingham's Rebellion", Archaeologia Cantiana, XXXVII.
[3] Tellers Rolls, E 405, 78, Mich. Term, 7 Henry VII, Pierson mem. 3.
[4] Ibid. mem. 3 dorso.   [5] Ibid.
[6] Ibid.:

		£	s.	d.	
Garth.	Arrows[a]	8	10	0	(last Pierson mem. dorso)
,,	Wages	7	10	0	Pierson mem. 3 dorso
,,	Food	6	5	0	Pierson mem. 3 ,,
,,	Wages	30	0	0	Pierson mem. 3 ,,
,,	,,	300	0	0	Pierson mem. 3 ,,
,,	,,	120	0	0	Stokes mem. 2
,,	Fee	66	13	4	Pierson mem. 3
Ormond.	Wages	200	0	0	Stokes mem. 2
,,	Fee	66	13	4	Pierson mem. 3
		£805	11	8	

[a] 120 garbels of arrows at 17d. the sheaf.

[7] Treasurer's Accounts, Scotland, I, 199, and Batten, Register of Fox, pp. 30–3.

accepted Charles VIII's invitation to the French Court. Kildare, in a letter to Thomas, Earl of Ormond, complaining of James Ormond, "your bace cosyn",[1] denied that he had ever helped the French lad; an assertion which conflicts with two statements of Perkin.[2] Perkin's assertions need not be believed, but his letters to Kildare and Desmond were said by Bacon and Ware to be extant in their day.[3] Ware's pronouncement that the charter of Cork was forfeited after this rebellion is not borne out by the text of its confirmation, in 1500, which excuses arrears of fee-farm rent in consideration of the town's poverty and decay.[4]

The departure of Warbeck did not bring peace, but was followed by a reorganisation of the Government in Ireland. Walter Fitzsymonds, Archbishop of Dublin, replaced Kildare as Deputy on June 11, 1492,[5] and on the same day James Ormond succeeded Roland Fitz Eustace, a brother-in-law of Kildare, as Lord Treasurer. The Earl was naturally outraged. Not only had he himself been dismissed from the practical kingship of Ireland, but his brother-in-law, degraded after forty years' service, was supplanted by the representative of the Butlers, the ancient enemy of his house. James Ormond's appointment could not fail to lead to fighting with the ex-Deputy. A letter written by Kildare to the Earl of Ormond on June 10, the day before he was supplanted by Fitzsymonds, described his proceedings in no measured vein.[6] James, anxious to consolidate his status as representative of the Earl of Ormond in the waning Butler domain of Kilkenny and Tipperary, had invaded it with the help of his mother's relatives, the Irish O'Briens. His successes in annexing lands of absentee landlords in these counties were secured to him by an Act of the Parliament which met at Dublin in the following year;[7] but on hearing that his violent proceedings in Kilkenny were not liked, he wrote to the new Deputy, Fitz-

---

[1] Gairdner, *Letters*, II, 55; February 11, 1493.
[2] His confession and a letter to Queen Isabella of Spain. *Archaeologia*, XXVII, 199.
[3] Ware, *Annals, Henry VII*, p. 22.
[4] *Cal. Pat. Rolls*, 1494–1509, p. 204.
[5] *Ibid.* 1485–94, p. 376.
[6] Gairdner, *Letters*, II, xxxviii. Published from a transcript of P.R.O. Ancient Correspondence, LVII, 119. The date is wrongly printed as January 16.
[7] Gilbert, *Viceroys*, p. 446.

symonds, that he had been accused of disloyalty and would immediately repair to Dublin to clear himself.[1]

The sweating sickness had broken out there in the spring of 1492,[2] and in the harvest following, James Ormond camped with a great host of Irishmen in St Thomas's Abbey,[3] the Dublin residence of the Lord Deputy. A native Irish chronicler[4] tells how Kildare burnt the Street of the Sheep in Dublin and how Geraldines and Butlers came to blows. In the summer James Ormond made a raid into the territory of O'Connor of Offaly, one of Kildare's Irish tributary chiefs, and killed his son.[5] James was supported in these adventures by Henry VII, who on November 26, 1492, gave him twenty pieces of blood-red cloth.[6] Garth seems to have outstayed the troops whom he had been sent to Ireland to command and helped Ormond in Offaly;[5] but in the winter of 1492–3 Kildare took Garth, "the King's Captain", prisoner in the Offaly country,[5] and hanged his son.[7]

This outrage to his captain at last forced Henry VII to take strong measures. A letter from Kildare in Dublin to the Earl of Ormond on February 11, 1493,[8] mentioned that the King had imprisoned Kildare's servants, sent to him with letters and instructions probably containing excuses for his presumption in taking Garth prisoner. Henry answered by despatching a fleet and armed force to Ireland under the leadership of Sir Roger Cotton,[9] who had proclaimed him King at York and at the beginning of the reign was Master of the Queen's Horse.[10]

---

[1] Gairdner, *Letters*, II, xxxix. I have not been able to trace the original, which Gairdner paraphrases. He may be copying Stanyhurst. See Holinshed, *Chronicles*, VI, 275.

[2] Fleming, Baron Slane, died of it in March, 1492. *Annals of Ulster*, III, 359. *Annals of Loch Cé*, II, 189.

[3] B.M. Add. MSS 4791, p. 135 (later pagination).

[4] Pollard, *Henry VII*, III, no. 95.

[5] *Annals of Ulster*, III, 365–7: "The Calbach, son of Ua Concobair Faly, was slain by some of the people of the son of the Earl of Ormond, namely of James, son of John, son of James Butler, that is by Master Gart. And Master Gart himself was taken in the same place by the Earl of Kildare in winter". See also *Annals of Loch Cé*, II, 189. The family of O'Connor Faly were perpetually at war with the Butlers. Mrs Green, *Making of Ireland*, chap. iii. See also Fitzgerald, *The Earls of Kildare*.

[6] Tellers Rolls, E 405, 78, Mich. Term, 8 Henry VII, Stokes mem. 2 dorso. The same entry in Exchequer T.R. E 36, 125, fol. 200, gives the day of the month.   [7] *State Papers, Henry VIII*, II, 174–5.

[8] Gairdner, *Letters*, II, 55.   [9] *Cal. Pat. Rolls*, 1485–94, p. 419 and App. LI.

[10] Tellers Rolls, Easter Term, 1 Henry VII, Pierson mem. 1 dorso.

Cotton left England in March, 1493, with eleven men-at-arms, 188 archers and £240 in two bags of £120 each.[1] Sir Richard Guildford, Master of the Ordnance, received ten days' wages for his "valet of ordnance", who had attended upon three wagon loads of munitions on the journey from London to Bristol with Sir Roger Cotton;[2] 3s. 4d. for his nightly vigil over the ordnance was paid him and an extra sum for the horse carriage of the barrels of powder for the cannon. The other captain, Henry Mountford, had 100 men under his command, who, with his own wages, cost the Exchequer £72. 2s. 0d. a month.[3] In the Michaelmas Term, William Hattecliffe, purveyor of oats to the King, who was afterwards Under-Treasurer of Ireland during the Poynings administration, acted as paymaster to the Army to the tune of £827. 14s. 8d.[4] Part of this sum was for the retinues of Cotton and Mountford at Bristol and £500 odd for their wages in Ireland. The total expenses of the army in 1493, paid from the Exchequer, were £2825. 0s. 8d.[4]

---

[1] Exchequer T.R. E 36, 125, fol. 233. Paid on March 12, 1493.
[2] Tellers Rolls, E 405, 78, Easter Term, 8 Henry VII, Hungate mem. 3.
[3] *Ibid.* Mich. Term, 8 Henry VII, Hungate mem. 1.
[4]

	£	s.	d.
To Cotton on departure	240	0	0[a]
To Cotton, Mich. Term	153	6	0[b]
,, ,, ,, ,,	85	0	0[b]
By hand of Hattecliffe—			
To Cotton and Mountford, for retinues at Bristol	235	2	6[c]
By hand of Hattecliffe—			
To Cotton and Mountford	500	10	2[d]
To Mountford for wages	92	2	0[e]
By hand of Wyatt—			
To Cotton for wages	200	0	0[f]
To Wyatt for soldiers' wages	534	18	0[g]
To Wyatt—Expenses in Ireland. "Circa negotia"	52	6	8[h]
To Wyatt—Carriage of money from London to Westchester	2	0	0[i]
To Wyatt—Payment of the Army	116	12	0[j]
To Wyatt—A fee for Garth	66	13	4[k]
To Wyatt—For wages for himself and his retinue in Ireland for 5 months	300	0	0[l]
To John Welsh—For Cotton's wages	246	10	0[m]
	£2825	0	8

[a] Exchequer T.R. E 36, 125, f. 233 and E 405,78, Mich. Term, 8 Henry VII, Warley mem. 1.
[b] *Ibid.* Warley mem. 1.
[c] *Ibid.*   [d] *Ibid.* Hungate mem. 1.   [e] *Ibid.*
[f] E 405, 78, Easter Term, 8 Henry VII, Warley mem. 1.
[g] *Ibid.* Easter Term, 8 Henry VII, Hungate mem. 1 dorso.
[h] *Ibid.*   [i] *Ibid.*   [j] *Ibid.* Hungate, mem. 3   [k] *Ibid.*
[l] *Ibid.* Stokes mem. 2   [m] Hungate mem. 1 dorso.

On March 30 a pardon was prepared for Kildare, conditional on his sending his son to England within six months,[1] and Cotton may have taken the letters patent to Ireland with him. Maurice, Earl of Desmond, Thomas de Desmond,[1] Hubert Burk,[2] and Edward Ormond were the subjects of letters of pardon in the spring, which Sir Richard Salkeld, Constable of Carlisle, probably carried out on the journey to Ireland for which he was paid £10[3] in the same Term. It is not known whether submissions and fines earned the actual bestowal of any of these pardons.

Early in the summer of 1493 the Geraldine-Butler feud assumed another threatening phase. It is briefly mentioned in a Dublin Chronicler's Register of the Mayors of Dublin under the year 1493,[4] which enters the occurrence of a fight on St Margaret's Day (June 10) on Oxmanton Green, in which William Tien, who had been Mayor in 1489, and Blanchfield, a Dublin citizen, were killed by the Kildare faction.[5] The Book of Howth deals with the same episode,[6] and Stanyhurst[7] gives a long account, reproduced in all the text-books of Irish history, of the reconciliation of Kildare and Ormond and their shaking of hands through a hole in the door of St Patrick's Cathedral.

It was probably due to this new quarrel and agreement that another pardon was enrolled for Kildare on June 22, 1493.[8] In the same month Henry Wyatt was on his way to Ireland[9]

---

[1] *Cal. Pat. Rolls*, 1485–94, p. 423.

[2] Hubert Burk is mentioned in Perkin's Confession, *Hall's Chronicle*, p. 489.

[3] Tellers Rolls, E 405, 78, Mich. Term, 8 Henry VII, Hungate, mem. 1.

[4] B.M. Add. MSS 4791, modern pagination 135: "till m [Michaelmas] 1493. Jo Serieant Mayor. Jo Blake & Wm Browne bailives. The Mayor was put to ward into ye kes Castle & then Rich. ffaland was Mayor till m & on St. Margretts die 19 Julij was the slaught given on Oxmanton greene & soe was slaine Wm Tien Ra Blanchfield & John Row".

The Dublin Assembly Roll gives John Sergaunt as Mayor, and William Brown and John Blake as bailiffs from Michaelmas 1492–3 (Gilbert, *Calendar of Dublin Records*, I, 377). The Mayor of Dublin was named on Holy Rood day (Sept. 14) and elected on Michaelmas Day (Gilbert, *ibid.* I, 367). Gairdner (*Letters*, II, xxxix) and Gilbert (*Viceroys*, p. 444) date this quarrel earlier, but the Register fixes it beyond dispute.

[5] A letter to Kildare's son, about 1533, says "thy fader killed them of Dublin, upon Oxmantowne Greene". *State Papers, Henry VIII*, II, 174–5.

[6] *Cal. Carew MSS*, "Book of Howth", p. 176.

[7] Holinshed, VI, 276.   [8] *Cal. Pat. Rolls*, 1485–94, p. 429.

[9] Tellers Rolls, E 405, 78, Easter Term, 8 Henry VII, Hungate mem. 1 dorso.

with a retinue costing £60 a month,[1] and stayed five months. His commission is not extant, but he doubtless went as commissioner to reinforce Cotton, and to negotiate with Kildare and receive his submission, in return for the new pardon, which he may have carried out. In the Easter Term, £1272. 10s. for wage payments passed through his hands,[2] and the appointment was a stepping-stone to the more important financial office of commissioner and auditor, held by him in 1495 during the Poynings régime.

Henry VII was at Kenilworth during part of June and July, 1493, with twelve gunners in attendance,[3] expecting Perkin's invasion from Flanders; and on June 16, Wyatt broke his journey to Dublin to pay the King a business visit at the castle in connection with the Mint of which he was Clerk.[4] Thomas Garth, Alexander Plunket, Thomas Butler, Fitzsymonds and the Archdeacon of Meath had their travelling expenses to Ireland paid at the same time as Wyatt.[5] As they were all officials in Ireland already, it is possible that they were travelling from Dublin to Kenilworth and back to consult with the King on Irish business. At this meeting the legislation of the approaching Parliament, held before Fitzsymonds at Dublin, may have been determined.

Kildare was under a cloud, and it is not surprising that the Statutes, 32 in number, passed in this Parliament, between the end of June and August 6, 1493, should all have been directed against him. Only one of these is in print.[6] The originals were

---

[1] Tellers Rolls, E 405, 78, Easter Term, 8 Henry VII, Stokes mem. 2.
[2] See p. 54.
[3] Tellers Rolls, E 405, 78, Easter Term, 8 Henry VII, Stokes mem. 1. It is written "Killingworth". See *Robert Laneham's Letter*, "Whearin part of the entertainment untoo the Queenz Maiesty at Killingwoorth Castle, in Warwick-Sheer in this Soomers Progress 1575 is signified". "The Castle hath name of Killingworth, but of truth grounded uppon feythfull stories Kenelworth."
[4] P.R.O. E 101, 413/2, part II, fol. 45.
[5] *Ibid.* fol. 46: "Item received by a warraunt of my lorde Tresourer by thande of Harry Wyott that is to say 17^li 6^s 8^d lent to Thomas Garthe at Duvelyn by the said harry Wiot xl^li to thomas Garthe 10^li to pluneket 6^li 13^s 4^d to buteler, c s. to Fitzsimonds 13^li 6^s 8^d for tharchedecon of methe and 26^li 13^s 4^d to harry Wiot for there costes going to Irelande. cxix^li". The passage money from Ireland to England for the auditor of the Duke of Norfolk in the time of Edward I was 6s. 8d.; *Journal Royal Society of Antiquaries of Ireland*, XXII, 52.
[6] *Statutes at Large, Ireland*, 1786, I, 40.

burnt in 1922; but a transcript of the Rolls made by the Record Commissioners more than a hundred years ago, was preserved in a safe, and salved.[1] The Carew MSS retain a list of the Statutes,[2] and Ware[3] and Gilbert[4] give some account of the measures passed. Fitz Eustace, Kildare's brother-in-law, the late Treasurer, was required to authenticate his accounts for the previous forty years, and remain in the custody of the Marshall until he had delivered his arrears. All the lands conquered by the Irish in Kilkenny and Tipperary were to become the absolute property of James Ormond unless the absentee claimants returned to reside upon them.[5] The Statutes against the citizens of Waterford, who had been condemned by Kildare for loyalty to the crown in the Simnel rebellion, were repealed, and a general resumption of grants and licences ordered from the first year of Henry VI, forestalling Poynings' Act of Resumption.

A municipal grant on September 3 for the purchase of bows and arrows, to be distributed among the commons of Dublin against the incursions of English and Irish rebels,[6] implies a stormy August in Dublin. This grant, attested by Fitzsymonds, is his last recorded act as Deputy. The grounds for his supersession by Robert Preston, Lord Gormanston, three days later, cannot be inferred from the general terms of his pardon in the following August, 1494,[7] which covered all transgressions as Deputy and ex-Deputy up to June 16, 1494.

In the matter of keeping peace in Ireland, his successor was certainly more competent. Gormanston's first act as Deputy was to summon a Parliament which met at Trim on September 12, 1493, consisting of peers from the four counties adjacent to the Pale. Wyatt and Garth were present as commissioners.[8] As the Statutes were burnt in 1922, the only record evidence for this Parliament is the Irish Close Roll.[9] This gives the recog-

---

[1] These transcripts are being prepared for publication, and include the prorogation of August 6.

[2] Lambeth, Carew MSS, vol. 608, fol. 113 verso.

[3] Ware, *Annals, Henry VII*, chapter ix.

[4] Gilbert, *Viceroys*, p. 446. See also *Liber Munerum Publicorum Hiberniae*, Part VI, p. 4.   [5] Gilbert, *Viceroys*, p. 446.

[6] Dublin, Liber Albus. Printed in Gilbert, *Calendar of Dublin Records*, I, 141–2.

[7] *Foedera*, XII, 556.   [8] Gilbert, *Viceroys*, p. 447.

[9] *Irish Patent and Close Rolls*, Record Commission, p. 270.

nisances into which certain lords and gentlemen of Ireland were commanded to enter, in order "to aid the Deputy in punishing those who might be found to have of late committed extortions, robberies and murders". They were to place hostages in the hands of the Deputy to be kept in the Royal Castles of Dublin and Trim, and Kildare was to be free of his debt of 1000 marks to the King if he fulfilled the articles in the Statutes.

These recognisances must have quietened the country, for before the end of the Easter Term of 1493, Cotton, the captain of the English army, had gone home,[1] and there was an exodus to England of Deputy and ex-Deputies. Fitzsymonds went to Court in October;[2] Ware recording his conversations with Henry VII.[2] Kildare followed in November,[3] "to purge himself to the King of the crimes which were laid to his charge",[4] and had arrived before Twelfth Day, 1493/4, on which occasion at a royal feast at Westminster two of his Irishmen were dubbed knights.[5] Henry VII lodged him and his household at a cost of £5 a week till the middle of May, 1494.[6] The Lord Deputy, Robert Gormanston, went next, leaving the government in the hands of his son,[7] and James Ormond wound up the rear after Christmas, "following the Earl of Kildare, to oppose him in the East".[8]

Not only the lords of the Pale, but even the obstreperous Earl of Desmond, whose doings in Munster from the time of Perkin's invasion in 1491–2 are obscure, were being brought into line. He took an oath of fealty to Henry VII in Ireland in March, 1494,[9] in the presence of Richard Salkeld, Groom of the Chamber, and Constable of Carlisle. Carlisle was conveniently

---

[1] Cotton is designated "late Captain of the King's Army in Ireland" in the Easter Term of 1493 (Tellers Rolls, E 405, 78, 8 Henry VII, Easter Term, Hungate mem. 1 dorso).
[2] Ware, *Annals, Henry VII*, pp. 25–7.
[3] *Annals of Ulster*, III, 369. [4] *Ibid.*
[5] Kingsford, *Chronicles of London*, p. 200.
[6] See Tellers Rolls, E 405, 79, Mich. Term 9 Henry VII, mem. 1 dorso, for payments from February 15–April 12, 1494; and Tellers Rolls, E 405, 79, mem. 2, for an allowance of £20 for a month in the Easter Term, 9 Henry VII.
[7] Cox, *Hibernia Anglicana*, 185.
[8] *Annals of Ulster*, III, 379. Post-dated by a year. See *Ibid.* footnote. Ware, *Annals, Henry VII*, pp. 25–6.
[9] Appendix VI.

placed geographically for visits to Ireland, and this, his second journey, "on the King's business", only cost the Exchequer 20 marks in the Michaelmas Term of 1493–4.[1] Henry Wyatt, the Captain of Carlisle, returned theré from Ireland in the same term,[2] as it was doubtless considered inadvisable that he and Salkeld should both be absent from their posts. Desmond's oath contained the reservation that he should not be obliged to appear before the King's Deputy in Ireland, unless (unlike his father) he were certain of getting away again in safety. He agreed to send his son and heir to the custody of Kildare, and an indenture between Henry VII and Kildare was made at Westminster in May, 1494.[3] Kildare bound himself to get Desmond's son into his possession as soon as possible, and hand him over to Henry should Desmond break his oath of March 18. The articles of Desmond's oath are repeated in the indenture.

Thus in May, 1494, Kildare, Desmond and Henry VII were in friendly relations with each other, cemented by documents as binding as could be made. The country seemed so safe that the idea was entertained of withdrawing all troops from Ireland. When the army, officered by Cotton, Wyatt and Mountford, was disbanded in the autumn of 1493, it is probable that a standing force of about a hundred soldiers remained in the country till the end of April and was paid for out of Irish revenue, since all English Exchequer payments cease. A small force such as this would correspond approximately with the eighty able yeomen archers and the forty spears whom Kildare, as Deputy under Edward IV, had been obliged to maintain out of his salary of £600 a year.[4]

The budget for the first year of the Poynings administration allowed a retrospective payment of £294 to Thomas Garth for the wages of a hundred soldiers in Ireland from June 24, 1494, till the landing of Poynings' army on October 13, 1494.[5] This sum must have been allotted in part payment of the contribution of £454, voted retrospectively to Captain Thomas Garth by the Poynings Parliament at Drogheda, for the service of his soldiers, whom, so the record runs,[5] he had kept together during the year

[1] Tellers Rolls, E 405, 79, Mich. Term, 9 Henry VII, mem. 1.
[2] P.R.O. E 403, 2558, fol. 43 v. Mich. Term, 9 Henry VII.
[3] Appendix VII.
[4] B.M. Cotton, Titus, B XI, vol. I, fol. 25.　　[5] Appendix XI.

for the defence of the country when they were about to disband or go to England.[1] £294 for sixteen weeks' wages (from June 24 to October 13) works out at an allowance of £18. 7s. 6d. a week, a wage of 6d. a day for 110 men; the complete sum of £454, on the same scale, would have paid the army from the end of April, 1494. This proves that entire disbandment must have been in contemplation at the beginning of May.

Garth returned to England in the Easter Term of 1494,[2] possibly to protest against this measure. In March, 1494, he was granted the office of Constable of Dublin Castle with £20 a year, and "of further grace" a sum of £46. 13s. 4d. annually.[3] With his up-to-date first-hand knowledge of Ireland Garth may have represented to the King that the oaths of Desmond and Kildare were not sufficient to make the land secure. Perhaps money from an Irish source was not immediately available to continue the payment of the troops, but would be voted by the next Parliament. Garth, on his own responsibility, bridged the gap, and was helped to do so by the King's grant. Such may be the explanation of the Poynings private Act.

A month later the situation in Ireland had completely changed. On June 16, 1494, Sir James Ormond was made Constable of Limerick with an additional grant of £100 for life.[4] Desmond had held the office of Constable since 1488[5] and it is unlikely that he would have been deprived of it by a rival Butler so soon after the acceptance of his oath of fealty on March 18, unless he had broken out into active rebellion since that date. A Munster uprising is mentioned in a commission to negotiate with Desmond, given to Richard Hatton on December 12, 1494.[6] The revolt probably began between May 14 and June 16, and with the reversal of Desmond's oath of fealty the whole settlement reached in the spring of 1494 must have become unstable. On August 8 a pardon was granted to Fitzsymonds for his offences committed before June 16, 1494, which tends to associate his name also with the Munster uprising of Desmond. The Annals of Ulster recount further disturbances in Cavan

---

[1] Poynings' Parliament, chap. xlvi, Lambeth, Carew MSS, 608, fol. 116. Appendix xxxvi.
[2] P.R.O. E 403, 2558, fol. 47 v.
[3] Cal. Pat. Rolls, 1485–94, p. 461.
[4] Ibid. p. 464.
[5] Ibid. p. 232.
[6] Ibid. 1494–1509, p. 27.

in the summer of 1494 in which O'Reilly slew "three score of the worthies of the Foreigners ".[1] At the same time the great Hugh O'Donnell, whose territories in Donegal were within easy reach of Scotland, was sheltering a Scottish leader.[2] To meet disturbances in Donegal or Munster there was probably only the standing army of a hundred Englishmen in Ireland under the command of Garth. Perkin's landing was expected any day throughout the summer of 1494, and Henry VII was confronted with a potentially Yorkist island on his flank, weakly governed from the Pale. The King seems suddenly to have decided that the time had come to take drastic action in Ireland. Since 1491 he had sent out two military expeditions and had tried to govern through three Anglo-Irish Deputies. They were jealous of each other and, with the exception of Kildare, on bad terms with the native Irish. The Anglo-Irish had themselves asked to have the "savage Irish" suppressed. Why not do so by armed force and at the same time make a temporary sweep, with their own consent, of the more important Anglo-Irish officials, replacing them with hardened English Lancastrians, tested in Buckingham's rebellion and the Bosworth expedition and trained in the law?

This policy, which was to be carried out under the Poynings administration, is clearly stated in the instructions of August 10, 1494, given to Richmond Herald for communication to Charles VIII of France.[3] As England was calm at home and at peace abroad, Henry said he had decided to put Ireland in order, especially the part peopled with the " Irlandois Sauvaiges " who were to be ruled in the future by the same laws as those in the English Pale. For this purpose he was about to send out a good and sufficient army, with important officers in command, both military and legal. He had been asked to do this by the chief Anglo-Irish ecclesiastics, barons and notables, who were as loyal now as they had ever been to any prince. For this

---

[1] *Annals of Ulster*, III, 381. *Four Masters*, IV, 1211.

[2] *Annals of Ulster*, III, 383. The Annals of Ulster, generally so meticulous as to chronology, go a year wrong about this time (see footnote, III, 379). As Christmas 1493 is transposed to 1494 in the Annals, it is possible that these two events, under the year 1494 in the Annals, relate to the summer of 1493, when open warfare was raging in Ireland.

[3] Printed in *Archaeologia*, XXVII, 200–204. The Irish paragraph is on p. 203.

purpose the [Archbishop]¹ of Dublin, and three or four other bishops and noblemen had come to England. These were in [agreement]¹ with the King and the army would be ready to start in September.

On September 12 the little Prince Henry, recently created Duke of York, was made Lieutenant of Ireland with Sir Edward Poynings as his Deputy.² Although the child was only four years of age, his two appointments were bestowed with the political object of discrediting the pretensions of Perkin Warbeck, the pseudo Duke of York, in the country that had proved itself ready to welcome every Yorkist claimant. They sounded in fact the keynote of an Irish administration primarily intended to forestall a threatened Yorkist movement. In the same year the Prince had succeeded his brother as Warden-General of the Scottish Marches. Henry's policy was identical in Ireland and on the Border. A centralised government of his royal officials was to take the place of the overgrown magnates beyond the King's control, who had established themselves on the outskirts of his realm. It was wise to attempt to associate Kildare with the new venture, although that soon turned out to be impracticable, and James Ormond, the Butler representative, was given a lavish grant of manors in Meath, Kilkenny and Tipperary on September 12,³ the day after Poynings' appointment. In the words of the Annals of Ulster for 1494: "The Earl of Kildare...and James Butler came from the house of the King of the Saxons to Ireland about November day of this year. And a Saxon knight came with them to Ireland, as Justiciary over the Foreigners of Ireland, namely Edward Poynill. And there was peace between themselves".⁴

---

¹ These words are missing in the original French.
² *Cal. Pat. Rolls*, 1494–1509, p. 12. Both patents are printed in full in Lascelles, *Liber Munerum*, IV, 101.
³ *Cal. Pat. Rolls*, 1494–1509, p. 8.
⁴ Pollard, *Henry VII*, III, 96, 97.

CHAPTER IV

THE FINANCIAL ASPECT OF THE POYNINGS ADMINISTRATION IN IRELAND, ILLUSTRATED BY THE HATTECLIFFE-WYATT ACCOUNTS

Sir Edward Poynings started life as a Kentish squire, the son of Robert Poynings, carver and sword-bearer of John Cade,[1] killed at the Battle of St Albans in 1461. From babyhood he was brought up by his mother, the same Elizabeth Paston, who at marriageable age "was sometimes beaten twice in one day and her head broken in 2 or 3 places".[2]

As a young man Edward Poynings took a prominent part in the Kentish sector of Buckingham's rebellion,[3] the Earl of Richmond's first abortive attempt to capture the crown, and had a price of £100 put upon his head.[4] Escaping to Brittany to join Henry, he landed with him two years later at Milford Haven and was dubbed a knight banneret on the field of Bosworth. The choice was for a fighting Deputy, who would at last suppress the "savage Irish" and prevent Yorkist pretenders from again using Ireland as a base.

Henry VII intended that the initial military phase in Ireland should be followed by an experiment in administrative government new in a dependency. Ireland was to be made to pay her way, and his instructions for the better regulation of the Irish Exchequer survive.[5] Poynings' civilian colleagues, who were to carry out this policy, were royal officials; the King's "new men"; free from feudal prejudices, trained to economy and efficiency and whose loyalty to the crown for the most part dated from the pre-Bosworth struggles of the Earl of Richmond.

Any study of this Irish experiment, military, politic or economic, must be based upon a copy of the accounts of the

---

[1] *D.N.B.* "Edward Poynings". [2] *Paston Letters*, 1, p. 90.
[3] Agnes Conway, "The Maidstone Sector of Buckingham's Rebellion", *Archaeologia Cantiana*, xxxvii.
[4] Gairdner, *Richard III*, p. 343.
[5] Gairdner, *Letters*, 11, 64.

two years' administration which probably belonged to Henry VII himself.[1] These are unprinted, apart from extracts,[2] and have never been used as a whole. The book, bound in modern times, is confused in arrangement; in some cases folios are separated from their context; and a detailed inventory[3] of them as they stand is an essential preliminary to their use. For convenience of reference their chronological sequence is also indicated.[4]

The salary of Poynings as Deputy was £500 a year,[5] the sum which had been customary for the office in the fourteenth century,[6] although in the fifteenth century larger salaries had been paid. Sir Hugh Conway was made Treasurer of Ireland[7] with a yearly fee of £66. 13s. 4d.;[7] Henry Deane, Bishop Elect of Bangor, Chancellor,[8] at a wage of £100,[9] and Thomas Butler, Master of the Rolls.[10] Thomas Bowring, Chief Justice of the King's Bench, and John Topcliffe, Chief Justice of the Common Bench, had salaries of £66. 13s. 4d. each.[9]

Sir Hugh Conway was one of the original four leaders of Buckingham's rebellion in 1483, carrying out the cash for that expedition to the Earl of Richmond in Brittany. Rewarded in 1485 with the office of Keeper of the King's Great Wardrobe[11] at a salary of £300 a year,[12] he had forfeited the post by 1488.[13] His appointment as Treasurer of Ireland may have marked his return to favour; for, although Henry obviously wished to promote him, his slackness in office made this difficult. He was not satisfactory in Ireland, and as Treasurer of Calais in 1504,[14] received no less than three pardons for failing to render his account at Westminster at the proper time.[15]

It is clear from Conway's accounts of the administration for the first year that he had received £7000 from Sir Reginald Bray, Treasurer of the Wars in Parts beyond the Sea,[16] for Irish

---

[1] B.M. Royal MSS, 18 C xiv.
[2] Gairdner, *Letters*, ii, 297–318.
[3] Appendix viii.
[4] Appendix ix.
[5] p. 187.
[6] Curtis, *Medieval Ireland*, p. 292.
[7] *Cal. Pat. Rolls*, 1494–1509, p. 15.
[8] p. 168.
[9] *Ibid.*
[10] *Cal. Pat. Rolls*, 1494–1509, p. 8.
[11] *Ibid.* 1485–94, p. 22.
[12] Tellers Rolls, E 405, 75, Easter Term, 1 Henry VII, Pierson mem. 4.
[13] *Cal. Pat. Rolls*, 1485–94, p. 226.
[14] *Ibid.* 1494–1509, p. 365.
[15] *Ibid.* pp. 442, 479, 583.
[16] *Ibid.* 1485–94, p. 424.

purposes, between August 12 and 29, 1494;[1] and was acting in the capacity of Treasurer a month before his official appointment, although his salary was paid as from September 12.[2] With this £7000 he defrayed the expenses of the Irish administration till June, 1495. These accounts are set out in his first report,[3] and in the audit upon it made in the following year.[4] The report is incomplete, but fuller in detail than the audit.

From Conway's accounts of his expenditure, the political sequence of events in Ireland from October 1494 to June 1495 can be followed in considerable detail. Although at Christmas Henry was able to report to Charles VIII of France that Ireland was quiet under the rule of Poynings,[5] that calm had not continued. Kildare's brother, James Fitzgerald, seized the royal Castle of Carlow in March 1495[6] and held it against the Deputy. Perkin Warbeck's invasion was expected at any moment. In the face of these dangers, the King sent out another army to Ireland in the spring of 1495 and was no longer satisfied to leave Conway in sole control of Irish finance. He appointed William Hattecliffe as Under-Treasurer on April 26, 1495.[7] On the day following Henry Wyatt and Hattecliffe were made commissioners and auditors of Conway's accounts,[8] and John Pympe became special Treasurer of the Wars in Ireland,[8] a new appointment,

---

[1] Appendix x, p. 165.
[2] Appendix xii, p. 173. As the whole expense of the administration for the first nine months was covered by this £7000, of which a surplus of £900 was carried on to the receipts for the following year, it is clear that Conway made a clerical error in his account as to the date of receipt of the moneys (Royal MSS, 18 C xiv, fol. 123; Appendix x). According to his statement, the £7000 was paid in six instalments between August 12 and 29 for the wages of the army in Ireland "per indenturam factam XIImo die mensis Augusti anno dicti Regis Xmo plenius continetur". August 12, 10 Henry VII, was August 12, 1495. Conway obviously meant 1494; but as the payments were made before and after August 22, the turn of the regnal year, the mistake is easily accounted for. (There is also a mistake in the margin of 18 C xiv, fol. 123, £8000 in error for £7000.)

The possibility that Conway received this £7000 by an indenture of August 12, 1495, for the expenses of the second year of the administration, is inadmissible, as all the receipts for that year are clearly set out in a later report.

[3] Appendix x.   [4] Appendix xi.
[5] Appendix xix.   [6] Appendix x, p. 168.
[7] *Cal. Pat. Rolls*, 1494–1509, p. 26.
[8] *Ibid.* p. 27. For their designation as "Commissionarii et auditores" see Royal MSS, 18 C xiv, fol. 133. The Chancery Warrant, P.R.O. (Series ii, bundle 133, no. 18) mentions no salary.

subdividing the work of Sir Reginald Bray. Hattecliffe, Wyatt and Pympe, in fact though not in name, superseded Conway's functions as Treasurer of Ireland.

Henceforth, Pympe received from Hattecliffe and paid out himself the moneys for the army, which formed the bulk of the Irish expenditure.

Poynings, by the terms of his appointment, was prevented from calling the Treasurer of Ireland to account;[1] Hattecliffe and Wyatt were sent over to do exactly that task; and, further, to investigate the sources of the King's revenue in Ireland in 1495 and to compare it in detail with the sums which had been received in earlier days. They were to take the musters of the second army, lately sent into Ireland against the rebels; and to audit and receive the moneys in the hands of Conway for its payment; they were also to deal with all the revenue from Irish sources and apply it towards the payment of the troops. The King's instructions on this matter[2] indicate the main reason for their appointment. No Irish revenue was mentioned in Conway's first report. It is true that he did more than make both ends meet, for he handed over a surplus of £900 to Wyatt and Hattecliffe in June and had a further balance of £342. 14s. 3d. at the end of the year. Furthermore it appears from a letter of Sir James Ormond to the Earl of Ormond, written on February 20, 1494/5,[3] and by another to him from William White of Waterford on April 12,[4] that Conway had already begun to enforce against the absentee Earl an Act of Resumption, passed by the Poynings Parliament;[5] and this although Ormond was away on official business as Chamberlain of the Queen. White advised him to send over writings from the King, exempting him on the ground of his service; and James Ormond told him to make a stand and be bought out, as "copper will appear where it is hastily".[3] On the estimates the Earl stood to lose two-thirds of his prise of wines in Waterford[6] and Limerick, and two-thirds of his lands, representing £80.[6]

In this matter Conway, who was accused by James Ormond

[1] See the text in full printed in Lascelles, *Liber Munerum*, IV, 101.
[2] Gairdner, *Letters*, II, 64–67.   [3] Appendix V.
[4] Appendix XV.   [5] Appendix XXIII.
[6] Appendix XVI, p. 188.

of being no friend to the Earl, had certainly not been dilatory. Nevertheless the task of tightening up the revenue from Irish sources, so that it should bear the expense of the internal administration of the country by English officials, was taken away from him and entrusted to two men who were probably better trained and more energetic financiers.

A digression into the question of Henry VII's financial arrangements at Westminster will account for the appointments of Wyatt and Hattecliffe in what was evidently an emergency. For the first two years of his reign the expenses of government had been discharged by the Treasurer and Chamberlains of the Exchequer, out of the ancient Exchequer of Receipt, according to the precedents of the previous hundred years. About one-quarter of the total receipts went on household expenses; five-twelfths to the general administration of government, the un-expended balance of one-third being paid over to the Treasurer of the King's Chamber.[1] Reconstruction of government finance was the absorbing occupation of a King who did his accounts with his own hand. Gradually and with some fluctuations he turned away from the machinery of the Exchequer and fixed upon an expansion of the thirteenth century methods of finance of the King's Chamber. By degrees all new revenues and some old ones were paid directly into the Chamber, the receipts of its Treasurer for a year, from September, 1487, being £10,811. Sixteen years later they had increased thirteen-fold.[2] In this way Henry gradually transformed the Chamber into a Treasury, which, during the next third of a century, was of vastly greater importance than the Exchequer of Receipt, and was kept under the control of the most able and trusted personal servants of the Crown as successive Treasurers.[3] The King's surplus in his Chamber account was spent on plate, jewels and rich stuffs; from 1491 to the end of the reign at least £128,441 being invested in jewels,[4] which, with the addition of bonds for

---

[1] Newton, "King's Chamber under the early Tudors", *E.H.R.* xxxii.
[2] Dietz, *English Government Finance*, pp. 80–2.
[3] *Ibid.* 87. A list of the extant account books of the Treasurer of the Chamber for the reign of Henry VII is given in the bibliography. For a description of the system of accounting in the Chamber by Henry VII see Statutes of the Realm, 3 Henry VIII, c. 23.
[4] Dietz, *op. cit.* p. 85.

obligations and recognisances, made up the bulk of the wealth left to Henry VIII at his death.[1]

Before September, 1486, Henry Wyatt was appointed Clerk of the King's Jewels,[2] probably as a reward for his services before Bosworth. The Household Ordinances of Edward IV[3] thus describe the post:

> The office of the Jewel House hath an architectour called Clerk of the Kings' or Keeper of the King's Jewels or Treasurer of the Chamber. This officer taketh by indenture betwixt him and the King, all that he finds in his office of gold, silver, precious stones and the marks of everything. Also he receiveth the yearly gifts by record of the Chamberlain.

From the middle of the fourteenth century onwards, the King's Chamber having deteriorated into a subsidiary part of the King's household, its Treasurer in the time of Edward IV may well have been the same official as the Clerk or Keeper of the Jewels, who literally carried out the simple duties described in the Ordinances. William Daubeney was Clerk of the Jewels to Edward IV.[4] Edmund Chaderton, Treasurer of the Chamber to Richard III, had also been Clerk of the Hanaper.[5] Henry VII, from the outset of his reign, subdivided offices, increasing the number of his officials. William Smyth was made Clerk of the Hanaper with a salary of £40 in 1485;[6] and a Master or Keeper of the Jewel House was appointed. This office of Keeper, with a salary of £50 a year, and £20 for two yeomen under him, was granted to Sir William Tyler in the same year.[7] Henry Wyatt as Clerk received £13. 6s. 8d., paid in instalments twice a year from the Exchequer of Receipt.[8]

[1] Dietz, op. cit. p. 87.

[2] Cal. Pat. Rolls, 1485–94, p. 136. The original grant of the office of Clerk of the Jewels does not seem to exist.

[3] Household Ordinances of Edward IV, Society of Antiquaries, 1790, p. 42. Edward IV modelled his household upon that of Charles the Bold. Olivier de la Marche composed L'État de la Maison du duc Charles de Bourgogne at the request of Edward IV to serve him for a model. Mémoires, ed. Beaune et d'Arbaumont, Société de l'histoire de France, 4 vols. 1883–8, vol. IV.

[4] Pollard, Henry VII, I, p. 100.   [5] Cal. Pat. Rolls, 1485–94, p. 41.
[6] Ibid. p. 48.   [7] Ibid. p. 110.
[8] This payment was entered on the Tellers Rolls for the first time in the Michaelmas Term of 4 Henry VII (E 405, 75, Pierson mem. 1 dorso). Sir William Tyler was paid £40 as part of his salary as Master of the Jewels in the same Term (ibid. Pierson mem. 4 dorso).

The business of the Jewel House was undertaken by Wyatt personally throughout the reign of Henry VII and most of that of Henry VIII. Sir William Tyler, the Keeper, was continuously employed in the north as Governor of Berwick, his name never appearing in connection with Jewel House business except as a recipient of salary.[1] Wyatt, as Clerk of the Jewels, shared the responsibility for the custody of the King's entire savings. The Jewel House was in the position of Bank to the Chamber, and although the Clerk, the Keeper, and the Treasurer of the Chamber were now three persons, the Clerk of the Jewels was the natural apprentice for the post of Keeper and ultimately for that of Treasurer of the Chamber. Such was in fact Wyatt's progression in the official hierarchy.

In May, 1488, Wyatt received the additional billet of Clerk of the Mint, Money and Exchange in the Tower of London and Usher of the Exchange.[2] On April 26, 1495, the day before he was made co-auditor with Hattecliffe in Ireland, he was promoted at the Mint, to the office of Keeper of the Exchange, Assayer of the Coinage and Comptroller, at a salary of £26. 13s. 4d.[3] There is no record of separate payment for his Irish work. This accumulation of offices illustrates Henry VII's method of rewarding the services of his friends, and was described in a note on Sir Henry Wyatt, in the handwriting of George Wyatt, his greatgrandson:[4]

His bountise to his sarvants were measured by ye perfect insight into their trust in discharge of their servicese and by difference of places of importance and neerenes. For ye most part he had them bestowed by promotions in successions to placese, seldome his threasure, more rarely his revenews supplied ye affect. This was apeered in this his servant. In his attendinges on him, ye kinge oft demanded how he thriv'd. His answere was his studise were to searve his Majestie. Saide ye Kinge, thy meaninge is that I should studie to make thee thrive; and thou saist wel, but ye kings my predicessors weakeninge their threasure have made themselves servants to their subiectes. Yet helpt he him with lones of mony on strickt devise of paiment.

[1] I have found no entry of the payment of this salary on the Tellers Rolls of the Exchequer after 1488.
[2] *Cal. Pat. Rolls*, 1485–94, p. 219.
[3] *Ibid.* 1494–1509, p. 16. The Chancery Warrant (Series II, bundle 133, no. 14) mentions the fees, profits, rewards and commodities of the office.
[4] Wyatt MSS, no. 21.

Hattecliffe's official status was that of Under-Treasurer of Ireland, the salary being equal to that authorised for Conway.[1] But although Conway's salary was nominally £66. 13s. 4d. he was actually paid £40 and an allowance of 6s. 8d. a day, making a total of £161. 13s. 4d. from September 12, 1494.[2] Hattecliffe's wife, Isabel, the daughter of Agnes Paston, was Poynings' aunt.[3] His father, William Hattecliffe, who died in 1480, had been physician and secretary to Edward IV.[4] The son, by 1492, was Clerk of the Marshalsea of the Household, and in this capacity kept the accounts of Henry VII's military expedition in that year against the French at Sluys,[5] which had been commanded by Poynings. He made all the payments, receiving the money from Sir Reginald Bray, Treasurer of the King's Wars, by the hand of William Cope the Cofferer. The return is beautifully written, and very different indeed from the rough notes subsidiary to the finished book, which alone have survived for the Poynings administration. William Hattecliffe bequeathed by will[6] the bed on which he lay in the Kings Court, and the book chest, which had belonged to his father, as well as all the books concerning the King's household. He was mentioned later, in 1500, as "clerk of the accounts of the household"[7] and in 1509 as "late accountant of the household".[8] By 1495, with the experience of the Sluys expedition behind him, he was already well qualified for his Irish task, under the same chief. The rough jottings for "a remembrance", before his journey, mention "all my books and in especiall my precedents".[9]

In 1491 and 1493 the payments for the English armies in Ireland had been made from the Exchequer, and in the Easter Term of 1493 they passed through the hands of Bray as

---

[1] Appendix XVI.   [2] Appendix XII, p. 173.   [3] *Paston Letters*, III, 471.
[4] Newton, *Tudor Reforms in the Royal Household*, Tudor Studies, p. 245.
[5] P.R.O. E 36, 208.
[6] P.C.C. 16 Ayloffe: "Item do et lego Thome hatcliff clerico et consanguineo meo quadraginta libras monete anglie et sterling una cum lecto meo proprio in quo iacebam in curia domini Regis cum omnibus suis pertinentiis ac cista una q erat Willelmi hattcliff pro libris imponendis libros omnes concern' compot' hospicii domini Regis precidencia que omnia quecumque fuerint scripta sive in pergameno aut papiro vel in libris aut Rotulis et generaliter omnes libros cujuscumque alterius compot' libris except' concernen' compot' domus mee".
[7] *Cal. Pat. Rolls*, 1494–1509, p. 202.   [8] *Ibid.* p. 598.
[9] Gairdner, *Letters*, II, 298.

Treasurer of the Wars.[1] A search in the Tellers Rolls for 1494 and 1495 has not revealed one entry relating to assignments for Ireland. A single payment of £4266. 13s. 4d. was made out of the King's Chamber in December, 1494,[2] and the remainder of the £7000 for which Conway accounted may have come from the revenues of the Duchy of Lancaster, of which Bray was Treasurer, or from the Household surplus. The Milanese secretary was told in 1496 that the only man who could do anything with Henry VII was named Master Bray and he controlled the King's treasure.[3] If the money for the Poynings administration was drawn from Henry's personal savings "banked" with his Chamber, it was natural enough that Wyatt and Hattecliffe, as Chamber and Household officials respectively, should be the auditors.

Hattecliffe landed at Dublin on June 7 and kept a Register of Receipts and Payments from June 15, 1495 onwards. It begins with an entry for June 13, preceding the regular Register, showing that the first thing Conway did was to hand his unexpended balance of £900 to Wyatt and Hattecliffe on their arrival in Ireland.[4] With it on June 20 they began to pay £897. 4s. to Pympe, the Treasurer of the Wars, and £2. 16s. to Captain John Mountford,[5] all in accordance with the terms of their commission.

Their first task was to audit Conway's accounts from October, 1494, to June, 1495.[6] His second report from June to December, 1495,[7] shows how much his powers as Treasurer had been curtailed. It is a truncated document in which the bulk of the army payments do not figure at all, these being transferred to Pympe. Conway's total receipts from June to December, 1495, were £813 odd, all from Irish sources, whereas Hattecliffe in the same period received £4035 odd, the sum of £2608 [8] being sent straight out to him by the King.[9] Of this he paid £3349 in

---

[1] Tellers Rolls, E 405, 78, Easter Term, 8 Henry VII, Stokes mem. 2.
[2] B.M. Add. MSS, 7099, December 19, 1494.
[3] Pollard, *Henry VII*, I, no. 99.
[4] Royal MSS, 18 C XIV, fol. 13. Appendix XIII, p. 176.
[5] Royal MSS, 18 C XIV, fol. 13, 13 v.
[6] Appendix XI.
[7] Appendix XII.
[8] £400 of this is unaccounted for. See Appendix XIV, p. 180 note 2.
[9] Appendix XIV, p. 180.

block sums direct to Pympe,[1] as Treasurer of the Wars, showing that his appointment had reduced that of Conway as Treasurer to comparative insignificance. Sir Hugh, in fact, left Ireland on November 7, 1495, and his diet allowance, which had been reduced to 3s. 4d. a day after September 12, was afterwards paid to Hattecliffe.[2]

The expenses incurred from June, 1495, till the following December are summarised in Hattecliffe's Declaration of his Receipts in Ireland.[3] The audit upon this Declaration, made perhaps by Wyatt, was concerned with the source of the cash rather than with the categories of expenditure and gives the same figures arranged under different headings.[1] On the receipt side it contains more items from Irish sources, as well as an extra £600 from the King.

Conway's second report, although it deals with small sums, is full of interest, as it gives the details of the expenses incurred by Hattecliffe in the process of carrying out the King's instructions for the tightening up of revenue from Irish sources. Poynings, with thirty horsemen for twelve days, and Conway, with twenty-four horsemen for thirty days, made separate expeditions, at a cost of £14, to assess the yield from the royal manors in all the counties of the Pale. At another time, Conway, with the Chief Justice, and the King's Attorney, and twenty-six horsemen, took nine days assessing ploughlands for the subsidy in Meath and county Dublin.[4] The finished record of this assessment, which cost £2. 4s. to write up, survives.[5] Meath was to yield £368 of subsidy (in lieu of coign and livery) from 276 ploughlands, at 26s. 8d. a ploughland.[5] Hattecliffe had previously copied a survey of Meath for the year 1413,[6] which assessed the county on a basis of 342 carucates. This first computation, probably made before the expedition and perhaps calculated with reference to the 1413 survey, was for a revenue of £480 from Meath, based on a return of 26s. 8d. from each of 360 carucates.[7] Other computations, on a similarly exaggerated

---

[1] Appendix XIV, p. 181.   [2] Royal MSS, 18 C XIV, fol. 67.
[3] See Appendix XIII.
[4] p. 175. See Poynings' Parliament, c. 4. Appendix XXI.
[5] Royal MSS, 18 C XIV, fol. 105 r. Appendix XVI, p. 186.
[6] p. 186 note 1.
[7] These figures are on fol. 109 r; Appendix XVI, p. 186 note 1.

basis, were made for Dublin, Louth and Kildare, amounting to a total estimate of £1739,[1] as against his later estimate of £1275. The sea-coast was scrutinised for customs; and the old records investigated and written up. The King's activities in this matter were not confined to Ireland, for in September, 1495, a census was taken throughout England and especially in the city of London, of the names, ages, and "faculties" of all men, women and children born in Ireland and not living there, which was certified in the King's Exchequer at Westminster.[2]

The result of all these investigations is seen in Hattecliffe's estimate of receipts and payments for 1496, made at the end of 1495.[3] The estimate of receipts was based upon many preliminary documents, recording the investigations undertaken in the autumn of 1495.[4] The yearly anticipated income from Irish sources was £2691. 4s. 4d.[5] of which £1719. 9s. fell due in the Hilary Term,[6] but had claims upon it of £622. 17s. 6½d. for arrears for 1495.[6] The forecast of expenses was only concerned with the salaries of the crown in Ireland, amounting to £1592. 13s. 11d.[7] and left the army out of account. The balance of income anticipated for 1496, and unallotted to salaries or debts, was only £475. 12s. 10½d.

No balance sheet for 1496, corresponding to those for 1495, was made up, although from the preliminary documents the actual receipts and payments for the Hilary, Easter and Trinity Terms can be calculated.[8] The total sum received from Irish sources for those three terms was £1283. 15s. 4¼d.; less than the estimated revenue for the Hilary Term alone, and not enough to pay the crown salaries. The money was actually spent on the army, only Hattecliffe's fee and that of Sir James Ormond appearing in the Register. Every item comprising the monthly totals of army wage payments[9] is given in the accounts. There is besides the check of Hattecliffe's daily register of Irish receipts and payments for the same terms,[10] in which lump appropriations

---

[1] Appendix XVI, p. 186 note 6.
[2] Kingsford, *Chronicles of London*, p. 207.   [3] Appendix XVI.
[4] Royal MSS, 18 C XIV, fols. 105–6 v., 109–13, and 115–20. The latter two documents served as the foundation for the estimate.
[5] Appendix XVI, p. 188.   [6] *Ibid*. p. 190.   [7] p. 189.
[8] Royal MSS, 18 C XIV, fol. 183. See Appendix XVI B.
[9] Royal MSS, 18 C XIV, fols. 94–9 v. and fol. 130. Appendix XVII.
[10] *Ibid*. Hilary Term, fols. 31 v.–48 v.; Easter Term, fols. 49–60; Trinity Term, fols. 61–70 v.

to Pympe of over £1000 figure. The Register is probably not a completely finished document, but its totals compare approximately with Hattecliffe's summary of receipts and payments over a period of five terms.[1]

The work of Hattecliffe and Wyatt, efficient as it appears to have been, was far from successful in making both ends meet. The Irish revenues for the first three terms of 1496 (£1283. 15*s.* 4¼*d.*)[2] fell short of the estimated Irish revenue for the year (£2691. 4*s.* 4*d.*)[3] by £2030. 6*s.* 6*d.*, allowing for the £622. 17*s.* 6½*d.* that had to come off it for arrears of salaries in 1495. The reasons can be given in Hattecliffe's own words, in the fragmentary draft of a letter, probably addressed to Bray, as late Treasurer of the Wars, in July or early August, 1496.[4]

Gairdner assigned this letter to Wyatt[5] because of the writer's mention of "my ready money from the Holt", the escheated property in Denbigh of the attainted Sir William Stanley, of which Wyatt was receiver. But Hattecliffe used the words loosely. There can be no doubt that he himself wrote the letter. The handwriting is the same as that of his accounts, and totally

[1] Royal MSS, 18 C XIV, fol. 183 (1) and my additions of the General Register of Receipts and Payments (2) compared:

Receipts

	(1) Hattecliffe's Summary, fol. 183			(2) General Register			
	£	s.	d.	£	s.	d.	
Trinity Term 1495	3272	6	3	3175	14	11	folios 14–21 v.
Mich. Term 1495	852	15	5	832	11	2½	,, 22–31
Hilary Term 1496	644	14	3	689	7	4½	,, 31 v.–48 v.
Easter Term 1496	442	15	9¼	541	9	11½	,, 49–60
Trinity Term 1496	196	5	4	368	1	9	,, 61–70 v.
	£5408	17	0¼[a]	£5607	5	2½	

Payments

	(1)			(2)			
Trinity Term 1495	2941	4	11½	2904	17	6½	folios 14–21 v.
Mich. Term 1495	1265	8	3	1291	10	11	,, 22–31
Hilary Term 1496	1022	12	0¼	887	8	2¼	,, 31 v.–48 v.
Easter Term 1496	532	4	0½	600	18	11	,, 49–60
Trinity Term 1496	187	11	9¼	308	15	11¼	,, 61–70 v.
	£5949	1	0½	£5993	11	6	

[a] The total of £5462. 3*s.* 8½*d.* given in Royal MSS, 18 C XIV, fol. 183, is wrong.

[2] Appendix XVI B, p. 190. [3] Appendix XVI A, p. 188.

[4] Gairdner, *Letters*, II, 67 and Pollard, *Henry VII*, III, no. 103.

[5] Gairdner, *Letters*, II, p. xlvi.

different from Wyatt's.[1] Moreover Wyatt is known to have been in Carlisle on June 4, 1496, on which date he wrote the King a letter showing his absorption as Captain of Carlisle Castle[2] in the affairs of the Border; he would hardly have returned to Ireland in the following month. Hattecliffe's letter, on the contrary, is that of a man working steadily at Irish administration up to the day on which it was written.

He had excellent excuses for his deficit. The first was the diminution of the Irish revenues by the wasting of the country owing to an "unnecessary war at Easter, waged on behalf of Sir James Ormond, Edmund Pierson and others". This campaign figures in the accounts of the army as aimed against the rebellion of Kildare's brother from January to June, 1496,[3] and contains frequent entries of payments to Sir James Ormond's galloglasses[4] for food and rewards, in addition to the regular sum of £56 a month for his forty horsemen or basnetts. Hattecliffe seems to have contented his creditors in January, 1496, about the time of the departure of Poynings, when he was not expecting a war in the spring. Moreover he had a promise from John Reding, who came out from England on April 10, that he would dispose of the ready money from the Holt, which had been in Wyatt's hands as receiver, a sum amounting in the previous May to £9062. 9s. 8d.[5]

John Reding, like Hattecliffe, was a Household official, seconded on public business outside the Court. In the autumn of 1489 he had received continual payments for expenses in connection with the French ambassador in London,[6] and in the following autumn was paid for victualling the army for Brittany.[7] In 1490 his position in the Household was that of purveyor of oats to the Queen,[8] and in 1496 he was termed Clerk of the Spices.[9] He went to England on May 18, 1496, with William

[1] Wyatt's signature can be seen in the margin of Royal MSS, 18 C xiv, fol. 18 v.
[2] Appendix xlv.
[3] Appendix xvii. [4] Scottish mercenaries.
[5] P.R.O. E 101, 413/2, part ii, fol. 85.
[6] Tellers Rolls, E 403, 78, Mich. Term, 5 Henry VII, Pierson mem. 5 and 6 and later.
[7] Ibid. Mich. Term, 6 Henry VII, Pierson mem. 3.
[8] "avenarius Regine." Tellers Rolls, Mich. Term, 5 Henry VII, Page mem. 7.
[9] Royal MSS, 18 C xiv, fol. 146.

Haulle and John Danyell,[1] two of Hattecliffe's servants, to bring back the treasure of the King for the King's army in Ireland.[2] £3000 was ordered to be paid out of the Chamber, for Irish purposes on May 26, 1496;[3] but the money must have been long in coming, for on July 18 Hattecliffe received letters from the King and from Bray, ratifying Reding's promise, but without any cash; and his servants had evidently not returned with the money before this letter was written.

On the assumption that it would still come, Hattecliffe had paid Gilbert Nugent, the Baron of Delvin (who had been appointed chief captain of the army on June 25, 1496)[4] and others, the uttermost penny of Irish revenue, obtainable from manors, subsidies and customs. The scale of payment to these persons, as authorised by the Deputies Council, was, in his opinion, unduly high and would have been higher still, had he not contested it. The yield of the customs had improved, but not to the extent it should have done had Hattecliffe obtained the "statutes and orders" from home for which he had asked. The war between France, Brittany and Spain and the presence of a man-of-war, which had lain off the coast since mid-Lent and prevented all stranger ships from landing, had also deprived the King of at least £100 in customs.

Between June, 1495, and August, 1496, Henry VII made five separate payments for Irish purposes out of his Chamber Account, amounting in all to £11,213. 13s. 4d.[5] Hattecliffe acknowledged £2608. 12s.[6] in receipts from the King between June and December, 1495; but the remainder of the money does not figure in the Irish accounts. Out of such a sum paid from

---

[1] John Danyell's name figures in the list of Hattecliffe's household at a salary of £2 a year. Royal MSS, 18 C xiv, fol. 225.
[2] Gairdner, *Letters*, ii, 311.
[3] B.M. Add. MSS, 7099 and P.R.O. E 101, 414/6.
[4] Gairdner, *Letters*, ii, p. xlviii.
[5] B.M. Add. MSS, 7099, fols. 27–35:

		£	s.	d.	
June 14	1495	200	0	0	fol. 27
Nov. 2	1495	2466	13	4	fol. 31
Dec. 1	1495	2600	0	0	fol. 32
Feb. 21	1496	2947	0	0	fol. 33
May 26	1496	3000	0	0	fol. 35
		£11,213	13	4	

[6] Appendix xiv.

the Chamber, there would have been many thousands of pounds over when the balance due on Irish salaries in 1496 had been met. This £11,000 must certainly have included all the expenses incident to Ireland, involving the payments made in England for the fleet of 1500 men destined for Ireland, under Sir Roger Cotton, who was appointed its admiral on July 26, 1495.[1]

Unfortunately only a few military commitments figure individually in the English accounts, but the payments made out of the Chamber from July 23-30, 1495,[2] for the victualling, shipping and sending over the sea of 200 men with 100 horses, must have been part of the expenses for the 1500 men of Cotton's fleet. It is unlikely that any of them reached Ireland in time for the siege of Waterford, which was raised by Perkin on August 3.

The army was reduced to half its size by June, 1496, and in August the English force had been disbanded and paid off, Hattecliffe signing the following general certificate of discharge for the gunners on August 8.[3]

Be it known to all men that A B C Gonner berer herof well and truly hath behad hym and our soverayn lord the Kynge in his service of warres within the land of Ireland in the company of Thomas Garth Squyer his capeteyn In witnesse whereof to the letters I, W. H.,[4] have subscrybyd my signe at Droghda the VIII day of August the XI yere of the regn of our soverayn Lord King Henry the VIIth.

Kildare was appointed Deputy on August 6 and Hattecliffe remained in Ireland to await his landing on September 27, being paid his fee as Under-Treasurer for the Michaelmas Term, 1496, as well as his diet of 3s. 4d. a day till September 28.[5] There is only one entry for the Michaelmas Term in the General Register of Receipts and Payments[6] and two entries of charges on the revenue,[7] both in his own handwriting. The latest item in the volume is a copy of John de Burgh's oath of fealty taken before Kildare on October 26, 1496.[8] With Hattecliffe's departure from Ireland the Poynings administration finally came to an end.

[1] *Cal. Pat. Rolls, 1494–1509,* 34.   [2] B.M. Add. MSS, 7099, fols. 28–9.
[3] Royal MSS, 18 C xiv, fol. 93 v.   [4] "I, William Hattecliffe."
[5] Royal MSS, 18 C xiv, fol. 67.   [6] *Ibid.* fol. 77.
[7] *Ibid.* fol. 76.   [8] Gairdner, *Letters,* ii, 326.

CHAPTER V

HENRY VII'S RELATIONS WITH SCOTLAND AND IRELAND DURING THE POYNINGS ADMINISTRATION—OCTOBER 1494– OCTOBER 1496

Poynings' first object was the military conquest of Ireland, but the force from England for which he drew pay from October 11 to November 8, 1494, consisted only of 5 lancers, 22 sub-captains and 400 archers. From November 8 onwards, the majority of these were distributed under the commands of officials and captains who each received the wages of their men in a lump sum. Thomas Garth continued to draw pay for 100 men from October 16 onwards, these being probably identical with the contingent he had commanded since June 24, 1494, and additional to the new army that came out with Poynings.[1] The Deputy retained 97 archers, 14 sub-captains and 8 lancers under his immediate command from November 9 to June 20, 1495. The entire English force in Ireland during the winter of 1494–5 would appear to have consisted of 32 lancers, 449 archers, 90 gunners and 36 soldiers and mariners; a complement of 653 men;[2] corresponding with the army "scarce amounting to 1000", mentioned by Ware, as led by Poynings, into Ulster, between October 13 and November 30, "against Perkin's abettors, who with other rebels had fled thither".[3] This force was supplemented by men, collected by Kildare and Sir James Ormond, who both accompanied him on this expedition.

The old earldom of Ulster had been reconquered by the "savage Irish", to which "wild colts Perkin showed himself first, easily persuading them to believe that he was the same very person whom he falsely fained and counterfeited!"[4] O'Hanlon

---

[1] See pp. 59–60.
[2] For all these figures see a summary of wages of soldiers in Ireland taken from Conway's first report. Appendix x.
[3] Ware, *Annals, Henry VII*, p. 27.
[4] *Hall's Chronicle*, 471, translating Polydore Vergil.

of Orior in Armagh rose against the Deputy and doubtless prevented him from going farther to attack the greatest Irish chief of the north, the notoriously disloyal Hugh O'Donnell of Tyrconnell, well known to be in league with James IV of Scotland against Henry VII. Record evidence for the Ulster campaign is to be found in the attainder of Kildare, which formed chapter 41 of the burnt Parliament Roll of Poynings' Parliament. A seventeenth-century copy of the attainder survives,[1] from which it is clear that the Earl's forfeiture was to date from November 10, 1494, the day on which he must have begun to plot openly with O'Hanlon against Poynings, whilst in his company in Ulster. Yet Kildare remained at large till February 27, 1495, when he was taken prisoner, and put in a ship "to be carried into Saxonland".[2]

There is yet another source for this period in a hitherto unnoticed letter from Sir James Ormond to the Earl of Ormond, written from Dublin on February 20, 1495, wherein he describes the cost he is at in Dublin, waiting upon the Deputy, "who is as good a man as he knows, for all the Irish in those parts had given up lands as their pledges for peace, and those who refused peace had had their lands destroyed".[3]

It has been assumed by every scholar of the period, following Ware, that the events mentioned in Kildare's attainder, including the siege of Carlow, occurred before the meeting of Poynings' Parliament at Drogheda on December 1, 1494. This Parliament lasted long enough to suffer "various Prorogacions and Adjornamentes".[4] The Parliament Roll was burnt in 1922 and has only been printed in part. A reconstruction of the text from a contemporary and slightly shortened copy of the chapters, at that time considered the most important,[5] in the order given by a seventeenth-century list of the complete chapter headings,[6] is appended[7]. Chapter 24, which acquits Kildare and Sir James Ormond of any offences done in Ireland, must date from before

---

[1] Lambeth, Carew MSS, 603, fol. 177. Appendix XXXI.
[2] *Annals of Ulster*, III, 387.
[3] Appendix V.
[4] *Rot. Parl.* VI, 481-2.
[5] P.R.O. E 30, 1548.
[6] Carew MSS, 608, folios 113 v.–116. Appendix XX.
[7] Appendices XXI–XXXVI.

his arrest on February 27.[1] Chapter 26,[2] authorising the Treasurer to act as Deputy, could scarcely have been framed after Conway fell out of favour in March or April. Chapter 33, giving authority to act as Deputy to the Chancellor, must belong to the period when Conway, as Treasurer, was a figurehead. Chapter 35, against coign and livery, was passed "notwithstanding the act late made in the said Parliament", which was chapter 4.[3] The attainder of Kildare is chapter 41. These instances imply that the chapters have survived in chronological order, Kildare's attainder being one of the latest acts of the Parliament.

Poynings' siege of the royal Castle of Carlow, occupied against the King by Kildare's brother, James Fitzgerald, can be dated from Conway's accounts and is mentioned in the attainder. Payments were made for wages, from March 2, 1494/5, onwards, for sixteen soldiers of the garrison of Carlow, driven out by James, brother of the Earl of Kildare, at the time of his treason;[4] and the Council repaid Sir James Ormond for expenses incurred at the siege of Carlow on April 11, 1495.[5] If James Fitzgerald captured Carlow about March 2, 1494/5, and Sir James Ormond was besieging it in April, the Bill of Attainder cannot have been passed till long after Kildare had been sent to England. Later in the year when the Earl petitioned in the English Parliament against his conviction and was reinstated,[6] O'Hanlon cleared him of his treachery upon oath.[7] The evidence of his guilt from the attainder must be given greater weight.[8]

Poynings was back from Ulster on December 1, 1494, for the opening of the Drogheda Parliament which passed Poynings' Law. By December 30, 1494, the Deputy appeared to the King to have made satisfactory progress in his task of Irish coercion. Such, at least, was the impression which Henry VII wished to make upon Charles VIII of France. His instructions to Rich-

[1] Appendix XXVI.
[2] Appendix XXVII.
[3] Appendix XXI.
[4] Appendix X, p. 168.
[5] Royal MSS, 18 C XIV, fol. 90 v.
[6] *Rot. Parl.* VI, 481-2, and Statutes of the Realm, 11 Henry VII, c. 44.
[7] Ware, *Annals, Henry VII*, p. 27.
[8] Busch, p. 342.

mond Herald[1] were to tell the French King that no monarch in England had ever been so well obeyed; that the savage Irish as well as those of the English tongue had done homage to Poynings and that it only remained to put the country "en bonne justice et police", a matter which would be accomplished soon and without difficulty. It was said that Scotland was sending a great embassy to England to sue for peace, which may have been the result of a premature Scots raid upon the Border timed to coincide with a rising in Ireland and with Perkin's expected invasion of England.[2] Henry dealt with the Scottish danger to some extent by appointing Richard Fox, the ablest statesman of his time, to the Bishopric of Durham on December 8,[3] where he remained as the backbone of English power in the north till a strong peace with Scotland had been secured.

However bold a complexion he might put upon it to the King of France, the danger of James IV's combination with the great Earl of Desmond and Hugh O'Donnell, mentioned in Kildare's attainder, was a black spot on Henry's horizon on New Year's Day, 1494/5. Tyrconnell and Munster were beyond the coercion of Poynings and still in open rebellion. Henry played with the idea of negotiation and authorised Richard Hatton in December, 1494, to deliver Desmond a pardon under the Great Seal if he could secure his eldest son as a hostage.[4] The pardon, dated on the same day as Hatton's commission, seems to have remained unused in his possession till 1496. Gilbert[5] says that his negotiations were unsuccessful, but there is no trace of Hatton's journey to Ireland till the following December, 1495, and Desmond made no submission till the March ensuing.

On the continent the combination of the Emperor Maximilian and the Dowager Duchess of Burgundy, in favour of Perkin, was growing in power and their courts were attracting more and more disaffected Yorkists from England. In the face of this increasing

---

[1] Appendix XIX.
[2] Tytler, *History of Scotland*, II, 117. Tytler, on the strength of notes to Sterling's MS Chronicle, which I have been unable to identify, says that the Armstrongs, Elwalds, Crossars, and Wighams took part in the raid. These persons are mentioned in a Scottish trial of March 2, 1494/5. Pitcairn's *Criminal Trials*, I, 21.
[3] *Cal. Pat. Rolls*, 1494–1509, p. 5.
[4] *Ibid.* p. 27.
[5] Gilbert, *Viceroys*, p. 457.

danger, Henry bribed Sir Robert Clifford, who had been sent to Flanders by Sir William Stanley in 1493,[1] with £500 to turn King's evidence,[2] and in February, Stanley, the brother-in-law of the King's mother and the richest gentleman in England was beheaded. Henry sent another embassy to Charles VIII in March which was less optimistic in tone than the one of the previous December.[3] Kildare's defection and the Irish revolt must have contributed to this change. It is obvious that Charles VIII was vacillating in his alliance with Henry VII, under pressure brought to bear upon him by Maximilian. In his appeal for Charles's neutrality Henry gave some curious secret instructions to Richmond Herald.[4] He was to tell the Cardinal of St Malo (Guillaume Briçonnet) who had previously held the rank of General under Louis XI, and was in Charles VIII's closest confidence,[5] that Henry had been informed that the Scottish King intended to make some movement against him that year. Of this he was not in the least afraid. Nevertheless, as certain French gentlemen had suggested to Sir Charles Somerset[6] (whom Henry had recently sent as ambassador to France), that in case of a Scottish attack, they might hand over to him the son of Alexander, Duke of Albany who was then in France (should the French King agree), he might say that, in acceding to this proposal Charles VIII would be doing him a favour. No other prince could so well help the Duke of Albany to secure his rights against James IV in Scotland as Henry himself, and he would treat him well, as befitted his rank, so that the King of France would be content.

This young boy was John, the son of Alexander, Duke of Albany, James III's treacherous brother,[7] who had been born

---

[1] Archbold, *E.H.R.* vol. xiv, for Stanley's inquisition.
[2] *Excerpta Historica*, January 20, 1495.
[3] The full instructions to Richmond Herald are in B.M. Cotton, Caligula, D vi, fols. 22–6 v. Part of the secret instructions on fol. 25 are printed in Gairdner (*Letters*, ii, 296–7), without a date. The additional instructions, given in Appendix xxxvii, are unprinted.
[4] Appendix xxxvii.
[5] "Lequel pour ce temps là avoit plus crédit qu'aucun autre auprès la personne du Roy." Godefrey, *Histoire de Charles VIII*, pp. 98, 638–9. See *Archaeologia*, xxvii, 180.
[6] The natural son of Henry Beaufort, Duke of Somerset. I can find no other trace of his embassy.
[7] See Chapter i.

of his father's second marriage with a French lady, in 1479, after divorcing his first wife for propinquity of blood.[1] He must have been about nine years of age at this time and could talk nothing but French. Alexander's three sons by his first wife were being brought up in Scotland;[2] but had been pronounced illegitimate. In this crisis Henry VII may well have thought that he could make excellent use of John, who was at least a real prince, whose father had been supported by Edward IV and Richard III as a candidate for the throne of Scotland. While James IV was backing Perkin's upstart claim to the English crown, why should not Henry reply by supporting a Scottish pretender? Nothing appears to have happened as the outcome of this suggestion, although in later years John, Duke of Albany, as Regent for James V, more than attained to his rights in Scotland.

The long siege of Carlow Castle was being waged in Ireland in the spring of 1495.[3] On March 20 Pympe "that came out of Ireland from Sir Edward Ponynges" was paid £10 by the King at Sheen.[4] His errand may have been a request for reinforcements for Poynings as his visit was followed by a strengthening of the administration in soldiers and officials. Pympe's appointment as Treasurer of the Wars in Ireland with 100 marks of salary, Hattecliffe's appointment as Under-Treasurer, and the joint billet of Wyatt and Hattecliffe as auditors followed on April 27.[5] On May 3 Wyatt and Pympe were paid £26. 13s. 4d. and £20 respectively for riding into Ireland.[6]

Wyatt was entrusted with Henry VII's verbal instructions to Sir James Ormond, his chief Anglo-Irish ally, as is shown by a letter from the King to James, written at Sheen on April 7.[7]

---

[1] G.E.C.
[2] See *Treasurer's Accounts*, I, cxlviii.
[3] Cox (*Hibernia Anglicana*, p. 186) says that Poynings had to patch up a peace with O'Hanlon and Magennis, so that he could go to relieve Carlow.
[4] *Excerpta Historica*, p. 102.
[5] *Cal. Pat. Rolls*, 1494–1509, pp. 26–7.
[6] *Excerpta Historica*, p. 102.
[7] P.R.O. Ancient Correspondence, LI, 114:
    "By the king.
Trusty and right Welbiloved We grete you Wele And Wol and desire you to yeve ful feith and credence to the relation of our trusty and Welbiloved servaunt henry Wyot clerc of our Jewelles in al such matiers and thinges as

Hattecliffe's entries of his travelling expenses on the same journey introduce his volume of accounts. He landed at Dublin on June 7, 1495, and on June 15 the Register of Irish Receipts and Payments, kept in his own handwriting, begins and continues till August 1496. From this Register the political events in Ireland can be followed almost day by day. Gairdner has printed extracts,[1] but these are far from complete, and the whole Register is well worth publication.

On June 15, 1495, a friar was sent to reconnoitre the O'Brien country near the southern limits of the Pale.[2] Other spies are said to have been despatched into Scotland,[3] but there are no references in the Register to any of these of an earlier date than January 1495/6.[4] The increased activity on all sides was caused by the imminence at long last of Perkin's invasion. In correspondence Henry expressed a contempt for the "garçon" but he was far too wise to leave a stone unturned in his preparations. Money and men were rushed out to Ireland in June.[5] Perkin's expedition to Deal on July 3,[6] with fourteen ships, was a shameful fiasco; but before the end of the month, he had appeared with a fleet of eleven ships off Desmond's territory of Munster, the old familiar ground of his first Irish welcome in 1491; one of the ships, the *Kekeout*, Gairdner believed to have been Scottish;[7] but the early seventeenth-century Dutch whalers named three capes in Spitzbergen "Kyckuit" or "Uitkyk", so Perkin's ship may have been supplied from Flanders.[8] Desmond and Perkin laid siege to Waterford, the "urbs intacta", which alone had remained loyal during Simnel's rebellion, and boasted in later years that it was never taken by Irish chief or Norman earl throughout the Geraldine-Butler feuds and the age of the Tudors. Waterford

we have commaunded hym to openne and declar unto you at this tyme on our behalve. As We perfaitely trust you. Yeven Undr our signet at our manoir of Shene the VIIth day of Aprile.
To our trusty & right Welbiloved knyght for our body *sir* James Ormond."
A grant from Henry VII to Sir Edward Stanley is dated from "o^r mano^r of Shene, the VIIth day of Aprill the Xth yer of our Reigne" (1495) (P.R.O. Chancery Warrants, Series II, file 133, no. 5).

[1] *Letters*, II, 298–314. [2] Gairdner, *Letters*, II, 298.
[3] Gilbert, *Viceroys*, p. 458. [4] Gairdner, *Letters*, II, 306.
[5] *Excerpta Historica*, p. 103.
[6] Gairdner, *Richard III*, p. 295, and Pollard, *Henry VII*, pp. 1, 79.
[7] Gairdner, *Richard III*, p. 298.
[8] Sir Martin Conway, *No Man's Land*, pp. 94, 347, 355.

was the second most important town in Ireland;[1] virtually a self-governing city-state of the continental type, electing its magistrates, declaring war and peace, and paying a small fee-farm to the Butlers.[2] The Book of Howth[3] gives a confused account of the siege, introducing the name of the Earl of Lincoln, long since dead, and ending with the story of Perkin's next departure from Waterford in 1497.[4] Help was sent to the citizens from the Pale, for, after June 24, ordinances were not enacted in the Dublin Assembly "because the Mayor, bailiffs and divers of the Commons were at Waterford in Munster with Sir Edward Poynings".[5] The siege lasted from July 23 to August 3, and was suddenly dropped owing to the activity of Poynings' gunners. The fleet destined for Ireland, of which Sir Roger Cotton was made Admiral on July 26, was too late.[6]

Payments of £394. 14s. 3d. were made to Captain John Morton[7] for himself and his retinue sent with Thomas Garth to Waterford.[8] The force consisted of 10 sub-captains and 289 archers, elaborate details of their pay for the months of August, September and October 1495 being given in Hattecliffe's accounts.[9] The total expense of the army in Ireland from June 20 to Michaelmas was £2770. 14s. 3d. Large payments for Ireland were made from the Chamber in July[10] and on the credit side there were assets from the capture of three of Perkin's ships before Waterford by the gunners, Edington and Warwick; for which deed and that of "breaking the siege" they were rewarded with £4.[11] It has been said that this was the first time that big

---

[1] Arthur Young, *A Tour in Ireland*, ed. Constantia Maxwell, p. 232. In a map of Great Britain of 1550, London, Oxford, Edinburgh and Waterford are the only cities marked. (Frontispiece to Hume Brown's *Scotland before 1700*.)

[2] Hattecliffe estimated that he would receive £10 from it in 1496 by resumption from the Earl of Ormond. Royal MSS, 18 C xiv, fol. 149. Appendix xvi, p. 188.

[3] Pollard, *Henry VII*, iii, no. 99.

[4] Gairdner disentangles these two accounts in *Richard III*, pp. 320–4.

[5] Gilbert, *Calendar of Ancient Records of Dublin*, i, 381.

[6] *Cal. Pat. Rolls*, 1494–1509, p. 34.

[7] John Morton was Sergeant of the King's Tents in 1497. His account as Sergeant is in P.R.O. E 101, 414/7.

[8] Appendix xiii, p. 177.

[9] Royal MSS, 18 C xiv, fols. 144 v. and 145.

[10] *Excerpta Historica*, p. 103.

[11] Gairdner, *Letters*, ii, 299.

guns were used in Ireland,[1] but the accounts show that they had been imported for the 1493 campaign.

Wyatt bought the *Kekeout* for £26. 13s. 4d. on August 14,[2] and on February 13, 1495/6, sent her from Dublin to Bristol on a venture of his own. He received a refund from Hattecliffe for the wages of her sailors for this trip, but the payment was afterwards struck out with the marginal words " quia non pro rege ".[3] Wyatt probably sailed in her himself, as he is not again mentioned in connection with Ireland and had returned to his post of Captain of Carlisle some time before June, 1496. John Clerk bought another of Perkin's men-of-war for £26. 13s. 4d. in cash and one called *Le Mare* for the equivalent of £40 in cloth.[4]

When Perkin escaped from Waterford, he did the first part of his journey in the company of Desmond.[5] The shipwrecks and trajects mentioned in the Book of Howth in connection with his flight in 1497 probably occurred in 1495 on his way to the Court of James IV in Scotland.[6] A letter written in October, 1496, describing Kildare's reception on his return to Ireland as Deputy,[7] gives some information as to the native Irish who had supported Perkin in the summer of 1495. After Desmond, John de Burgh of Galway (Shane Burke), O'Donnell, and O'Neill of Clandeboy[8] were the greatest succour Warbeck had had. In July, 1495, James had received O'Donnell at his Court and treated him with great consideration.[9] He was back in Donegal on August 7,[10] and had probably arranged for Perkin's regal reception in Scotland. Without Shane Burke's help and that of O'Donnell, Warbeck could never have made his way through the wild fastnesses of Connaught and Donegal.

---

[1] Curtis, *History of Medieval Ireland*, p. 406. In 1506 Henry VII was planning an expedition into Ireland with "3 great pieces, four hundred Harquebushes, three score Fawkins, & 500 Handgunnes"—Scofield, *Star Chamber*, p. 24.

[2] Gairdner, *Letters*, II, 299.

[3] *Ibid.* II, 308.   [4] *Ibid.* II, 300.

[5] Royal MSS, 18 C xiv, fol. 144. Owen Eton was sent from Waterford to the King in England with letters about rumours of the journey of Desmond and Perkin in August. See p. 175.

[6] Gairdner, *Richard III*, pp. 320–4.   [7] Appendix XLIII.

[8] He is called "McBoye" in the letter. The O'Neills of Tyrone divided into two branches in the fourteenth century. The senior branch was called by the English "O'Neill the Great". The second branch founded Clannaboy, with its capital seat at Castlereagh.

[9] *Treasurer's Accounts*, I, 227.   [10] *Annals of Ulster*, III, 389–91.

The summer after Perkin's departure was a quiet one, and the officials of the Poynings administration put their affairs in order and paid off their debts contracted during the crisis. The mayor and citizens of Waterford were reimbursed £100 for payments made by them while the Deputies' army was there.[1] During August and September Wyatt was repaid loans of £44. 6s. 8d. which he had incurred on behalf of the Irish Exchequer,[2] and he initialed the receipt of £20 on Hattecliffe's accounts.[3] On October 11 he was still in Waterford, where he received letters from the King,[4] but had returned to Dublin by November 5.[5] In the autumn Hattecliffe was able to set to work in earnest to carry out the King's instructions for the reform of Irish finance. Several new subordinate officials were appointed, and the country was so quiet that Poynings may well have thought his work was done. In mid-December he left Ireland in triumph. £12. 10s. was paid for the passage of his soldiers back to England and £20 for conducting his ship.[6] The approximate date can be inferred from a warrant issued on December 12, for the payment of £5. 12s. to William MacMahon, which was not honoured "because before this time the Lord Deputy had gone to England".[7]

The rule of Poynings had achieved its main object, the rout of the Yorkist faction, and the year 1495 ended with Ireland calmed and Henry's reputation considerably higher upon the continent. The Chancellor, Henry Deane, who had taken Poynings' place in Parliament during his absence, was appointed Deputy on January 1, 1496,[8] and Hattecliffe's accounts give full information from January 4[9] onwards as to the army left behind in Ireland. The complement consisted of 330 Englishmen, 100 kerns and 1 trumpeter, costing £294. 11s. 1d. a month. There

---

[1] Royal MSS, 18 C xiv, fol. 145, p. 179.
[2] *Ibid.* fols. 18 v., 22 v., p. 179.
[3] *Ibid.* fol. 18 v.
[4] *Ibid.* fol. 22.   [5] *Ibid.* fol. 20 v.
[6] Gairdner, *Letters*, ii, 308–9.
[7] *Ibid.* ii, 304. See also *Annals of Ulster*, iii, 397. In 1495–6 the city of Canterbury made him a present of wine on his return from Ireland; *Hist. MSS Com. 9th Report*, i, 146.
[8] *Cal. Pat. Rolls*, 1494–1509, p. 65. The Chancellor was paid his diet allowance of 6s. 8d. a day till Easter; Royal MSS, 18 C xiv, fol. 131.
[9] *Ibid.* fol. 129. Printed in Gilbert's *Viceroys*, pp. 610–11.

were 110 English basnetts,[1] 150 foot archers, 60 horse archers, 6 petty captains and 2 "spears". Garth commanded 188 Englishmen and 100 kerns and Sir James Ormond led 40 of the basnetts. The force was smaller by half than that existing in Ireland at the beginning of the Poynings administration.

In August, 1495, the foolish Emperor Maximilian was still eagerly awaiting the result of "the Duke of York's invasion", financed largely by himself, in the hope that Perkin might become King of England and be admitted to the Holy League in the place of Henry VII.[2] This Holy League, of which Maximilian was the leading promoter, was to be a concert of Europe directed against France for her aggressive policy in Italy. Its formation was the main international question of the day, England being the doubtful Power which Spain, Venice and Milan alike wished to persuade to membership. Henry was still on friendly terms with Charles VIII and made it clear that until the affair of Perkin was settled he would come to no decision in the matter. This caused Spain to further an Anglo-Scottish peace. Maximilian realised that England's membership of the League was essential to its success, but hoped against hope that his vassal Perkin might yet become King. By September he was disillusioned, and had named Henry as a member of the League,[3] with a reservation concerning the so-called "Duke of York". By December he was content to drop the reservation "although he could expect neither benefit nor favour from the King of England".[4] By January, 1495/6, he had invited him to join the League unconditionally with no mention of Warbeck,[5] and Henry declined the invitation.[6]

Maximilian's change of front measures the growth of England's prestige upon the continent. Yet even after the Deal and Waterford invasions James IV remained Perkin's firm friend. It was said that "James did not admit the stranger into his kingdom until Henry had treated with manifest scorn the

---

[1] A "basnett", alternatively called a "spear", was a mounted man to whom three horses were assigned during the campaign (Gairdner, *Letters*, II, 316). He must have taken his name from the "basnet", a helmet terminating in a point and closed in front with a visor. The secondary meaning is not given in the *N.E.D.*

[2] *Venetian Calendar*, I, 652.   [3] *Ibid*. I, 657.
[4] *Ibid*. I, 660.   [5] *Ibid*. I, 665.
[6] *Ibid*. I, 666.

Scottish heralds, who, in the name of their country and relying on existing treaties, demanded restitution of stolen property and satisfaction for injuries done ".[1] Safe-conducts had been issued in May, 1495, to commissioners of the King of Scots[2] and to Sir William Tyler to meet and discuss peace and other matters. In August £40 was paid to an ambassador from Scotland[3] and it is possible that Boece may have been referring to these frustrated deliberations of which nothing is known.

After the departure of Poynings a renewal of attacks upon the English was made by the same James Fitzgerald, brother of Kildare, who had seized Carlow the year before. The new Deputy, Henry Deane, sent out letters on February 9 ordering fires to be kindled on various parts of the hills of Tara, Lyons, Athboy and Slane, to warn the King's people when James Earleson, with other Irish enemies, should be descried advancing on the English territories.[4] On the last day of February the royal Castle of Carrickfergus was strengthened for two months by the presence of Sir Richard Salkeld, Constable of Carlisle, with an extra garrison of twelve men.[5] A messenger was paid on March 15 for carrying missives to various barons asking them to prepare to fight against James and other rebels,[6] and on the 24th, Garth, who was with the King's army at Naas, sent letters with rumours about him to the Chancellor.[7] James was still resisting the King in April and May.[8] On July 4 mention was first made of a tripartite indenture of peace drawn up between him and the King's Council.[9]

In this campaign some of the native Irish were helping the English, notably William MacMahon,[10] to whom Henry VII was paying black-rents.[10] Hugh MacMahon and John O'Reilly were said to have slain sixty Englishmen in the summer of 1494.[11] Since that time John O'Reilly had changed sides and Hugh MacMahon followed his example after O'Hanlon had slain his son in May, 1496.[12] O'Donnell, in revenge, pursued the Irish

[1] Moir, *Boece's Lives*, p. 81. [2] *Rot. Scot.* II, 516, 517.
[3] *Excerpta Historica*, p. 104. [4] Gairdner, *Letters*, II, 307.
[5] Royal MSS, 18 C XIV, fol. 99, p. 195. [6] Gairdner, *Letters*, II, 309.
[7] *Ibid.* II, 309–10. [8] *Ibid.* II, 311–12.
[9] *Ibid.* II, 312–13. [10] Royal MSS, 18 C XIV, fol. 102, p. 194.
[11] *Annals of the Four Masters*, IV, 1211.
[12] *Ibid.* IV, 1225, and *Annals of Ulster*, III, 405.

chief, who dared to be loyal to the English King, into Cavan; burnt O'Reilly's territories and sacked, destroyed and pillaged the English settlements in Louth.[1] This incessant warfare in the Marches of the Pale necessitated the construction of the dyke and raised fence around the frontiers of the four partially English counties, ordered by Poynings' Parliament;[2] and writs were issued enjoining the sheriffs and justices to compel the land-holders near the borders to complete the work under penalties.[3]

Garth distributed his force under the command of several captains, only two of whom were the same as those of the previous year. Every detail of the wages of the troops from January to June 24 is to be found in Hattecliffe's accounts,[4] with the exception of the four weeks from April 25 to May 24, which are missing altogether. The additional incidental payments made by John Joseph, Pympe's deputy, throw light on the operations of the campaign. The payments for the army from May 24 to June 22 had decreased by more than half since January, indicating the approach of the peace treaty on July 4 between James, brother of Kildare, and the Council.

Gilbert Nugent, Baron of Delvin, was appointed chief captain of the King's forces in Ireland,[5] at a salary of £200 a year,[6] on June 25, three days after the entries of payment of army wages in Hattecliffe's accounts stop. He must have succeeded Thomas Garth, who, when the Irish war was over, was urgently needed on the Scottish Border to organise resistance to James IV's expected invasion. Henceforth, till his death in 1505, when he was Marshal of Berwick, Garth's activities were confined to the north. The appointment of an Anglo-Irish baron, as commander of the King's forces in Ireland, is the first sign of the approaching withdrawal of the English administration in favour of a modified return to the previous form of government.

The warfare on the borders of the Pale did not affect Munster, for at last, on March 12, 1495/6, Desmond made his first sign

[1] *Annals of the Four Masters*, IV, 1225.   [2] Appendix xxx.
[3] Gilbert, *Viceroys*, p. 459. No reference.
[4] Appendix xvii.
[5] Gairdner, *Letters*, II, p. xlviii. Ware, *Annals, Henry VII*, p. 33.
[6] B.M. Royal Roll, 14 B xliv.
"m[d] that thes bene the syngments that the barrown off delwyn hade off the tresowrer off the 11cli that the ffor seyd tressower promyste hym ffor h[s] wages." In Hattecliffe's handwriting.

of surrender to the King. Hatton had gone out to Ireland in December, 1495,[1] and, by virtue of his commission of December, 1494, made an indenture with Desmond[2] in his own town of Youghal, embodying the King's proviso of the previous year, that his son and heir should be handed over as a hostage. His guardians were to be the mayor and bailiffs of Cork, a city in Desmond's sphere of influence, with whom the Earl no doubt knew that the boy would be perfectly safe. It cannot be said that his submission was more than a gesture towards peace, better than nothing, but far from satisfactory. He was still the independent sovereign, treating with Henry VII as an equal and able to make and enforce his own conditions, which, if not carried out within two years, should automatically result in the delivery of his son to Kildare. Otherwise, young FitzMaurice was to remain at Cork for three years "on behalf of the King". The four conditions named were the return of Kildare to his lands in Ireland; the observance by Henry of the same relation towards Desmond that Edward IV had maintained with his predecessors; his freedom from compulsion to attend Parliament or Grand Council in Ireland; and immunity from the appointment of a Deputy or Lieutenant unfriendly to himself. The two years' time limit was reduced to one year in the case of the second and third conditions. On March 14, the mayor, bailiffs and commons of Youghal swore to influence Desmond, to the best of their power, to keep his indenture; and in case of default to help the mayor, bailiffs and commons of Cork.[3] On the following day Desmond took his oath of allegiance to the King.[4]

The size to which the army was reduced by May, 1496, shows the comparative calm of the country. It is universally assumed by historians that Kildare's reappointment as Deputy in August proves the Poynings administration to have been a costly failure. It is also said that Kildare ruled Ireland for nothing. Both statements are inaccurate. Whereas Poynings received a salary of £500 a year, Kildare under Edward IV had had £600 "for thexercise of his office of deputy and for the finding of 80 archers & 40 horsemen called spears".[5] Henry VII had raised

---

[1] Bentley, *Excerpta Historica*, p. 106.
[2] Appendix xxxviii. [3] P.R.O. E 30, 1565. [4] Appendix xxxix.
[5] B.M. Cotton, Titus, B xi, vol. i, modern pagination 25. An indenture between Edward IV and Kildare. The £600 is to be paid out of the revenues

this sum to £1000 in 1485.[1] But if Kildare continued to receive such a salary, as he probably did, he also became responsible for a local army[2] and this was the crux of the whole matter.

With the departure of Perkin to the Court of James IV, Henry was naturally anxious to economise in Ireland, and concentrate his energies on the Border. The Poynings administration had not been successful in making Ireland pay her way, but the emergency which had brought it about had been surmounted; and there is no sign whatsoever of an anticipated general Irish rising with which Kildare might be expected to cope more efficiently than Poynings. The army that had been sent to Ireland was needed for the Border, military preparations on a very large scale being made in England during the next two years. Without an English army in Ireland the bureaucratic régime of government could not have been enforced. Henry was wise not to attempt it, and to fall back upon Kildare, the best of the Anglo-Irish nobles, as Deputy; a man for whose return within two years the influential Desmond had stipulated before he would take an oath of homage to the King.

The stories told in the Book of Howth show that Henry had a personal liking for the gruff and outspoken rebel. "This old Earl, being soon hot and soon cold, was of the English well beloved", writes one of his contemporaries.[3] When the Bishop of Meath said to him: "All England cannot rule yonder gentleman", the King answered: "No? Then he is mete to rule all Ireland".[4] To the Irish of a later date, Henry's reappointment of Kildare as Deputy seemed merely pusillanimous. In 1533 his son was incited to rebellion in Ireland on the ground that he would be more esteemed if he took part against the King like his father. "What wouldst thou have been if thy father had not done so? How was he considered, until he crowned a King? Took Garth, the King's captain, prisoner; hanged his son; resisted Poynings and all Deputies; killed them of Dublin upon

of Ireland, unless they amount to less; in which case it is to be supplemented from the English Exchequer.

[1] Gairdner, *Letters*, I, 91–3 and xxxi. Pollard, *Henry VII*, III, no. 87.
[2] See Appendix XLIX.
[3] "MSS of Duke of Leinster", *Hist. MSS Com. 9th Report*, Part II, App. II, p. 263.
[4] *Cal. Carew MSS*, Book of Howth, p. 180 and Pollard, *Henry VII*, III, 120.

Oxmanton Green; and would suffer no man to rule here for the King, but himself? Then the King considered him, made him Deputy and married thy mother to him. Otherwise thou wouldest never have had a foot of land, while now thou canst spend 400 marks a year or more."[1]

It is important to note that the cessation of the Geraldine-Butler feud was made the first condition of Kildare's reinstatement.[2] On August 6, Kildare, on the one part, and Fitzsymonds, Thomas, Earl of Ormond, and Sir James Ormond, on the other, swore, at great length and on the Gospels, in the presence of Henry VII and his Council at Salisbury, that the old enmity between the "two noble blodes" of the Geraldines and Butlers should cease.[3] The four parties set their seals and signs manual to the document, Kildare's signature consisting of laboriously drawn initials. The seal of the Earl of Ormond has dropped off. The other witnesses "of the said kinges Counsaill then being present" all signed the indenture in their own handwriting.[4] They were Thomas Savage, Bishop of Rochester; Henry Deane, Bishop of Bangor and ex-Deputy; Reginald Bray, ex-Treasurer of the Wars in Ireland; Thomas Lovell, Treasurer of the Chamber; Giles Daubeney, the King's Chamberlain; Sir Robert Willoughby de Broke, the Lord Steward; and three lawyers; Robert Middleton, Richard Hatton, who had negotiated Desmond's submission, and John Kingsmill.

Although the document is not dated, the Articles which the Earl of Kildare promised in the presence of the King and Council to observe must have been sworn to at the same meeting.[5] These show the results of the Poynings administration in the new demands that could be made on Kildare as Deputy. The first two Articles dealt with Poynings' Law. The Earl was not to summon any Parliament or pass any Act without the licence of the King. He was to catch and imprison English rebels taking refuge in Ireland, and send to England any rebels or traitors asked for by the King. If the Earl of Desmond or any other

---

[1] Paraphrased from *State Papers, Henry VIII*, ii, 174–5.
[2] For the story of his reappointment see Pollard, *Henry VII*, iii, no. 102.
[3] Appendix XL.
[4] Appendix XLI. See "The Seal of the Privy Council" by Labaree and Moody, *E.H.R.* XLIII, 191.
[5] Appendix XLII.

man in Ireland should rebel, whether English, Irish, wild Irish or a foreigner, he was to repress him to the utmost of his power and defend Ireland against Scots or French invaders.

The codicil to the Articles dealt with the finance of Kildare's recent marriage to the King's cousin, Elizabeth St John, his first wife having died of grief while he was in England.[1] Henry is said to have already given Kildare lands to the yearly value of 200 marks, half in England[2] and half in Ireland, as well as 600 marks sterling, 400 of which were paid on August 17;[3] in return he was to endow his wife with an income of £200 in Ireland. Henry hoped to recoup some of this money, for as early as April 1, 1496,[4] Lady Kildare's kinsfolk, at the instigation of Sir Reginald Bray, had promised to repay him for his expenses in connection with her marriage. Hattecliffe noted in his accounts an assignment to the Countess of Kildare of manors in Meath, Dublin, Kildare and Limerick to the annual value of £253. 6s. 8d.,[5] proving that she was well provided for. As an additional safeguard, Kildare's son remained in England for eight years[6] and £2 were paid by the King to a "surgeon that heled him" in the following year.[7]

On August 26 a pardon was issued to all Perkin's supporters in Ireland, except Water and Lord Barry,[8] and on August 28 Kildare set sail.[9] An animated description of his reception on landing survives in a letter from Sir Ralph Verney to Sir Reginald Bray.[9] Verney's wife was first cousin to the new Lady Kildare and to the King,[10] and held a post in the Queen's household. Ralph Verney acted as Chamberlain to Princess Margaret till her marriage to James IV, and afterwards to Princess Mary.

---

[1] Ware, *Annals, Henry VII*, p. 32.

[2] On August 25, 1496, he granted several manors in England to Kildare and his wife jointly. *Cal. Pat. Rolls*, 1494–1509, p. 84.

[3] P.R.O. E 101, 414/6.

[4] *Ibid.* fol. 5 verso, of the section "Kings debts" at the end of the volume:

"my lady kildare kynsfolk promysed to pay unto the kinges grace for hir mariage by the labor of Master bray for suche money as his grace hath payed and layed oute for hir said mariage. C. marcas."

[5] Royal MSS, 18 C xiv, fol. 216.

[6] Pollard, *Henry VII*, iii, no. 106.

[7] *Excerpta Historica*, p. 115.   [8] *Foedera*, xii, 634.

[9] Appendix xliii.

[10] See Genealogical Table, compiled from *Annals of Ulster*, iii, 608, and *Letters and Papers of the Verney Family*, pp. 29–34.

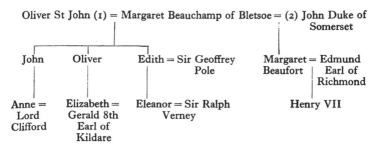

Both were eminently suitable relatives to accompany the Countess of Kildare to her new home. From internal evidence there is no doubt as to the year of the letter; and this is confirmed by the discovery in another part of the Public Record Office, of the indentures between Kildare and O'Reilly; and Kildare and Bernard MacMahon; dated October 2, 1496, and mentioned as enclosed in the letter, together with the names of the pledges of the Irish chiefs.[1]

Verney wrote to Bray from Dublin on October 31 that after a terrible voyage of twenty-one days the party had landed at Howth on September 17. Kildare held a council in St Peter's Church, Drogheda, on the 21st and took the oath; and an assignation was made with the messengers of the great Irish gentlemen of the north and the four counties of Ulster, for their masters to meet with the Deputy at Dundalk (the northern limit of the Pale) on Michaelmas Day. The elder and the younger MacMahon,[2] Magennis,[3] O'Reilly,[4] and O'Hanlon[5] took the oath, gave up their eldest sons as hostages, renounced their black-rents and signed indentures with the Deputy.[6] Donal O'Neill came to Dundalk, but Henry O'Neill[7] broke his tryst; so Kildare would not indent with Donal till he saw what Henry O'Neill would do. Each was struggling to be *the* O'Neill. Henry

---

[1] P.R.O. E 30, 1542. Appendix XLIV.

[2] MacMahon possessed the Irish part of Uriel, now part of the County of Monaghan; "State of Ireland", p. 2.

[3] Magennis of Upper Iveagh in Down; "State of Ireland", p. 2.

[4] O'Reilly of East Brenny, which extended over a great part of the County of Cavan; "State of Ireland", p. 4.

[5] O'Hanlon of Orior in Armagh; "State of Ireland", p. 2.

[6] O'Reilly's specimen indenture and the list of hostages (all enclosed in Verney's letter) are given in Appendix XLIV.

[7] He received £40 as black-rent; Gairdner, *Letters*, II, 308.

O'Neill had killed his eldest brother Conn treacherously, the son-in-law of Kildare, in order to be chief himself,[1] and the Deputy was waiting to know which of the two would do the King best service before taking sides. As yet he had heard nothing from Henry O'Neill, although in the meantime he had taken Donal O'Neill's oath and hostages. Moreover O'Donnell and O'Neill of Clandeboy, the two chief Irishmen from the coast opposite Scotland and the Outer Isles, had sent letters to the Deputy at Dundalk, asking for peace and promising to come to him wherever he wished in Ireland and to be ruled by him. Kildare had answered that, as they had taken part with James IV of Scotland, and helped Perkin Warbeck against Henry VII, they should have no favour from him till they had taken an oath to the King and sued for their pardon. John of the Outer Isles[2] had recently come into O'Neill of Clandeboy's country near Carrickfergus Castle with 1000 Scots and keteriks.[3] He said he had come to get back his son, who had been taken prisoner by an Irishman in those parts; but, although he had recovered him, John was still there and many of the Scots were living near to the country of the savage Irish. Kildare had sent secretly to him and wanted to entice him into the King's service away from that of the King of Scots; as he thought that if Henry VII were at war with the Scots, he and O'Neill of Clandeboy would be useful to him. But as yet there had been no answer. The same course had been taken with the Irish of the south and west; so that now, thanks be to God, the King had peace throughout Ireland, without great cost to himself. All were glad to submit themselves to him of their own free will except Macmurrough[4]

[1] This was in January 1492/3, and till 1498 Tyrone was divided between Henry and Donal O'Neill, and there was perpetual warfare. In August, 1498, Henry was killed by his nephews, the sons of Conn. Ware, *Annals, Henry VII*, p. 38.

[2] Sir John Mor MacDonald of Isla, with his son John, is thought to have been executed in 1494, on the evidence, inferential only, of the *Lord High Treasurer's Accounts*, I, 238–9. In the *Annals of Ulster*, III, 443, the date is given as 1499. The Annals are meticulously accurate. See also *The Clan Donald*, III, p. 375, by Angus MacDonald.

[3] "Keteriks" = "Ceithearnaigh" = "kerns." They were light-armed Irish soldiery.

[4] Macmurrough (also called Kavanagh) of Idrone, in the west part of Carlow ("State of Ireland," p. 2). He received £26. 13s. 4d. in part payment of black-rent for 1495 (Gairdner, *Letters*, II, 301), and £53. 6s. 8d. for 1496 (Royal MSS, 18 C xiv, fol. 151).

and O'Conor,[1] who would not give up Carlow Castle. So two expeditions against it had been made, and now that castle, their hostages, their oaths and their indentures were secured. The Earl of Desmond had sent several letters to the Deputy engaging to keep the promises he made to the King;[2] but Verney himself saw no sign of his submission as yet, for which reason he was remaining so long in Dublin, as he wished to have definite information about him to give the King before he left. The Earl of Desmond had promised to meet Kildare at Waterford the following week, after All Hallows, and to conclude all matters with him then.

Also John de Burgh,[3] a great Irishman, who ruled all the country about Galway, and was the best succour Perkin had had in Ireland, after the Earl of Desmond, had come in and made his submission to the King, beseeching Kildare to sue for his pardon.[4] He offered to travel to England under the protection of Lady Verney and so did several others who had offended likewise. The decision was deferred till the King's pleasure in the matter might be known. Nevertheless the Deputy had taken John de Burgh's oath[4] to be true to the King.

Verney excused himself for not having written before, but he had had no certain news till now. He asked for his excuses to be made to the King, to whom he dared not presume to write. He thought that his Grace could have put no man other than Kildare in authority in Ireland who would, in so short a time and with so little cost, have set the country in such good order, and trusted he had found a great treasure in him.

In a different ink and with a different pen Verney added that the Earl of Desmond had broken one appointment with the Deputy. Would to God he might keep the next one! If not, Verney thought there would be little satisfaction to be got from him. His words sounded well but must be proved by deeds.

The indenture made with O'Reilly[5] and enclosed in the letter was no doubt typical of many others, and was followed by a longer one made with Bernard MacMahon. The curious wording of the documents is due to the fact that the Irish

---

[1] O'Conor of Offaly (Kings County); "State of Ireland", p. 2.
[2] Appendix xxxix. [3] Shane Burke.
[4] Gairdner, *Letters*, ii, 326. [5] E 30, 1542. Appendix xliv.

chieftains neither understood nor tried to understand English, carrying on their correspondence in monkish Latin supplied by their priests.[1]

Kildare's success in securing submissions from the greater Irish chiefs as well as from the Irish of the south and west was very striking. Since Richard II's visit to Ireland no English King had received so many oaths of fealty from the Irish. It was no wonder Verney thought Kildare's new Deputyship promised well, and it is fair to consider that the close of the year 1496 saw the Irish question relegated to the background of Henry's mind, for the first time during his reign.

[1] Introduction to "State of Ireland", *State Papers, Henry VIII*, vol. II, Part III.

CHAPTER VI

ANGLO-SCOTTISH AND ANGLO-IRISH RELATIONS, 1496–98

James IV had begun preparations for the reception of Perkin, after his failure in Ireland, early in November, 1495, when arras was transported in his honour from Edinburgh to Stirling.[1] In December he and his royal host made offerings together in church,[1] and the next month James gave him the hand of Lady Katharine Gordon, the beautiful sister of the Earl of Huntley, and a kinswoman of his own, in marriage. The Scottish burghs contributed a quota to his allowance of over £1200 a year,[2] and he was treated in every respect as a royal prince.

"Him of Ireland", his royal patron, James IV, and Henry VII's relations with them both, riveted the attention of Europe. Ferdinand and Isabella of Spain considered any pretender an impediment to the proposed marriage of their daughter, Katharine, with Arthur, Prince of Wales; and were anxious too that Henry should be freed from danger at home, so that he might join the Holy League and concentrate his forces against France.[3] England's problems were not her own, and she was forced so clearly into the limelight of European gossip and intrigue that the calendars of foreign State papers become for a time valuable sources of information as to Anglo-Scottish relations.

Throughout the spring and summer of 1496 Henry was impressing men and making preparations of all kinds to secure the Border against the dreaded Scottish invasion of James IV and Perkin.[4] At the same time he had not given up hope of a peaceful solution, for on May 5 he nominated Bishop Fox to treat with the King of Scots for marriage with his daughter Margaret, then aged six, James's future wife.[5] This was followed by three

---

[1] Gairdner, *Letters*, II, 327–35.
[2] *Burgh Records of Aberdeen* (Spalding Club), July 5, 1495. (Error for 1496.)
[3] Their policy is fully stated in a letter to De Puebla of April 26, 1496. *Spanish Cal.* I, p. 96.
[4] *Cal. Pat. Rolls*, 1494–1509. [5] *Rot. Scot.* II, 520.

similar commissions during the summer.[1] A letter from Henry Wyatt to Henry VII, written from Carlisle on June 4, 1496, where he was Captain, has survived among the Wyatt MSS[2] in a transcript of the mid-sixteenth century. Although it is in uncouth English, lacks a beginning, and presents difficulties of interpretation, it gives the only description of conditions on the English side of the Border at this period and is worth study. In language it affords an astonishing contrast to the accomplishment of his son, illustrating at a glance the gulf in one generation between the Middle Ages and the Renaissance.

Wyatt had been appointed to the new office of Captain and Governor of Carlisle in June, 1491,[3] which entrenched upon the powers of Sir Richard Salkeld of Corby Castle, Cumberland, as Constable, and seems to have been held for a few years only during the acute stage of Anglo-Scottish relations. Carlisle commanded the only road in Cumberland practicable for wheeled vehicles.[4] The city had been totally destroyed in the Wars of the Roses and half the fee rent remitted ever since by Edward IV, Richard III and Henry VII successively.[5] Richard III had made additions to the castle, and Henry VII had repaired it in 1488.[6] Previous to Wyatt's appointment the functions of Captain had been performed by the Constable, an old Yorkist, considerably Wyatt's senior, who in 1487 was responsible for the keeping of the West Marches as well as of Carlisle.[7] After Lord Dacre's appointment as Warden, he was mentioned alternatively as Constable or Captain of Carlisle Castle[8] receiving payments from the Exchequer for the wages of himself and a retinue of twenty men for its defence at the rate of 300 marks a year.[9] Salkeld had also been Constable of Leixlip Castle in Ireland, and at the end of April, 1496, was strengthening the garrison of

---

[1] *Rot. Scot.* II, 521, 522. [2] Appendix XLV.
[3] *Rot. Scot.* II, 500 b. [4] Creighton, *Carlisle*.
[5] Ferguson, *Charters of Carlisle*, A.D. 1461, 1483 and 1488, pp. 53, 67, 79.
[6] Tellers Rolls, E 405, 76, Easter Term, 3 Henry VII, mem. 4 dorso.
[7] See p. 33.
[8] Campbell, *Materials*, I, 231, 233.
[9] P.R.O. E 405, 75, Easter Term, 4 Henry VII, Page mem. 1 dorso: "Ricardo Salkeld militi C marcas de illis CCC marcis sibi per dominum Regem appunctuatis pro salva custodia ville et castri Karlioli...per breve de privato sigillo hoc termino LXVI li XIIIs IIIId".
The Privy Seal authorisation for 300 marks is in P.R.O. E 403, 2558, fol. 16 v.

the royal Castle of Carrickfergus.[1] The imminent danger of James IV's invasion of England brought both Wyatt and Salkeld back from Ireland, before the end of the Poynings administration, and then the question arose of dismissing Salkeld on the ground of advancing age.

Wyatt's petition to the King was a two-fold one. The first suit, of which the beginning is missing, was for an additional retinue of some kind, supplementary on occasion to that of Salkeld, for the safeguard of Carlisle, but also to be used to attend upon Lord Dacre, or to defend the surrounding country. The existence of this garrison under the command of someone else would have the advantage of making Salkeld's position as Constable of Carlisle of less importance, since he "was not so able for it as he had been". Wyatt himself was probably to command this extra force.

The second suit was for the payment of the usual annual fee of 100 marks to Sir Richard Salkeld. The Parliament, which met in October, 1495,[2] assigned the income of certain royal manors for the upkeep of Carlisle, entailing that the payment of 306 marks a year for the Constable and his retinue should be made in future by the Receiver-General of the King's manors, instead of by the Exchequer at Westminster. As up to June 4, 1496, the act had not functioned in the case of Carlisle, and the King had had no time to concern himself with its enforcement, Sir Richard had received no fee and was thrown upon his own resources.

The letter then passes to the doings of John Musgrave, the Captain of Bewcastle in the English West Marches.[3] The West March extended from Kershope Bridge to Carlisle. In later years the Warden resided at Carlisle, and from the reign of Mary onwards combined the office with that of Constable. But in 1496, when both Salkeld and Wyatt had functions at Carlisle Castle, it is probable that Lord Dacre was living in his own keep at Naworth. The Captain of Bewcastle was appointed by the crown to keep watch over Liddesdale in the Scottish Marches,

---

[1] Gairdner, *Letters*, II, 316.   [2] Statutes, II Henry VII, c. 61.

[3] *Ibid.* Pease, *Lord Wardens of the Marches*, pp. 48–9. For maps of the West March and photographs see D. L. W. Tough, *The Last Years of a Frontier*. Bowes' Survey of 1541 is the earliest record of the Border Line on the Middle March. Hodgson's *Northumberland*, II, Part III. Bates (*Border Holds*, pp. 29–49) prints a portion of this more accurately.

as the junction of the Lidd and the Esk was the weakest spot for defence along the whole border. John Musgrave's post was in the extreme east of the West March. Teviotdale, where Musgrave's men were fighting, was in the Scottish Middle Marches, with Jedburgh as its chief town; and in 1521 John Major wrote that the boundary between Teviotdale and the Solway still remained doubtful and was matter for contention between Scots and Englishmen.[1] Wyatt considered Musgrave's work unsatisfactory. Even Sir William Tyler, the Captain of Berwick, and Wyatt's titular Chief at the Jewel House, needed quickening in his estimation, and by writing to him of their doings in the West March, he hoped to spur them to greater efforts in the East.

Wyatt also held a poor opinion of Lord Clifford,[2] the hereditary Sheriff of Westmorland, who had been a child of four in 1461, when his father, the thirteenth Baron, was attainted and executed. Brought up of necessity in hiding, in the mountains, by a shepherd, he had become rough and illiterate. On Henry VII's accession the attainder was reversed, too late to polish Lord Clifford. Wyatt considered him inefficient and inferior to his wife, the King's cousin.[3] He was not self-seeking in this letter, giving only the intimate advice as to Border conditions, supplemented by the "plain speech" of his bearer, incumbent upon his office as servant and councillor of the King. From Carlisle he could keep in touch with his old associates Buchan and Bothwell, with whom he had worked on James III's behalf in 1488, and who, now as then, were acting as Henry VII's spies in Scotland. Bothwell continually crossed the Border, and Wyatt's presence in the north must have been a help to his machinations.

Bothwell's well-known letter to Henry VII,[4] written a few months later, supplements Wyatt's story of Border conditions from the Scottish point of view. From internal evidence it seems to have been written from Scotland between August 28 and September 2, 1496, and is only intelligible in the light of Bothwell and Buchan's previous relations with Henry VII.

[1] John Major, *History of Greater Britain*, p. 20. [2] See *G.E.C.*
[3] Appendix xlv, p. 238 and p. 95.
[4] Pollard, *Henry VII*, I, no. 100.

Bothwell said he had been busy about that little matter of kidnapping Perkin, which Wyatt had suggested to him, and that Buchan agreed to carry it out, if possible, during the middle of the night when Perkin had no guard about him save the King's. He had given Buchan Henry VII's letter, with which he was well content.[1] Bothwell had then gone on to St Andrews and had had a long talk with James IV's brother, the Archbishop, and had given him a crossbow. He, at any rate, would not fight against England; and Andrew Stewart, Bishop of Moray, Buchan's brother,[2] would come over to Henry, if James still insisted on invasion against the advice of the barons and all his people, as Bothwell thought he would. The Bishop of Moray would do his best to enlist James's brother on the English side.[3] On August 28 a man had come from Carlisle to see Perkin, and Bothwell remained in the room when Perkin brought him to an audience with the King. He was secretly informed that the man came from Randall of Dacre, brother of Lord Dacre (Warden of the West Marches), and from the Skeltons; for Michael Skelton, who was there, had brought him up.[4] Undoubtedly the men of Northumberland were in continual communication with the Scots, and every day vagabonds escaped and joined Perkin, letters passing to and fro. Recently a certain Hatfield, who used to dwell with the Earl of Oxford, came and brought much news. After the last interview held between the Scottish commissioners and the Bishop of Durham in Berwick,[5] the King of Scots had become set on invasion, although this was contrary to the wish of his whole people and they were not properly prepared for it. Bothwell hoped that about a dozen English leaders and men of authority, together with the people, already in Scotland, who were on his side, would win for Henry the greatest day of triumph over his enemies that any King of

---

[1] This letter must have contained a bribe.

[2] He had identified himself with James III's party, before Sauchieburn, which was backed by Henry VII. See pp. 13, 15.

[3] He was not successful, for the King's brother contributed to the raid on Norham in July, 1497. *Treasurer's Accounts*, I, 313–14.

[4] Edward Skelton was with Perkin at Beaulieu. See Henry VII's letter to the citizens of Waterford, October 17, 1497. Pollard, *Henry VII*, I, nos. 120, 123.

[5] These were in connection with the marriage negotiations. *Rot. Scot.* II, 520, 521, 522.

England had had for a hundred years. Bothwell ended by saying that he had shown James IV the Earl of Desmond's bond of submission to Henry VII,[1] which the King could scarcely believe was real.

James and Desmond had worked in unison as backers of Perkin in 1492 and 1495.[2] Desmond had accompanied Perkin through Ireland on his flight towards Scotland in August, 1495, after the siege of Waterford.[3] The news of his change of side must have been a bitter blow to James and it was difficult for him to believe that the bond could be genuine. A payment of £10 was made to Bothwell from his Chamber Account by Henry VII in May, 1496.[4] He may have been at the English Court at that time, and have received his instructions from the King, together with Desmond's actual bond,[5] given him to show to James IV, and which he returned by a bearer with this letter.

Wyatt's difficulties as Captain of Carlisle emerge more clearly from Bothwell's letter than from his own. If the brother of the Warden of the English West Marches, Wyatt's own chief, was in communication with Perkin at the Scottish Court, he must have been in an impossible position. Yet no complaint was made. James IV's reported interview with Bishop Fox was in connection with the marriage negotiations set on foot by Henry VII's four commissions of the previous summer. Bothwell's letter tends to prove that no progress had been made, although another letter written by an anonymous member of Henry VII's Council in September, 1496, mentions an agreement lately come to between the Scots and the Bishop of Durham.[6]

A second letter was written by Bothwell to Henry VII on September 8, 1496,[7] after he had crossed the Border and come to Berwick. It begins by assuring the King that he had spent a long time in Scotland, mostly at James IV's court, doing his best to wean him from support of Perkin. To his efforts James had always replied that he hoped to conclude satisfactory terms with

---

[1] The bond signed at Youghal in March, 1496. Appendices XXXVIII, XXXIX.
[2] See Chapters III and V.
[3] Appendix XII, p. 175.
[4] *Excerpta Historica*, p. 108. [5] Appendix XXXVIII.
[6] *Milanese Cal.* no. 510 and *Venetian Cal.* III, pp. 634–5.
[7] Pollard, *Henry VII*, I, no. 101.

Bishop Fox; but should the negotiations fall through he intended to invade England with Perkin and 1400 men on September 17. That was now his definite plan, in spite of the opposition of his nobles and people, and neither the bad time of year, nor advice to the contrary could stop him. Bothwell hoped that God would punish him by Henry VII's means for his cruel consent to the murder of his father.

The letter tells how James IV had held a Council meeting, on September 2, to which he called Perkin, demanding, as a condition of his help, the restoration of the seven sheriffdoms,[1] the delivery of the Castle and Town of Berwick, and the payment of 100,000 marks, within five years, for military expenses. Perkin considered these terms overnight, and the next morning took Sir George Neville,[2] Lounde,[3] a priest, and Heron,[4] to the Council with him. After long consultation he bound himself in writing to deliver Berwick and to pay 50,000 marks for costs within two years.

Bothwell then went to Saint Andrews with the King and there witnessed his reception of the Sieur de Concressault[5], the French ambassador, who was a Scot by birth, and had commanded Perkin's guard of honour at the Court of Charles VIII. A few weeks earlier Henry VII had said to the Spanish ambassador, De Puebla, that if Concressault should travel by way of England he would retain him a whole year and not permit him to go to Scotland.[6] Bothwell was able to read the letter he had brought from the King of France, which said, in effect, that Charles VIII understood there was great dissension between Henry VII and James IV and had sent Concressault to Scotland so that he might understand James's point of view, and decide as to whether he or Henry were at fault. Because of his friendship

[1] See Gairdner, *Richard III*, p. 309, who suggests that this may mean seven English counties.

[2] Sir George Neville was a Yorkist, who had been at the French Court with Perkin in 1492 (*Hall's Chronicle*, p. 463) and was attainted by the Parliament which met in October, 1495 (*Rot. Parl.* VI, 504).

[3] Sir William Lounde was Perkin's chaplain, sometime chaplain and steward to Sir Ralph Hastings, Kt. See Pollard, *Henry VII*, I, p. 182.

[4] John Heron fled to sanctuary at Beaulieu with Perkin. *Ibid.* p. 182.

[5] "Lord Monypenny." *Treasurer's Accounts*, I, 303. See also Scofield, *Edward IV*, I, 251 and De Wavrin, *Chroniques*, III, 186 footnote, for William de Mennypeny, Sieur de Concressault, who was probably his father.

[6] *Spanish Cal.* I, p. 111.

with both parties, he asked James whether he might mediate and arrange a peace between them, for he understood from the envoys Henry had sent to France that much of the trouble was due to the King of Scots. After this reception James took Concressault to a council meeting and explained how all the fault was England's, and that he had lost ships and droves of cattle on the Border. Concressault then said to Bothwell it was no wonder the King felt so strongly against Henry. Bothwell also understood from Concressault that Charles VIII had asked James to send Perkin to France, and had offered him 100,000 crowns. This Bothwell knew was true, although he could not understand the reason, except that Charles VIII did not want James IV to marry Henry's daughter. Concressault told him of the inquiries that had been made into Perkin's origin, and Bothwell showed him the document he had received from De Meautis, which proved his Flemish birth.[1] Concressault did not believe this and in effect his embassy had done little good, for he and Perkin were together in Council every day.[2] Bothwell then assured the King that he was his servant, although a Scot, and would prove his good faith to him when he came to England.

Sir George Neville could be bribed on both sides, for in a previous letter (now lost) Bothwell had written to Henry that Neville and his accomplices "were bonded" before Andrew Stewart, Bishop of Moray and himself. After he had received Henry VII's letter of advice, Bothwell had sounded Sir George Neville, the latter answering that he was inclined to be on the side of the King of Scots; but if the English King and he could come to terms he would be quit of Perkin. Neville and Perkin had now made a new arrangement. Bothwell wrote that he would not destroy the King's letter, but thought that Neville would repent his action. In James IV's Council Neville had desired that the meeting should be put off till next summer, and this he said was done to please the King of England. Bothwell answered that the King did not care what he did.

Should Henry fail in coming to an agreement with James IV (and it seemed to Bothwell that he had no real need of one), the

---

[1] See Gairdner, *Richard III*, p. 311, for a description of this.
[2] Concressault set sail from Scotland on October 19, 1496. *Treasurer's Accounts*, I, 303.

impetuosity of the young King would probably endanger himself, Perkin and all the Scots people. He considered that the invasion would be regretted in Scotland even a hundred years hence; and no Englishman would be more anxious to ruin James than Bothwell himself, because he found him unreasonable, lacking in virtue, mischief-making and cruel, unless he could get his own way in everything. And Henry might have as much success with Scotland as Edward IV had had, for the King of Scots did not possess £100 when he coined his chains,[1] his plate and his cupboards, and people were never worse content with the Government than they were now. Although Bothwell had so long desired his friendship, yet now, seeing that the King of Scots was at fault, he was willing to desert him, and so would others be. There were many of his father's servants who would still like to see some retribution for James III's death.

Bothwell begged Henry to send him word of any work he could do, for he had come to England to wait upon the King or upon anyone else he might appoint, and would not fail by God's grace to do good and acceptable service in this business. And nothing should happen, however secret, about James IV's person or in his army, that Henry should not hear of; for all arrangements to that effect were made before Bothwell left Scotland.

Roderick de Lalain[2] with two small ships and sixty Germans had arrived from Flanders. Bothwell was there when James IV received him in the presence of Perkin and heard Roderick say in French:

Sir, I am come here according to my promise, to do your Highness service, and for no other man's sake am I come here; and if I had not had your letter of warrant, I should have been arrested in Flanders and put to great trouble for Perkin's sake.

Lalain did not go near Perkin, but Perkin went up to him and saluted him and asked how his aunt[3] was, and he answered

---

[1] See *Treasurer's Accounts*, I, 314, for the coining of the great chain on July 26, 1497.

[2] Roderic de Lalain, a Burgundian of good family. For his ancestors see Michel, *Les Écossais en France*, I, 207. He was paid 100 marks by James IV on October 7, 1496. *Treasurer's Accounts*, I, 301.

[3] The Dowager Duchess Margaret of Burgundy.

"Well". And Perkin inquired if he had any letters from her to him, and Roderick said he dared not bring them, but had some for the King. He had certainly brought James much useful equipment for the war, both for man and horse. If Henry could put a good army on the sea, he would do much; for all the sailors and inhabitants of the coast towns of Scotland were to march by land with James IV, and so their whole navy might be destroyed and the harbour towns burned.

Bothwell had been to Edinburgh Castle, and had seen the provision of ordnance there, which was not plentiful; it consisted of two great curtalds[1] that were sent from France; ten falcons or little serpentines;[2] thirty "cart" guns[3] of iron with chambers, and sixteen closed carts for spears, powder, stones and other material for the guns. Bothwell considered that the Scots, when they came to invade England, would be so weary in four or five nights, through lack of food and sleep, that Henry would be able to make James return home without a battle. When the Scots entered England, the people of Northumberland and those of the Diocese of Durham should march westwards to the head of Northumberland and then northwards; not straight upon the Scots army, but sideways, until they came upon them from north and south simultaneously; then the Northumbrians should attack them from behind and the men of Yorkshire from the front. And so, whichever way they went, the Scots would not be able to escape, but must fight. Considering the long nights, the amount of baggage and the number of carriages, 20,000 men would be as good as 100,000; and the folk behind them would frighten them more than twice as many in front. Bothwell had listened to the deliberations of his countrymen and could therefore give this advice.

His information was correct, for, on September 17, Perkin, under the name of Richard IV, did invade England. Three reliable accounts[4] of the much-dreaded expedition show exactly how negligible it was. He penetrated four miles beyond the frontier and cast down two small towers. The news of his defeat

---

[1] Short pieces of ordnance. [2] Small artillery.
[3] Small guns on wheels.
[4] *Hall's Chronicle*, p. 475; Pollard, *Henry VII*, I, no. 102 and Registrum Annalium Collegii Mertonensis. See C. H. Williams, *England under the Early Tudors*, no. 36.

was carried to Ireland by one of O'Donnell of Tyrconnell's men, who was paid £7. 4s. on October 15 by James IV.[1]

The story of the following year has been fully told from the Scottish and English standpoints.[2] If the burden of taxation imposed upon the country for defence against the Scots was a measure of the danger involved, it had never been so great as in October, 1496, when a Great Council granted £120,000[3] and a loan of £40,000 for the Scots war. Yet this danger was more fancied than real, for in the words of the Venetian ambassador, "under the pretence of war the King amassed much money".[4] He had done the same with France in 1492, securing a pension of 50,000 crowns from the Peace of Étaples, and is unique among monarchs for turning military outlay to profit. Yet his preparations were thorough.[5] The Earl of Surrey was appointed Lieutenant in the North by special Commission[6] and Lord Willoughby de Broke took the *Regent* to sea to support him from May 14 to September 17.[7]

On June 8 James IV got tidings of the Battle of Duns, in the Merse, from a servant of the Humes by whom the English were repulsed.[8]

These were trifling events compared with the rising of the Cornishmen against the payment of the subsidy imposed for the Scots war. Their march on London, ending in a pitched battle at Blackheath on June 17, 1497,[9] an utter rout for the rebels, involved the withdrawal southwards of the bulk of the army which was in Yorkshire on its way to Scotland, under the command of Sir Giles Daubeney.[10] Henry Wyatt was among the men mentioned by Polydore Vergil as present at Blackheath. He was paid £12. 18s. 6½d. for conducting two demi-launces and

[1] *Treasurer's Accounts*, 1, 303.
[2] For Scotland see Dickson, Preface to the *Lord Treasurer's Accounts*, pp. cxliv–clviii. For England see Gairdner, *Richard III*, pp. 307–34. For other references see Busch, pp. 346–7.
[3] Kingsford, *Chronicles*, 211.
[4] *Venetian Cal.* 1, 743.
[5] P.R.O. E 101, 414/6 and P.R.O. E 36, vol. 126, fol. 40.
[6] *Hall's Chronicle*, p. 478.
[7] Oppenheim, *Accounts and Inventories of Henry VII*, pp. xlii and 82–132.
[8] *Treasurer's Accounts*, 1, 341.
[9] See Kingsford, *Chronicle of London*, p. 214, and *Chronicle of the Grey Friars*, p. 25. The *V.C.H.* for Surrey gives an excellent account of the battle.
[10] *Hall's Chronicle*, p. 477 and Oppenheim, *op. cit.* p. xliv.

thirteen archers and bills, 186 miles; and fifteen bowes and bills 240 miles,[1] back to the Border, after the battle, in the company of Daubeney. The southward withdrawal of the army had for the first time left James IV a free field for the invasion of England. That he took no advantage of this, although he raided Norham three weeks later, when the English army had marched north again, shows that his heart was no longer in the war. He had at last realised that no good could come from backing Perkin, whom he had genuinely believed to be the real Duke of York.[2] A letter from Ferdinand and Isabella to De Puebla[3] implies that Warbeck behaved foolishly to James after the débacle of September, 1496, "since he went away without being advised to do so, and the King of Scots looks upon him since his return almost as a prisoner". He was strongly influenced, no doubt, by the representations of the Spanish minister Ayala, who was working hard for an Anglo-Scottish peace, in order that Henry VII might be free to pull his weight in the Holy League.

Henry did not realise the extent to which Perkin had fallen out of favour with James when he issued his famous double set of instructions to Fox, on July 5,[4] for negotiating a peace with Scotland. The Bishop was to begin by asking for the actual person of Warbeck; should this prove impossible of attainment, "we, havyng consideracion to the loving mynde of our seid cousin in the tyme of the rebellion of dyvers of our subjects (at Blackheath), will be content to take another way". The other way was to accept the conditions agreed upon at the meeting at Jenyn Haugh in the previous spring, when the Earl of Angus and Lord Hume had made offers to Henry on James's behalf. This mention is the only evidence of the Jenyn Haugh meeting.

On the very day after Fox's instructions were issued Perkin left Scotland for ever in a Breton vessel hired by James for the

---

[1] Tellers Rolls, E 405, 79, Easter Term, 12 Henry VII, Stokes mem. 3 dorso. This occurs on the "Liber compotorum de Termino Pasche Anno XIImo Regis Henrici VIImi. Roberto Lytton militi. Thes. Guerre".
[2] Pollard, *Henry VII*, I, no. 121.
[3] *Spanish Cal.* I, p. 140.
[4] Gairdner, *Letters*, I, 104–9. Pollard, *Henry VII*, III, 37. For a commentary see Gairdner, *Letters*, I, p. xxix.

purpose.[1] On July 26 he landed at Cork,[2] at the invitation, according to Piers Butler, of Sir James Ormond, who had turned traitor, although, from 1491 till Kildare's return as Deputy in 1496, he was Henry's mainstay in Ireland. James Ormond and Kildare had sworn in the presence of the King in 1496 to let their ancient feud drop and co-operate in Ireland. But when the old rebel Kildare actually played the part of Henry VII's loyal viceroy, jealousy and Geraldine hatred welled up afresh in Sir James, and drove him to seek revenge by backing the Pretender, whom he had helped to oust in 1491 and 1495.

Perkin's luck had at last deserted him, nor could his visit have been more ill-timed; for, nine days before he landed in Ireland, Sir James Ormond met his death by the hand of Piers Butler, his ancient rival, in the open country near Kilkenny.[3] Warbeck's Irish welcome was in any case worn out. Tradition has it that from the castle at Ardmore, on a promontory attached to the mainland as it were by a thread, and overlooking the magnificent bay, Perkin sent in vain to Waterford to demand its surrender,[4] and then sailed away for ever with his wife and children, pursued by four great ships equipped at the charge of the citizens of Waterford.[5] Later he experienced the adventures and tempests described in the Book of Howth.[6] Henry VII wrote to Sir Gilbert Talbot[7] that Kildare and Desmond would have seized him had he not stolen away to Cornwall. This change of heart on the part of Desmond, Warbeck's former mainstay, is a strong tribute to the growing respect felt for the King even in Ireland.

Kildare and the Earl of Ormond, James Ormond's patron, had carried out in full their pledges of friendship given in the presence of Henry VII on August 6, 1496.[8] A friendly letter from

[1] The expenses of his outfit are all given in the *Treasurer's Accounts*. See also Gairdner, *Richard III*, p. 318.
[2] Henry VII's letter to the Mayor and Citizens of Waterford, August 6, 1497. Pollard, *Henry VII*, I, no. 109.
[3] Gairdner, *Letters*, II, pp. xl, xli. He prints Piers Butler's letter, describing the murder, in full. The original has recently been acquired for the B.M. (Add. Charters, 56,453). Pollard (*Henry VII*, III, no. 94) does not give the right date. See also *Cal. Carew MSS*, "Book of Howth", p. 177.
[4] *Fraser's Magazine*, 1845, p. 299. Article on Ardmore.
[5] Letter of 1499 from the citizens of Waterford to Henry VII. Charles Smith, *History of Waterford*, 138.
[6] Pollard, *Henry VII*, III, no. 99.   [7] *Ibid.* I, no. 113.
[8] Appendix XL.

the Earl in London to Lady Kildare, offering to do commissions for her, shows the excellent terms upon which they associated.[1] The letter to her husband, in which this was enclosed, in answer to Kildare's complaint of James Ormond, regrets that his kinsman should not have kept his bond of loyalty to the King and Kildare.[2] Another of March, 1497/8, from Kildare to Ormond, accusing one O'Brien of being the most maliciously disposed Irishman he ever knew, says that he had been associated with Sir James "to destroy Englishmen".[3] Both men in this correspondence appear as loyal servants of the crown, dissociating themselves from the memory of Black James.

In January, 1497/8, Kildare pressed the claim of his son-in-law Piers Butler to succeed his victim as representative of the Earl of Ormond in Ireland.[4] For many years Piers and his wife lived "in great civilitie" at Kilkenny Castle, introducing Flemish tapestry weavers to set a pattern to the workers of the countryside.[5] Some of their products hang to-day on the walls of the castle. Their sculptured effigies in Kilkenny Cathedral are of beautiful workmanship, Piers wearing chain-armour of a fashion a hundred years behind that of England.[6] He ultimately succeeded Anne Boleyn's father as ninth Earl of Ormond.

In spite of the opportunity lost three weeks earlier, James IV began to prepare for a raid upon England immediately after Perkin's departure from Scotland.[7] It may have been undertaken in ignorance of Fox's commission to negotiate with him, and as a feint to save his face with his own subjects, who did not at this stage want peace. The object of attack was Norham Castle, of which Thomas Garth was captain under Fox, himself the Governor. The castle had been newly fortified by Fox and withstood a siege for two weeks. The Bishop, in spite of criticism, made an annual grant to Garth in reward for his services during the siege.[8] The news of Surrey's approach with a formidable army caused James to retreat into Scotland, followed by Surrey,

[1] Appendix XLVII. [2] Appendix XLVI.
[3] Appendix XLIX. [4] Appendix XLVIII.
[5] *State Papers, Henry VIII*, III, 146 note.
[6] Illustrated in Graves and Prim, I, 183.
[7] *Treasurer's Accounts*, I, p. cliv.
[8] *Calendar of Chancery Enrollments. Rolls of Bishop Fox as Bishop of Durham*, 36th Report of Deputy Keeper, App. I, Roll 2, mem. 5. Allen, *Letters of Fox*, nos. 13 and 14.

who captured Ayton Castle in the Merse.[1] Dacre, still Warden of the West Marches in 1513, wrote of this episode, sixteen years later, as "the last war", and said that Surrey, with Fox, Conyers, Sir William Bulmer and others, and 1000 soldiers, supported by Berwick and Norham Castles, found it as much as they could do to make a raid on Teviotdale.[2] On August 20, Sir William Tyler and James had an interview at Dunbar,[3] and the next day, the Scottish King sent letters to the sheriffs of the Border counties, warning them of the departure of the English[3]. Henry VII informed the Milanese ambassador at Woodstock, on September 3, "with great modesty" of his victory over the Scots.[4] Bothwell's ability as a spy was remarkable, for his favour in Scotland remained constant and his information to Henry accurate and reliable. On August 24 at Holyrood, he received a payment of £5. 8s. by James IV's command,[5] as recompense for the satisfaction he had given in the ending of the strife.

Meanwhile Perkin had wasted his time in Ireland, and landed at Whitesand Bay in Cornwall as late as September 7.[6] Cornwall, still thoroughly hostile to Henry VII, was the only good base remaining for the operations of a pretender. On landing he issued a proclamation giving the history of his life.[7] A paragraph mentions the nineteen persons who had been most active against his cause in Scotland and in England, amongst whom are the names of Garth and Wyatt, the typical "new men" to whom he objected.

He [Henry VII] hath none in favour and trust about his person but Bishop Fox,[8] Smith,[9] Bray,[10] Lovell[11] Oliver King,[12] Sir Charles

---

[1] Oppenheim, *Naval Accounts*, p. 129. *Milanese Cal.* no. 544.
[2] *L. and P. Henry VIII*, I, pt II, 2382.
[3] *Treasurer's Accounts*, I, 353.
[4] *Milanese Cal.* p. 323.
[5] *Treasurer's Accounts*, I, 354.
[6] *Rot. Parl.* VI, 545.
[7] Pollard, *Henry VII*, I, no. 108.
[8] Bishop of Durham, December 1494–1501.
[9] William Smyth, made Bishop of Lincoln in 1496, and President of the Council of Arthur Prince of Wales.
[10] Sir Reginald Bray, Henry VII's chief adviser.
[11] Sir Thomas Lovell, Treasurer of the Chamber.
[12] Bishop of Bath and Wells (1495–1504) and formerly Henry VII's chief secretary "always in attendance on our person". (*Venetian Cal.* I, no. 583.)

Somerset,[1] David Owen,[2] Rysley,[3] Sir James Turborville,[4] Tylere,[5] Robert Litton,[6] Guildeforde,[7] Chumley,[8] Empson,[9] James Hobard,[10] John Cutte,[11] Garthe,[12] Hansey,[13] Wyat,[14] and such others, caitiffs and villains of simple birth, which by subtle inventions and pilling of the people have been the principal finders, occasioners and counsellors of the misrule and mischief now reigning in England.

This invasion was as disastrous as the rest,[15] ending in the ignominy of Perkin's surrender at Taunton, and his execution in 1499. Although the total failure of his cause had become plain to James IV a year before the Peace of Ayton, the negotiations leading up to the treaty were still long, tedious and complicated. Fox, Warham and Cartington acted for Henry by virtue of their commission of the previous July 4.[16] The Scottish commission to Bishop Elphinstone, Andrew Forman (the Protonotary who had been in continual attendance on Perkin in Scotland) and others was dated September 17.[17] But on September 5, a different commission, almost a duplicate of the one to Fox, and not mentioned in the final text of the Treaty of Ayton, had been given to William, Bishop of Carlisle, Thomas Dacre, William Warham and Henry Wyatt.[18] The safe-conduct of September 16,[18] for the English ambassadors, leaves blank spaces

[1] See p. 82, Ambassador to France.
[2] Chief carver, with a salary of £50, and appointed Constable of Winchester in 1489. (*Cal. Pat. Rolls*, 1485–94, p. 268.)
[3] M.P. in 1491 and Councillor. (*Bulletin of Institute of Hist. Research*, III, 172.)
[4] Treasurer of Calais. "James" must be an ancient error for "John".
[5] Sir William Tyler, Captain of Berwick since 1488.
[6] Sir Robert Lytton, Under-Treasurer of England.
[7] Sir Richard Guildford, Controller of the Household and Master of the Ordnance.
[8] Sir Richard Cholmley, Chamberlain of Berwick and knighted by Surrey in 1497 for his services against the Scots.
[9] Richard Empson, General Attorney of the Duchy of Lancaster; P.R.O. D.L. 42, no. 21, fol. 1.
[10] Sir James Hobart, Attorney-General.
[11] Receiver-General of the profits and revenues of the Duchy of Lancaster; P.R.O. D.L. 42, no. 21, fol. 1.
[12] Thomas Garth, chief captain of the King's Army in Ireland before and under the Poynings' Administration, 1491–2, 1493–6, and Castellan of Norham in 1497.
[13] John Hussey? Controller of Henry VII's Household.
[14] Henry Wyatt, Captain of Carlisle, and Clerk of the Jewels.
[15] See Gairdner, *Richard III*, 325–32.
[16] *Rot. Scot.* II, 528 b.   [17] *Ibid.* II, 528 b.
[18] *Ibid.* II, 524.

for their names; but Wyatt was in Scotland, or approaching it, on September 9 when "Halis pursewant", bringing news of "Hari Wiot", was given 27s.[1] by James IV. Perhaps the King intended to supersede his earlier commission to Fox by one to Warham, Dacre, Wyatt and Bishop Severs, and then changed his mind.

The indenture of truce for seven years was sealed on September 30 in Ayton Church,[2] Ayala, the Spanish ambassador, acting as mediator. It was to be ratified within two months by letters patent on each side, and James IV's letters patent, confirming the truce, were conveyed to Henry by Lyon Herald, who arrived in London on November 25, with the Spaniard Ayala and thirty horses. Ayala had brought with him a new commission, to conclude a still longer truce for any length of time he thought well,[3] and on December 14 Warham was authorised to treat afresh with him. Four days later they came to an agreement, prolonging the truce for the lifetime of either King.[5] De Soncino wrote to Milan that the peace was honourably proclaimed on December 7 and that the Scottish ambassador was leaving for home with it the next day.[6] Yet on December 12 Richard Middleton received still another commission to treat with the King of Scots;[7] and the next day Ayala was named by Henry, a final arbiter,[8] as representative of the King and Queen of Spain, with regard to the breach of all treaties between England and Scotland, as to invasion and robberies committed by either side. Henry was still unsatisfied. Among the Cotton MSS are some undated original instructions to Norroy, signed with the sign manual,[9] which order him to attempt to procure a change in the fourth article and the deletion of two sentences which remain incorporated in the sixth article of the final Treaty of

---

[1] *Treasurer's Accounts*, I, 357.

[2] *Rot. Scot.* II, 526. Henry VII wrote to the citizens of Waterford on October 17 that he had heard from Fox that a truce was made with Scotland, and that an Embassy was to come for peace "during both our lives". Pollard, *Henry VII*, I, no. 120.

[3] *Foedera*, XII, 680. [4] *Ibid.* XII, 679.

[5] *Ibid.* XII, 680. [6] *Milanese Cal.* p. 335.

[7] *Rot. Scot.* II, 525. *Foedera*, XII, 671.

[8] *Rot. Scot.* II, 526. *Foedera*, XII, 671. *Spanish Cal.* I, no. 186.

[9] B.M. Cotton, Vespasian, C XVI, fol. 118. Appendix L. Gairdner, *Letters*, I, 424, gives an abstract.

Ayton. As Henry mentioned the arrival of Lyon Herald, the instructions must date between November 25, 1497, and the final ratification of the peace. The King furnished Norroy with a copy of the amended letters patent which he was to do his best to get James to accept, without in word or deed offending his cousin. If unsuccessful he was to deliver instead an exact duplicate of the letters patent James IV had sent by Lyon.

Norroy failed to secure the alterations, and the instructions have a certain interest as demonstrating Henry VII's meticulous personal oversight of detail. Norroy and Warham took the alternative versions of the letters patent, confirming the extended truce, to Scotland and were rewarded with £16. 13s. 4d. at St Andrews on February 12,[1] the day on which James IV ratified the peace. His letters patent of confirmation were carried back to London by Warham in March, 1498.[2]

Ayala, the intimate eye-witness of these negotiations, says that James made the treaty against the wishes of the majority of his kingdom,[3] and in great matters acted on his own judgment. The peace may not have seemed much more important at the time than any of the other many treaties; but it did actually mark the most notable stage in the improvement of Anglo-Scottish relations during the reign of Henry VII. Minor disputes did not cease during the next three years; but the Scottish King had at last learnt to respect Henry VII, and time had mitigated Henry's feeling against James as an instrument of his father's murder.

The marriage of Margaret Tudor with James Stewart in 1502 had far-reaching and unforeseeable results, making possible the ultimate political union of England and Scotland. That his slow and patient statecraft should have had such weighty consequences would surely have surprised no one more than Henry VII himself, as it hinged on the death without issue of all his surviving son's children.

The foreign transactions and negotiations of the reign are most important and most tedious; most important because they are closely connected with the opening of the new drama, the equipment of England for her part on the stage; most tedious because they go on

---

[1] *Treasurer's Accounts*, I, 377.   [2] *Milanese Cal.* no. 557.
[3] Pollard, *Henry VII*, I, p. 198.

without crisises and without issues, like a game at chess which has a charm only for an adept, or a well-contested game of croquet which never comes to an end.[1]

For the tediousness of six chapters analysing what are in truth foreign transactions, the author can only plead for mercy.

[1] Stubbs, *Medieval and Modern History*, p. 419.

CHAPTER VII

THE ACTS OF THE DROGHEDA PARLIA-
MENT, 1494–5, OR "POYNINGS' LAWS"

Sir Edward Poynings is most memorable in Irish history for the measures passed in the Parliament that he summoned to Drogheda on December 1, 1494. The general object of these was to restore the royal authority which had two hundred years before under Edward I covered the greater part of Ireland and seemed likely to make of this island a second England. The immediate object was to deal with abuses or dangerous opponents of the time, and the greater and the smaller object were well blended.

Of the forty-nine acts passed by the Drogheda Parliament, the more important have been printed several times among the Statutes of the realm of Ireland.[1] Some, of a more immediate and particular nature, which were enacted though they have never been printed, are to be found only in manuscript transcripts in two great depositories of imperial records.[2]

The acts of Poynings' Parliament are described in the printed Statutes as:

Statuta, ordinationes et actus in quodam parliamento apud Drogheda die Lunae proximo post festum Sancti Andreae Apostoli anno regni Regis Henrici septimi decimo coram Edwardo Poynings milite Deputato ipsius Domini Regis terrae suae Hiberniae edita in haec verba anno Domini 1495.

A summary will enable us to estimate the purpose and importance of these enactments, which were at once a commentary

---

[1] Bolton, *Statutes of Ireland* (Dublin, 1621). *A Collection of all the Statutes now in use in the Kingdom of Ireland* (Dublin, 1678). *The Statutes at Large, passed in Parliaments held in Ireland* (1786), vol. 1. There are twenty-three Acts in the printed Statutes out of forty-nine.
[2] Namely, Lambeth (Carew MSS, vol. 603, fol. 177 and vol. 608, fol. 113) and the Public Record Office, London (E 30, 1548). The original Rolls of Parliament having perished in the Dublin Record Office in 1922, the P.R.O. and Lambeth transcripts are our best, if not our only, authority for the unpublished Statutes.

on the state of Ireland for a hundred and fifty years back, and a programme of reform. Reading and analysing them in order, we shall be able to discern their general character.[1]

The first three, which are in Norman-French and of traditional character, confirm to the Church, the land of Ireland, and the towns of Ireland their liberties, franchises and usages as of old. The rest are in English.

The fourth is described as: "for extortion of coign, livery and pay". Its language explains clearly the evils referred to and the remedies prescribed.[2]

The fifth act authorises the Treasurer of Ireland to make all officers as the Treasurer of England does, namely, to appoint all customers, controllers, farmers and other officers accounting for the King's revenue. All manner of acts formerly made for the election of sheriffs, escheators and other such officers, contrary to the present Act, are revoked. The Treasurer shall henceforth every year make a declaration of his account for the revenues before the Barons of the Exchequer in Ireland and members of the Council, which shall further be certified into the King's Exchequer in England.[3]

The sixth declares that the Chancellor and Treasurer, the judges of the King's Bench and Common Pleas, the chief and second Barons of the Exchequer, the Master of the Rolls and all officers accountant, shall have their offices solely at the King's will and pleasure. This is at the request of the Commons, "in consideration of the great and manifold inconveniences that late were attempted contrary to all national allegiance by the pro-curement, counsel and exhortation of such officers as late had administration under the King and had their offices granted unto them by patent for term of life".[4]

---

[1] For the text of the published Statutes I refer to *Statutes at Large* (Ireland), vol. I. For the full text of the unpublished ones (of which I only make a summary) see Appendices XXI–XXXVI.
[2] See Appendix XXI.
[3] Cap. I, *Statutes at Large.*
[4] Cap. II, *Statutes at Large.*

The seventh is for "annulling a prescription which traitors and rebels claimed within this land". Of late all sorts of rebels and traitors, coming into Ireland, have remained there without molestation notwithstanding any writ, letters missive, or commandment from the King under the Great or Privy Seal directed against such persons. This has been under a "pretensed prescription", which in fact never existed up to the time of Henry the Sixth, but which was approved and confirmed by authority of a Parliament held before Richard, Duke of York, then Lieutenant of Ireland. By authority of this Parliament it was made high treason for any person to bring any writs, privy seals or commandments over from England to attach any person so remaining in Ireland. Hence the abuses and inconveniences that have ensued from "the said feigned unlawful prescription" and the act confirming it, as for example in the maintaining of the two "lads", contrary to all faithful and natural allegiance. Therefore the "pretensed prescription" and the Act of ratification are now revoked and annulled, and anyone who receives or maintains such rebels and traitors shall be adjudged an open traitor to the King. It is also enacted that the King's Great Seal, Privy Seal and letters missive under his signet, sent out of his realm of England, shall be duly obeyed, the said "pretensed prescription" and confirmation notwithstanding.[1]

The eighth, entitled: "a grant of 12d. of every pounde of merchandise during five years to the King", imposes a duty of that amount upon all goods brought into or taken out of the country, whether by strangers or denizens, excepting the freemen of Dublin, Waterford and Drogheda.[2]

The ninth act, entitled "that no parliament be holden in this land until the acts be certified into England", declares that at the next Parliament that shall be held by the King's licence (wherein among other things his Grace intends to have a general resumption of his whole revenue since the last day of Edward II's

---

[1] Cap. III, *Statutes at Large.*
[2] See Appendix XXII. The Carew MSS, vol. 608, fol. 114 adds "hydes & wyne excepted" and ends with "a repeal of all grant to all persons of any poundage to this time".

reign) no Parliament shall be held hereafter in the said land save at such season as the King's Lieutenant and Council there do first certify the King, under the Great Seal of Ireland, what acts it seems good to them should pass in the said Parliament after which, when the King and his Council [in England] have approved of such said acts to be passed as seem to them good and expedient for that land [Ireland] and the King's licence obtained under the Great Seal of England for a Parliament to meet in Ireland, a Parliament shall be held after the form and manner afore rehearsed, and any Parliament held hereafter contrary to such form and provision shall be deemed void and of no effect.[1]

The tenth re-enacts and puts into force the Statutes against papal provisions made in England and Ireland in past times.[2]

The eleventh is for a resumption of lands and lordships to the crown. It is enacted that there be taken into the King's hand all honours, manors, lordships, castles, rents, services, etc., etc., and all other profits and inheritances whereof he or any of his said progenitors, Kings of England, were at any time seised from the last day of Edward the Second till now.[3]

So many exemptions however are made from this terrific "Act of Resumption" as to leave it little force.

The twelfth declares that no citizen shall receive livery or wages of any lord or gentleman. The reflection is made that the cities and great towns, especially Dublin, have neglected their natural faith and allegiance to the King and such as his Grace did commit his authority unto, for amity and favour of divers lords and gentlemen, and were retained with the said lords, contrary to their own laws and customs. Therefore any citizen, burgess or freeman so offending shall be deprived of his freedom or liberty and be expelled out of the said city for ever. Any

---

[1] This is here given in summarised form. It is Cap. IV in *Statutes at Large*. See *Facsimiles of National Manuscripts of Ireland*, Part III, p. liii.

[2] Cap. V, *Statutes at Large*.

[3] See Appendix XXIII. This important Act is not included in the published Statutes. Another copy, without the exemptions, is in B.M. Harl. MSS, 2058, fol. 301.

mayor or other head officers not executing this ordinance to forfeit to the King twenty pounds. It is also enacted that no lord or gentleman shall retain by livery or wages any person or persons but only to such as are or shall be his officers, bailiffs or servants of his household. This act not to extend to the Marches, so that those of the Marches shall present the names of such as they have in their retinue, such as they shall answer for to the King's Lieutenant or his Deputy.[1]

The thirteenth act declares that none shall be admitted alderman, juror or freeman in any town but such as have been apprentice or inhabitant in the same. The intention is that town councils shall not elect as mayor, officer, councillor or freeman, lords and others who are not true men of the King, having a serious mind for the common weal. Further any acts made or to be made in such cities and towns, contrary to the King's majesty and jurisdiction royal, shall be revoked and deemed of no effect in law.[2]

The fourteenth cancels and revokes all the records, processes and pardons done in the name of the pretended king, Lambert Simnel.[3]

Acts fifteen, sixteen, seventeen and eighteen deal with Kilmainham and with the Order of St John of Jerusalem in Ireland, whose rich possessions have been aliened and squandered by Sir James Keating, Prior, and his predecessor, Sir Thomas Talbot.[4]

The nineteenth is for the confirmation of the Statutes of Kilkenny [1366], and all other acts, made in that land [Ireland] for the common weal. The words relating to the famous Statutes may be quoted in full:

Item. Prayen the commons that forasmuch as the Statutes of Kilkenny were made and ordeyned for the publicke weal of the King's subjects of Ireland to keep them under the order and obeysance, and all the season that the said statutes were set in use and duly executed

---

[1] Cap. VI, *Statutes at Large.*   [2] Cap. VII, *Statutes at Large.*
[3] See Appendix XXIV.   [4] See Appendix XXV.

the land continued in prosperitie and honour, and sith [since] the time that they were not executed the foresaid subjects rebelled and digressed from their allegiance and the land did fall to ruine and desolation—be it ordeyned, enacted, and established by authority of this present parliament that all and every of the foresaid statutes (those that will that every subject shall ride in a saddle and those that speaketh of the language of the Irish only excepted) be authorised, approved, confirmed, and deemed good and effectual in law.[1]

The twentieth enacts that as the subjects of Ireland have not, as they had in times past, English bows and arrows to resist rebels and enemies, they shall have arms suitable to their status, that is, every subject having property to the value of £10 to keep a bow and sheaf of arrows; every subject having property to the value of £20 to keep a jack,[2] salett,[3] bow and sheaf of arrows; every freeholder, having land to the value of £4 yearly, to keep horse, jack, salett, bow, and sheaf of arrows; every lord, knight and squire to have for every yeoman in their household jack, salett, bow and arrows. Neglect of this is to entail a fine for each occasion of 6s. 8d. In every barony in each shire there shall be two wardens of the peace, having authority as of old times, and in every parish constables, and butts to be provided in each parish and all constables to see that the subjects practise archery thereat on every holy day and to have power to amerce those who neglect it at 4d. on each occasion.[4]

Act twenty-one ordains that no one shall take money or amends for death or murder of friend or kinsman, other than the King's laws allow. The reference is to the adoption of Irish law by "divers of the land", i.e. the border Englishry. "Whereas on a man being slain his heir should sue appeal of death in the King's courts according to law, many of this land for the death of a kinsman or friend are used to burn, slay or rob as many as bear the name of him that is slain."[5] To remedy this, the Statute of Winchester is directed to be put into full force as it

---

[1] Cap. VIII, *Statutes at Large.*   [2] Breastplate.
[3] Helmet.   [4] Cap. IX, *Statutes at Large.*
[5] The sense would seem to be "are used, as many as bear the name of him that is slain, to burn, slay and rob", i.e. if a Bermingham were slain all of his name and kindred would share in avenging it on say the O'Connors of Offaly, if one of them did the deed.

hath been in old time past within the said land, and whenever murder or robbery shall chance to be done, the Hue and Cry shall be raised according to that Statute.[1]

Act twenty-two directs that the Captains of the Marches shall certify the names of their retainers. The commons say that the inhabitants of the Marches are wont to let the King's enemies and rebels through to rob and spoil his liege subjects, and are even privy to the same. Therefore every Marcher and English captain within the Marches shall certify to the King's Lieutenant the names of all such as they have in their retinues, so that they may answer for the defaults of the same when complained of. Every inhabitant of the Marches who receives or succours such enemies and rebels passing and re-passing shall be attainted and the Warden of the March shall endeavour to bring him to justice. Every person having land in the March parts is to dwell on or to put sufficient guard on their lands there to defend them, otherwise after proclamation made the King may enter upon and seize such lands and take the profits thereof for the maintenance of his wars in Ireland. Every man between sixteen and sixty dwelling in any county, city or town adjoining the Marches shall upon reasonable summons be ready in their best defensible array for war to aid and defend the said Marches.[2]

By the twenty-third it is enacted by the King with the advice and assent of his lords, spiritual and temporal, and the proctors and commons and by the authority of the same that no one shall from this time forward retain or keep in his house, garrison or place, any ordnance or artillery, that is to say, great gun or handgun except only long bows, arrows and bills, on pain of forfeiting the same, and anyone who, within a month after due proclamation made does not surrender such ordnance to the King's Lieutenant, but without licence from the latter retains them, shall forfeit to the King £20.[3]

The twenty-fourth act acquits the Earl of Kildare, Sir James of Ormond, and all persons adherent to them of all actions, suits

---

[1] Cap. XI, *Statutes at Large.*   [2] Cap. X, *Statutes at Large.*
[3] Cap. XII, *Statutes at Large.*

and vexations for murder, robbery or any other offence done in these quarters.[1]

The twenty-fifth enacts that, inasmuch as divers persons have assembled with banners displayed against the King's Lieutenant, not knowing it was treason to do so, whosoever shall stir up Irishry or Englishry to make war against the King's Lieutenant or Deputy or shall procure the Irish to make war on the English shall be deemed a traitor attainted of high treason.[2]

The twenty-sixth enacts that the Treasurer shall be governor in the absence of the Deputy. It recites that the King—considering how the land of Ireland has often been in great jeopardy because the Lieutenant or his deputy has voided his office before any provision could be made out of the realm of England—has with the assent of the present Parliament ordained and enacted that whenever in future such voidance shall take place the Treasurer of Ireland for the time being shall be Justice and Governor until such time as the King shall send his Lieutenant or Deputy, all other usages of election of a Justice at such voidance to be repealed and of no effect.[3]

Act twenty-seven, "for discharge of annuities, coign and livery granted by compulsion out of the March lands", vividly and sufficiently describes the evils it tries to deal with.[4]

The twenty-eighth is "an act that one born in the realm of England shall be Constable of Dublin, Trim, Athlone, Wicklow, Greencastle, Carlingford and Carrickfergus". These are described as the chief castles of the land, of right appertaining to the King, but they have been negligently kept and those that have been committed to the keepers of them for treason, felony and other offences, have been suffered to escape. Therefore it is ordained that henceforth in each of the aforesaid castles there shall be a Constable who shall be an able and sufficient person of the realm of England.[5]

---

[1] This is found only in Carew MSS, vol. 608, fol. 115, and compares curiously with the attainder of Kildare in Act forty-one, *infra*. Appendices XXVI and XXXI.
[2] Cap. XIII, *Statutes at Large*.
[3] See Appendix XXVII.
[4] See Appendix XXVIII.
[5] Cap. XIV, *Statutes at Large*.

The twenty-ninth act recites that the earldom of March and Ulster and the lordships of Trim and Connaught have been annexed to the Crown and that all such records and rolls, etc., were remaining in the Treasury at Trim as should entitle the King to all such lordships, domains, manors, services, etc., as were appurtenant to the said lordships, but that these records were of late taken and embezzled. It is therefore enacted that after public proclamation whatever person or persons have records, etc., or know where they are, shall within two months reveal or deliver them or be deemed traitors attainted. It is further enacted that the King may enter upon all such lordships, manors, etc., "whereof any maner lefull title or discharge of our said soveraign lord's interest cannot be shewed".[1]

The thirtieth act directs that the lords, spiritual and temporal, of Parliament shall wear robes in like manner as the lords of England, and as they were wont to do up to the time of twenty or twenty-five years ago.[2]

The thirty-first begins: "item, that the acte agaynst Lollardes and heretikes be auctoryzed by this present parliament".[3]

The thirty-second is: "an act that no peace or war be made with any man without licence of the Governor". It recites that divers lords and gentlemen have been used to make peace with the King's Irish enemies and yet, when the peace was ratified by his Lieutenant, they have broken it and entered into the countries of such Irish enemies being under the protection of our sovereign Lord, and have robbed, spoiled and hurt there, whereupon the said Irish enemies have entered into the English country and robbed and spoiled the true English subjects. Therefore it is enacted that henceforth no peace or war shall be made without the Lieutenant's licence, but only by the Lieutenant or his deputy, and whoever shall break such peace shall forfeit £100 to the King.[4]

---

[1] Cap. xv, *Statutes at Large.* [2] Cap. xvi, *Statutes at Large.*
[3] Only the heading is given in P.R.O. E 30, 1548, and in the Carew MSS, vol. 608. See Appendix xxix.
[4] Cap. xvii, *Statutes at Large.*

The thirty-third enacts, "that the Chancellor shall have authoritie to continew, adiourne, prorogue and dissolve this parliament, in the absence of the Lord Deputie, and shall have like authoritie for all things to be done therein as if the Lord Deputie were present".[1]

The thirty-fourth act, "for ditches to be made about the English Pale", recites that the Marches of the four shires are open and not fencible, whereby the Irishmen make great preys in the English land. Therefore it is enacted that every earth-tiller and occupier in the said Marches—that is to say, in the Counties of Dublin, from the water of Annaliffey to the mountain in Kildare, in Kildare from the water of Annaliffey to Trim and so into Meath and Uriell [county Louth]—shall build and make a double ditch of six foot of earth above the ground at that end of the said land that he occupies which joins next unto Irishmen before next Lammas. The said ditches so builded to be kept up and repaired as long as they shall occupy the same land upon pain of 40s. by him who shall be found negligent therein. The lord of the land to allow the old rent to the said builder and maker of the ditches for one year upon the said pain. The Archbishop of Dublin and the Sheriff of the county of Dublin to be commissioners, overseers and wardens thereof in that shire and other commissioners to be assigned to the other shires, who shall cause the inhabitants of the four shires to make ditches in the wastes or "fasagh"[2] lands without the said Marches at such times and places as they shall think most expedient.[3]

Act thirty-five, "for extirpation of a new manner of coign and livery", recites that, notwithstanding the Act lately made in this same Parliament against this custom, many evil-disposed persons continue to take daily by colour of gift and reward from some husbandmen for them and their servants 8d. and of some less, and of some more, besides sheaves of corn, oats and other grain for their horses, and so daily ride about the country from one husbandman to another, menacing to be revenged upon them in

---

[1] See Appendix xxix.
[2] Irish "fásach" = waste or rugged ground.
[3] See Appendix xxx. This is not in the *Statutes at Large*.

times to come if that they be denied—the which is equivalent to coign and livery. Therefore such practice is forbidden upon pain contained in the Statute of Kilkenny for taking of coign and livery, and no husbandman shall make such gift or reward upon pain of forfeiting 100s.; commissioners to inquire into such offences.[1]

The thirty-sixth act provides for the payment of Poynings' army, sent into this land to subdue the King's rebels and enemies. It is ordained that whenever they shall ride into the enemy's country or whenever the latter shall invade the English country, then the subjects shall lodge the soldiers in their houses, the soldiers to receive meat and drink reasonable as the governor of the house shall fortune to have, and the latter not to take of each soldier more than $1\frac{1}{2}d$. for one meal and for his servant $1d$., and for every horse not more than $1d$. for six field sheaves with a double band with litter according. Further whoever shall refuse to lodge such soldiers (lords and gentlemen of 20 marks of land and more, and cities and borough towns alone excepted) shall forfeit to the King $12d$. for each occasion.[2]

Act thirty-seven declares that, "forasmuch as there hath been universal murder by malice prepensed used and had within this land by divers persons contrary to the laws of Almighty God and the King without any fear or due punishment", it is ordained that henceforth any person of whatsoever estate or degree, who of malice prepensed do slay or murder or procure to be murdered any of the King's subjects, shall be "deemed a traitor attainted of haute treason likewise as it should extend to our said soveraign Lord's person and to his royal Majesty".[3]

The thirty-eighth is an act to abolish the words "Cromabo" and "Butlerabo", and such Irish war cries, which have been used by one party and the other in the great variances, malices, and debates between divers lords and gentlemen and their retainers. Therefore the use of such words and all such maintaining of variances, etc., is forbidden, and subjects are to call

[1] Cap. XVIII, *Statutes at Large.* [2] Cap. XIX, *Statutes at Large.*
[3] Cap. XXI, *Statutes at Large.*

only on St George or the name of their sovereign Lord the King, on pain of stated penalties.[1]

Act thirty-nine, considering how the wealth and prosperity of England are due to the many and divers good and profitable statutes late made there by great labour, study and policy, as well in the time of our sovereign Lord the King as in the time of his progenitors, Kings of England, by advice of his and their Council, ordains that all statutes late made within the realm of England, concerning or belonging to the common and public weal of the same, shall from henceforth be deemed good and effectual in law and be accepted, used and executed within this land of Ireland.[2]

The fortieth is an act for repealing a Parliament held at Drogheda in 1493 before Robert Preston, Viscount Gormanston, Deputy to the Lord Lieutenant, Jasper, Duke of Bedford. It was declared void because, first, the Duke surrendered his letters patent of office before the said Parliament was summoned; secondly there was no general summons to all the shires, but only to four; thirdly because the said Deputy had no power by his commission to hold Parliaments.[3]

Act forty-one is for the attainder of the Earl of Kildare.[4]

Act forty-two is for the attainder of James fitz Thomas Gerald and many others for divers treasons, felonies, murders, robberies, insurrections, extortions, coigns and liveries, etc.[5]

Act forty-three is for giving authority to the Deputy and Council to examine into alienations, grants, leases, etc., made by prelates and other spiritual persons.[6]

Forty-four is an act giving authority to the Chancellor to examine into annuities granted by spiritual persons, in pursuance

[1] Cap. xx, *Statutes at Large.*   [2] Cap. xxii, *Statutes at Large.*
[3] Cap. xxiii, *Statutes at Large.* With this the printed Statutes end.
[4] Carew MSS, vol. 603, fol. 177. See Appendix xxxi for text.
[5] See Appendix xxxii.   [6] Appendix xxxiii.

of a former act of this same Parliament declaring void such annuities and pensions.[1]

Forty-five is an act restoring to all religious houses such possessions as have been taken from them and yearly mis-charged extortionately by mighty men of this land of Ireland.[2]

Acts forty-six to forty-nine are only of minor importance. One orders the payment to Thomas Garth, commander of Poynings' army, of £454 for wages of soldiers; another repeals pensions and grants made to the Earl of Kildare and other attainted persons by the Archbishops of Armagh and Dublin; another revokes all alienations and grants made by the House of St John beside Waterford from the ninth year of Henry VI.[3]

THE PURPOSE AND IMPORTANCE OF "POYNINGS' ACTS"

In law and in theory Henry VII, as King of England, was also Lord of all Ireland. In fact of actual sovereignty only a fragment of the island was actually his. The area variously called "the land of peace", "the obedient shires", "the English land", was reckoned as the Pale, or four counties of Dublin, Kildare, Louth and Meath, with southern Wexford and a few cities and towns such as Dublin, Drogheda and Waterford. Even in the four counties, outlying portions were given over to Gaelic mountaineers or "degenerate" feudal English. Everywhere but in this Pale the Lordship of Ireland, which in 1300 had embraced twelve great counties, had practically slipped out of the King's hands and ceased to obey English law or preserve the tradition of English speech and loyalty. A large part of the land had gone back to the old native princes. The earldoms of Desmond, Kildare and Ormond covered most of Munster and a large part of Leinster, and old English families ruled the greater part of Connaught and Eastern Ulster, but these feudal areas were almost independent of State control. The King himself, in right of his wife, Elizabeth of York, heiress to the houses of De Burgo and Mortimer, was titular Earl of Ulster and Lord of Connaught,

---

[1] Appendix xxxiv.   [2] Appendix xxxv.   [3] See Appendix xxxvi.

Trim and Leix, but these lordships for the most part were now enjoyed by Gaelic chiefs and hibernicised English. The decay of English sovereignty was at once political, legal, racial and linguistic. The earldoms and feudal areas were not altogether lost, but their chartered liberties excluded direct control from Dublin and Westminster, and Irish custom prevailed more and more among them. Many of the Anglo-Normans of Ireland with the lapse of time preferred Brehon law to English law, and adapted also a "March law" to the relations of their Norman and Gaelic tenants, which seems to have been a convenient mixture of Irish and feudal customs. Being for the most part only an upper crust of English ascendancy among a dominant Celtic population, they retained great numbers of Irish on the soil and in later times preferred them to their less responsive English tenantry. In direct defiance of the Statutes of Kilkenny (1366), which aimed at keeping the English blood, language and law pure, they had come freely to intermarry with the Irish and adopt their speech and customs. Instead of the Norman conquerors gallicising or anglicising "the Irish", the Irish gaelicised the Normans, and by 1500 the Celtic speech was dominant in Ireland, not only among the natives but among the colonists, even in the towns themselves.

Such was the general result of two centuries of English rule. If we can attribute any one single cause to this decay, we must find it in the absence of the King from his lordship of Ireland. Between the visit of King John in 1210 to the visit of Richard II, nearly two centuries had elapsed, and since Richard II no English monarch had set foot on Irish soil, though several royal princes had landed as viceroys. The English monarchy had its eyes fixed upon Scotland and France, while in Ireland native chiefs who hated the English as a race, and Norman conquistadors who hated royal authority, established in the ruins of the Anglo-Irish State their tribal and feudal independence.

Poynings was commissioned to end this state of things and restore to Henry his "Dominium Hiberniae". But what *terminus a quo* was to be fixed for the Crown's decline and the usurpation of its prerogatives? A remote date was indicated as a time when the decline began, and a nearer one as a time when the monarchy let slip from its hands what remained of the Irish heritage. The accession of Edward III was the first date, the outbreak of the Wars of the Roses was the second. In the early years of Edward, the Mortimer party, by creating the Ormond, Desmond and Kildare palatinates, had endowed the feudal power in Ireland to the detriment of the Crown. Edward III had later striven to rescue Anglo-Ireland from the baronage, but without real determination, and therefore without success. Henry VI had inherited an Irish lordship which was great at least *de jure*, but forty years of civil war and unsteady monarchy in England had allowed Ireland to assume a practical independence. Irish Home Rule, as run by the Geraldines and Lords of the Pale for their own interest, and favoured by the English Yorkists, who needed the help of Irish allies, had resulted in an Ireland independent in its own Parliament and law courts and firmly attached to the Yorkist cause.

The first Tudor sovereign was obliged to consider Ireland as a home for White Rose candidates and a hatching-ground for Yorkist plots and foreign intervention. He was thus impelled to clip the wings of the Anglo-Irish nobility. But further he believed that at least the *de jure* claims of English sovereignty could be reasserted and some essential features of it recovered *de facto*. To go back to 1327 as the *fons et origo* of English decay was a bold act of the higher policy and a clear pronouncement of indefeasible right. It rings through the whole of "Poynings' Acts". But to end the Wars of the Roses, in Ireland as in England, was an aim nearer to hand and easier to achieve.

Before the boy Henry VI ascended the throne in 1422, the Dublin government, ruled in the interests of England by English-born viceroys, had still a chance to recover Ireland from the native princes and from the "great chieftains of English lineage" who enjoyed in the fairest parts of Ireland the wide liberties of their ancestors, continually enhanced. The Gaels were "Irish enemies", not comprehended in the law or government of the Englishry. But the Anglo-Irish, though fallen away from English law and speech, and no longer paying taxes or rendering homage, were still subjects and might be recalled, certainly in the nearer parts, to an allegiance they had rendered under the Plantagenets.

But supposing that government fell into the hands of an

Irish-minded nobility and a succession of native Deputies, the very citadel and hope of English authority was in danger. And that is what happened. From 1422 to 1485 the monarchy had no time to spare in its other realm, and the control of affairs in Dublin and the feudal ownership of half the island passed into the hands of three Anglo-Irish nobles, "English to the Irish but Irish to the English", the Earls of Kildare, Desmond and Ormond. Home Rule rather than independence was their aim, but Home Rule would mean control of the government, of the Parliament, of the law, of the revenues. The Irish, becoming reconciled to those "mighty men of Ireland" who spoke Gaelic and patronised the bards, became their allies and were proud to marry their daughters. The pride of the lesser Englishry was gratified at the thought of a sort of colonial nationalism in which a distant over-lord in Westminster would respect the "Customs of Ireland", and leave intact the feudal, ecclesiastical and civic liberties of the Anglo-Irish colony. A fortunate *entente* with the House of York put the Anglo-Irish patriots into the saddle. Richard, founder of that house, was lineally and personally popular in Ireland as heir to the Lacys, De Burgos and Mortimers, and as titular Earl of Ulster and Lord of Connaught and Trim. Sent over as Lord Lieutenant in 1449, he won the hearts of almost all Ireland, saving the Butlers who, under their head the Earl of Ormond, preserved in their wide country of Tipperary and Kilkenny a Lancastrian enclave. England's misfortunes became Ireland's opportunity, and an implicit bargain was struck between the House of York and the Anglo-Irish by which Ireland fought for the White Rose and got her parliamentary independence in return. A Parliament at Dublin in 1460, held under Duke Richard, declared Ireland to be bound only by laws enacted in her own Parliament, and the decisions of her law courts. The King's authority could not be openly impugned, but it was to all intents laid down that only a command under the Great Seal of England, and perhaps not even this, could take effect against an Irish subject or an Englishman, that is a Yorkist, resident in Ireland. The Duke became a sort of native king, and Ireland was made a safe retreat for the supporters of York from their Lancastrian enemies.

Richard fell at Wakefield, but his son Edward by a lightning stroke won the throne. The new King of England was a sort of Irishman, and hereditary Lord of Ulster, Connaught and Trim. Blood has always counted in Ireland; the Yorkists were believed to be the rightful line; and good looks, splendid stature and affable ways, which were the heritage of the dynasty, further enkindled the devotion of Ireland. York's son, George, later Duke of Clarence, saw the light of day in Dublin; he was therefore considered there as "one of ourselves", and later his unfortunate child Edward, Earl of Warwick, was the nation's hope. Out of the three Earls who between them owned almost a half of Ireland, the Leinster Geraldine emerged the leading figure. Duke Richard had made Thomas, seventh Earl of Kildare, his Deputy in 1457, and Edward IV could do no less than take him into permanent favour. The "Fitzgerald Supremacy" or "all-but-Kingship" of Ireland was now founded, and became firmly established under Gerald, "the Great Earl of Kildare". In its essential features, though with much vicissitude, it lasted till 1534.

Till 1485 the Anglo-Irish nobility maintained intact their colonial nationhood. They dominated government, Parliament, the law and the Church; and, if we can believe the charges of Poynings' Parliament, their rule was selfish and oligarchic. One class, at least, seems to have strongly objected to it, namely the old English population of the four counties, the burgesses in the lesser towns, and the loyal element in the Church. The hopes of this anti-feudal, anti-Gaelic element had always been fixed on a viceroy of English blood and in the direct intervention, or even the personal advent, of the crown. It was from them that Sir Edward Poynings was able to draw his Parliament of Drogheda and secure the condemnation of fifty years of Home Rule. But the tiny Parliament of Dublin, never numbering more than a hundred and fifty, whether peers or commoners, and drawn from a limited area of the original colony, was in fact a mere registering machine which any strong faction or viceroy in Ireland could in turn control.

When Richard III fell at Bosworth, Gerald, Earl of Kildare, and the Anglo-Irish found they had no longer at Westminster a "king of their own". In truth, neither Edward IV nor his successor, Richard, had ever loved to see the Prerogative so abased in their second realm, and any strong King of England was bound to end the scandal of English decay there. To prolong Home Rule under the former conditions was naturally the object of Kildare, and had he at once declared for the victor of Bosworth, Henry VII might have been content to leave the reformation of Ireland to his successor. But Kildare could not be blamed for thinking that Henry's title might be reversed by some scion of the fallen house, and when so many believed in Simnel and Warbeck, he can hardly be condemned for believing too. Doubtless the continuance of the Yorkist-Kildare understanding was the prime consideration. In Lambert Simnel, crowned in Dublin on May 24, 1487, as Edward VI of England, the Home Rule lords seemed again to have a king of their own. How this enterprise and that of Warbeck failed need not be recapitulated. Sir Edward Poynings' rule was at least effective in ending the Wars of the Roses in Ireland.

The problem of Ireland, as faced in Poynings' Acts, came under several heads: the government, the Parliament, the law, the revenue and the armed forces. The "Irish enemies" who owned more than a third of the land might for a time be disregarded, for never yet had they combined to make a final conquest of the colony. Another third was a mass of Norman feudalism gone strangely Irish, but even that did not directly menace sovereignty. What was most serious and immediately to be faced was the seizure of the State by the "mighty men", who had made Dublin the capital of an Anglo-Irish nation, as an Irish aristocracy were to do again in the eighteenth century. In the Parliament that Kildare and his supporters controlled a king according to Irish ideas might be elected, or treaties passed with foreign powers to England's disadvantage, if not to the actual peril of Henry's throne.

To unseat the colonial oligarchy and to restore the mere prerogatives of the Crown was the first and most necessary step. Hence the Acts that resumed to the King the appointing of officers of State, and invested in men that Henry could control the exercise of a deputed power.[1] During the weakness of

---

[1] Acts V, VI, XXXIII.

England there had been many intervals between English-appointed viceroys; the gap had been filled up by native Governors, and an Irish Act of 1471 had given to the Irish Council in a vacancy power to elect a Justiciar till the royal pleasure should be known. The so-called "Statute of Henry Fitz Empress", a traditional usage which that Act confirmed, was now annulled.

Another Act restored to the King the appointing of constables to the royal castles and restricted the office to men of English birth.[1] Henry did not trust the Anglo-Irish, and this distrust is expressed through all these Statutes. They had held power for fifty years and abused it, and it was his intention, had it then been possible, to have Ireland ruled once more by English viceroys who would put the offices of State and the control of essential points into the hands of Englishmen, or at least of men who could be trusted to be both loyal and conscientious. But where almost none were loyal in the new Tudor sense, such a programme was as yet impossible, and actually for forty years after Poynings, Kildare and his son after him ruled Ireland according to Irish ideas. To recover the lost revenues of State was imperative if the new monarchy designed to reduce the land to whole and perfect obeisance. Such revenues as remained were contemptible, hardly enough to pay the working staff that ran the skeleton government at Dublin. Almost no royal demesnes or parliamentary subsidy, no regular yield from feudal reliefs, homages, wardships, courts of justice, customs or merchandise. To fill up the empty Treasury there was designed a vast and sweeping Act of Resumption, by which all royal rights since 1327 were reasserted.[2] This was in essence to declare two centuries and a half a period of usurpation and embezzlement of royal property. But it was rather a case of stating a claim than of making it good. Numerous saving clauses mitigated the Act of Resumption, and how could the crown at this stage have assailed the vested rights of three earls and a whole landlordry built on feudal grants or prescriptive right? Of the Mortimer lands in Ulster, Connaught and Meath, only the lordship of Trim yielded any profits, and persons interested in concealing

---

[1] Act XXVIII.   [2] Acts XI and XXIX.

the royal prerogatives over these inheritances had embezzled or destroyed the records.[1]

The Act of Resumption was a failure, and had lapsed before the Statutes were printed. The Irish revenues of the time were small and there is little evidence that from this time to that of Henry VIII they increased in any considerable degree. And if they did, it profited the King little when Kildare recovered power, for it had long been the practice to appropriate all the State revenue to the upkeep of the Deputy and his government.

Poynings' real success was in the sterilising of the Dublin Parliament and the organising of the Pale as a garrison for the English interest. After all, the King in his high court of Parliament was the legal and supreme authority in Ireland. However threatened that authority might be, nothing could be binding and legal that was done without it. Hence the Act which became famous and infamous as "Poynings'" until it was abolished by the eighteenth century Patriots in 1782.[2]

This enactment made it impossible for a native Lord Deputy to make the Dublin Parliament his creature, or for that assembly to offer to a native Earl, a Yorkist claimant, a Scottish or French King, the crown of Ireland. Henceforth whatever laws might be legally enacted in Ireland were subject to a double veto, that of the King and his Council in Ireland, and that of the King and his Council in England exercising final and imperial control. Often as it was and has been denounced, "Poynings' Act" was only an assertion of the new monarchy; the English Parliament itself was almost equally shackled.[3]

An Act usually coupled with "Poynings'" made *de cursu* in Ireland the Statutes "formerly made for the common weal" in England. With this provision, the crown remained content for

---

[1] The records of Trim, Ulster and other Mortimer estates were never recovered, and are probably not extant; a sore loss to Irish history.

[2] Act IX (or IV in the *Statutes at Large*). See Curtis, *History of Mediaeval Ireland*, pp. 399–402.

[3] "The statute known as Poynings' law came later to interfere very seriously with the liberty of the Irish parliament, but at the time of its adoption it enacted nothing which was not also true of England. No English parliament could meet without the approval of the King and his Council, and when it met it still had no initiative, at least before the very end of the [Tudor] period, and only passed what would be called to-day government bills"; Adams, *Constitutional History of England*, p. 252.

the future with the imperial veto. Ireland still retained the power of internal legislation. But what these Statutes made for the common weal were, was left vague. No one knew how far the great enactments of English law had been applied to or re-enacted in Ireland, but it is certain that many of them had never been formally extended there. From some of them Ireland might well boast of being free. It was not till this Parliament passed an Act "against Lollards and heretics" that the ferocious statute *De heretico comburendo* of 1401 was made known in this happier realm and curiously enough it remained on the statutes there till the seventh of William III.[1]

In the legal, as in the legislative field, the independence of Ireland had been declared in the Home Rule parliament of 1460, which practically made the two realms into a dual monarchy. On no point would a Tudor King feel more outraged than by that "pretensed prescription" for shielding traitors and rebels which is denounced in one of these acts and emphatically annulled.[2] Henceforth every royal writ or commandment under Great or Privy Seal or by letters missive is to be as sacred as in England.

So far for the royal or prerogative law which under the new monarchy was to rival or even override common law. The Anglo-Irish colony among other pleasing immunities had so far, or for a long time, known little of the law of treason and the dreadful penalties it entailed, and the introduction of it into several of these Statutes is a striking fact.

As for the common law of England, it had in its earlier forms at least been made a heritage of Anglo-Irish freemen equally with those of England, and the liberties of Magna Carta were a possession of both lands. But the common law area had dwindled away in Ireland down to the home counties. In seven-eighths of the island, what between "March lands" and "Irish counties" Gaelic law and feudal-Gaelic custom held the field. The Tudors were well acquainted with Wales, its Cymric natives, and its many and variegated Marcher lordships. To Henry most of Ireland might well seem to be a Welsh March-land on a vaster scale. The same remedies naturally suggested

---

[1] See Appendix XXIX. It is not in the *Statutes at Large*.
[2] Acts VII and III, *Statutes at Large*.

themselves; hence the strong enactments against the use of Irish law or that mixture of Irish and feudal custom which former Statutes had called "law of the Marches". Ireland was predominantly the home of an unfettered landlordry, whom no resident monarch could bridle or had bridled, and who had become tyrants exercising in the "poor true liege subjects many and ruinous extortions of coign, livery, kerntye", and other impositions learned from their Gaelic neighbours.[1] By such "extortions" the lords and gentlemen had driven out their English tenantry who could not or would not endure them and drawn in an Irish tenantry who did not object to them. The Gaelic law of compensation for murder, or a worse thing, the blood feud and vendetta, had displaced with many of the marchers the English law on homicide. Against all this collapse of common law several of Poynings' statutes are emphatically directed.[2]

Having secured the citadel of power, the next step was to provide for the defence of what was after all a garrison, the English Pale, and to seize such strategic points in Ireland as could immediately be controlled. The King's army must be as in England the only army and really his. Hence the royal castles must be committed to trustworthy commanders. No one but the King and his Deputy may legally keep ordnance and great guns. No subjects may assemble in arms with banners displayed against the State or make war or peace with Irish enemies or others but by government licence. The royal army sent under Poynings was but a small force, but it was a mighty efficient force, armed with modern weapons, and more than a match for many times its number of feudal or Gaelic levies. It struck the terror of the royal name and was to be maintained by the State and the people. But for the defence of the loyal counties every subject must be armed after English fashion and called on to do his military duty as by ancient statutes.[2]

The picture given of the former times suggests an unwarlike population of earth-tillers in the Pale, grown unfamiliar with

---

[1] For the meaning of "coign and livery", etc. see Wilson, *Beginnings of Modern Ireland*, pp. 58–72, and Curtis, *History of Mediaeval Ireland (passim)*.
[2] For these provisions of defence see Acts IV, XI, XX, XXI, XXIII, XXV, XXXVI, XXXVII, XLVI.

English weapons and unable to cope with Marcher lords and Gaelic kerns and galloglass, and accustomed to being invaded and terrorised by both. But in reality most of Ireland, native and English, was a land of war. The Marcher English appear as a military class, and the great earls and lords had, like their fellows in England before 1485, mustered armies of retainers wearing their livery and raising their war cries, "Butler to victory", or "Fitzgerald to victory." The very cities had entered into these great factions, and Waterford was a Butler preserve as Dublin was a Geraldine preserve. Henceforth, if law could avail, such factions and maintaining of factions, and the aristocratic domination of tenants and townsmen must cease. There should be no forces but those of the King, and no party in the State save his. It was an impossible demand, but then it was worth stating. Men, even March rebels, could not be left defenceless against Irish and other enemies; so the Marchers were to be allowed to keep retainers, but only under State licence.[1]

Poynings' Acts, like many medieval statutes, are really more valuable for the contemporary picture they draw than for the remedies they provide. In them we see the "March English" riding from house to house of their tenantry and vexing them with manifold burdens, foreign to common law and the rights of their English ancestors.[2] Or we behold the "mighty men" of Ireland attending the Home Rule Parliament, no longer in the robes of peers met in civil consultation, but in their factions and arrayed in the armour and weapons of their feudal pride.[3] In the eyes of the crown this was all a vast offence. In the eyes of the Gaels and the long-established English it was a great age of liberty and civilisation, highly acceptable to the feudal and traditional mind of both races. The fifteenth century was in fact a remarkable period in Irish history, when the blending of the two races, which had long been proceeding, was bearing fruit in a garnering and a revival of Irish literature and Irish culture. The official mind, bent on the King's business, could not be expected to sympathise with this, and it is only natural that in the dry statutes of an obsequious Parliament the official view should be strongly emphasised.

[1] Acts XII, XIII, XXII.   [2] Act XXXV.   [3] Act XXX.

After all, the main care and the main hope of Henry VII's policy in Ireland lay in the more English land, its towns and its English tenantry, on which the hopes of a forward movement rested. Several of the enactments aim at delivering them from the double scourge of Irish inroads and the oppressions of Marcher lords. An act which could hardly have been paralleled in Europe at that time directed that a double ditch should be raised about the Pale, so that Irish rievers could not, even if they slipped past into the English land, drive out again the cattle they had raided.[1] Only four counties, or rather half-counties, were thus legislated for, the poor remnant of an "English land" which once covered more than half of Ireland.

In Ireland, no more than in Wales or Cornwall, was the Tudor monarchy likely to favour Celtic speech and custom. As well as being delivered materially, the Palesmen were to be saved spiritually from the Irish population that pressed upon them. The Statutes of Kilkenny, originally designed to keep the colony English-speaking and English-minded, were once more re-enacted, but it shows how far the native language had penetrated even into the Pale and the towns that the former provision against the use of Irish had now to be abandoned.[2]

For the great world of Gaelic kings and chiefs and of the "mere Irish" who had practically recovered the independence of their ancestors before 1172, Poynings' parliament had little comment to make. Peaceful persuasion which would make State subjects of these proud chieftains was hardly to be conceived, and for a forcible subjection no means were available, in spite of big words about a complete reduction of Ireland. How was a feeble Government to deal with a whole race which spoke no English, was outside the legal and governmental system of Dublin, and fiercely defended its liberty? The Gaelic people had been for over a century outside the law; Poynings' parliament had no power or wish to end that state of things, and outside the law the native race of Ireland remained till 1603.[3]

---

[1] Act XXXIV.   [2] Act XIX.

[3] The "mere Irish" had ever since the Statutes of Kilkenny (1366) been considered as excluded from the benefits of English law. By occasional treaties with chiefs, however, or individual grants of denization considerable numbers of the native race had been admitted to the protection of the common law. Henry VII made no general pronouncement of enfranchise-

It would be easy to exaggerate the importance of "Poynings' Acts". Actually when this vigorous servant of a new régime departed, the Earl of Kildare resumed his former state, and till 1534 his house ruled Ireland almost as separately as before, though with a crippled Parliament and with ever-growing reminders from England that the old order was not to be tolerated for ever. Under the restored Kildare supremacy much of Poynings' legislation was bound to be rendered inoperative or even actually to play into Kildare's hands. The famous Statutes bringing Dublin's government and Parliament under imperial control remained intact, and were Poynings' most lasting achievement. The provisions for the maintenance of the army and for defence provide a model which lasted all through Tudor times. How the revenue could be increased had been indicated, but in fact, until the overthrow of the House of Kildare enabled Henry VIII to take Leinster in hand, any increase that there was in crown rents, subsidies and customs, was slow and insignificant. The tide of the Irish revival, which had captured so much of Ireland and embraced so many of the Old English in speech, law and sympathy, continued to flow steadily even up to Elizabeth's days.

As for coign and livery and such "damnable Irish extortions", and all the oppressions of landlordry at once feudal and gaelicised, Poynings' Acts scarcely struck a blow at them, and they continued to oppress the husbandman and exasperate the Government until the final reduction of Ireland, Gaelic and Norman, in 1603. As the English power spread after 1534 more and more country from the east outwards was brought under the common law, but as late as 1583 inquisitions into the vast principality of the Earl of Desmond, perhaps the greatest example of a Norman-Irish Marcher, revealed a whole labyrinth of "chargeable lands", "customary rents", "Irish exactions", and duties called variously "shragh, kerntye, coign, livery, cuddies, Bonaghtbur and Bonnaghtbeg, sorohen, musteroon", etc., which were the same as those condemned in 1495.

ment, but continued the issuing of particular grants of liberty. In 1488 two Munster chiefs, Florence MacCarthy and Cormac MacTaig, were by letters patent "emancipated from Irish servitude" and given the laws and privileges of Englishmen (*Materials for the Reign of Henry VII*, Campbell, vol. II, pp. 309, 313, 496).

The reduction of Ireland as Henry VII contemplated it was in fact a task that demanded more statesmanship, attention and resources than he had or cared to devote to Ireland. Nevertheless the work of Poynings was of momentous importance, as cutting off medieval Ireland from modern Ireland, and giving a headline to the Irish policy of his successors, even though the execution of it was deferred for forty years and more.

E. CURTIS

APPENDIX I

Extracts from the Summons of Lord Bothwell, and the recitals of the treasonable acts of James, Earl of Buchan and John Ross

The following narrative is composed of a translation of the whole summons of John Ramsay, Lord Bothwell, together with supplementary extracts from the indictment of James, Earl of Buchan and the summons of John Ross of Montgrenan, all taken from *The Acts of the Parliament of Scotland*. When the three complete documents are placed in parallel columns it is easy to see where there is overlapping in the recital of the same facts. Only the relevant portions, without recapitulation, are here translated, and should be read as giving a chronological story of the crisis.

SUMMONS OF BOTHWELL BY JAMES IV
(Acts Parl. Scot. ii, 201)[1]

We order you to summon John, Lord Bothwell...to appear personally to answer to us, in our Parliament, for his treason in seducing and setting James, King of Scots, our deceased Father,[2] against the commonweal and our Realm; causing him to oppress his Prelates, Barons, burgesses and lieges by the common selling and buying of justice, to their final undoing; by reason of which foreign merchants coming to our realm were destroyed and preyed upon, so that none of them dared to enter our kingdom for its refreshing. Also (to answer for)[3] his treason in art, part, counsel and assistance given and shown to James, Earl of Buchan, in his treasonable journey into England.[4] Also for his treasonable intercourse with the King of England and his part in the importation of certain Englishmen for the destruction of our realm and our lieges. Also for his treasonable part, together with the Earl of Buchan, in instigating, as far as in him lay, the said King of England, to enter our realm in his own person,[5] with arms and many men, for our

---

[1] Printed without contractions in Pitcairn's *Criminal Trials*, i, 5–7.
[2] James III.
[3] "To answer for" governs all the remaining paragraphs of this appendix.
[4] Buchan had been banished for three years in March, 1483. He was in England in December, 1487. (Campbell, *Materials*, ii, 219.)
[5] Buchan's indictment in this particular is phrased less ambiguously: "Et pro instigatione et causacione dicti Regis Anglie in propria persona cum suis armis et copia virorum in regnum Scocie advenisse".

destruction and that of our lieges. And for the treasonable journeys into England made by John himself, divers times.[1]

Also for his treason in art, part, counsel and assistance given and shown to Andrew Bishop of Moray, James Earl of Buchan, and Alexander Lord Forbes,[2] in forging a commission and other documents taken to the King of England by you, John Bothwell, and *Henry Wyatt*, Englishman, in order to break the peace and truce made by our late Father, and his Parliament and the King of England,[3] against the common weal and for the perpetual destruction of our realm; by virtue of which war was proclaimed in one part of our realm, and divers of our lieges in that part, were ravaged. killed and burnt out.

And for his treason in the delivery of the said commission and documents to the King of England for the perpetual subjection of our realm to the obedience of the English King. And for his treason in art, part and counsel, in the framing of that Commission and the sending of it to the Earl of Northumberland and Sir William Tyler,[4] Englishman and Knight, stating that they, by virtue of the said Commission, should give pardons to all Scots fighting against us on the side of the English.

EXTRACT FROM THE INDICTMENT OF BUCHAN
(Acts Parl. Scot. II, 201)[5]

And for his treason in art, part, counsel and assistance given and shown to John Ross of Halkhede[6] Knight, John Ross of Montgrenan and Thomas Fotheringham of Powrie, in the leading out of our late Father, the King, with arms and a force of men, at Blackness, for the destruction of our supreme lord the King,[7] and the Lords adhering to him. It being observed that our said Lord the King[7] at that time, as at every other, stood ready and offered to fulfil the promises,[8] sent and signed with his[9] sign manual, to our King,[7] then Prince, which were broken, violated and despised by Buchan's advice; because of which

---

[1] John Ramsay, Lord Bothwell, was at Windsor on April 27, 1488 (Leland, *Collectanea*, IV, 240). He was not witnessing James III's charters between October 10, 1487, and December 16, 1487 *(Great Seal Register)*, and may have been in England at that time with Buchan.

[2] The recital of Buchan's criminal acts adds the names of John Ross of Montgrenan, John Murray of Touchadam, Stephen Lockart of Cleghorn and James Hommyll, tailor.

[3] This must be the truce of December 20, 1487. *Rot. Scot.* II, 480.

[4] Tyler was appointed Captain of Berwick on February 10, 1488. *Rot. Scot.* II, 484.

[5] Printed without contractions in Pitcairn's *Criminal Trials*, I, 3–4.

[6] John Ross of Halkhede had the custody of Blackness Castle. *Exchequer Rolls*, X, 33.

[7] James IV.

[8] These were the Terms of Blackness, quoted in *Acts Parl. Scot.* II, 210.

[9] James III.

APPENDICES

the Earls of Huntley, Eroll, Marischal and Lord Glamis, then with the said James,[1] changed their minds and went back to their own homes.[2] And for his treason in art, part, counsel and assistance given and shown to the said persons in preparing and arraying the field of battle against our said supreme lord the King[3] at Blackness, after which again there was a pact;[4] and for the carrying out of the beforenamed promised pacts, the said James Earl of Buchan, William Lord Ruthven, Thomas Fotheringham of Powrie and William Murray of Tullibardine were offered as sureties.[5]

SUMMONS OF JOHN ROSS OF MONTGRENAN
(*Acts Parl. Scot.* II, 204)[6]

And for his treason in art, part, counsel and assistance given to the said persons in breaking the said pacts, made for the tranquillity, peace and concord of the realm, after which our late Father[1] went to the Castle of Edinburgh....And for his treason in art, part, counsel and assistance given to the said persons in advising our then Father to come out of the Castle of Edinburgh with arms and a force of men to invade us at Stirling, and for his treason in pursuing and persecuting our person beyond the bridge of Stirling. At that place burning, destruction and killing took place. Also for his treason in art, part, counsel and assistance given and shown to the said persons in making our Father rise against us for the destruction of our person on the battlefield of Stirling on June 11 last past, after divers agreements and pacts had been made between us and our Father. And we were ready then as always to be on bended knees, between the conflicts, and we offered to carry out the bonds broken by his advice;[7] by whose counsel, together with that of others, at the beginning of the battle, our Father left the field, fell into the hands of vile persons and was killed.

[1] James III.
[2] From the Terms of Blackness, *Acts Parl. Scot.* II, 210: "The quhilk being read and shewn that the said articles were diverse times granted and broken by the perverse counsel of divers persons being with him at the time, which counselled and assisted him in the inbringing of Englishmen...for which Huntley, Marischal etc. left him and adhered to our sovereign lord that now is".
[3] James IV.
[4] This must have been a new pact after the skirmish at Blackness. It seems clear that there were two pacts at Blackness and two sets of hostages; one pact arranged without fighting and the other after a battle.
[5] This is the end of Buchan's indictment, which is complete.
[6] Printed without contractions in Pitcairn's *Criminal Trials*, I, 9.
[7] John Ross.

146

APPENDIX II

Corrections of Rymer's *Foedera* and Bain's *Calendar of Documents relating to Scotland*, 1485–94

CORRECTIONS OF RYMER'S *FOEDERA*[1]

	Subject	Rymer's *Foedera*	*Rot. Scot.* (Record Commission edition)
1.	Safe-conduct for Bishops of Dunkeld, Aberdeen, etc.	XII, 325: Sept. 22, 3 Henry VII	II, 469: Sept. 22, 1 Henry VII
2.	Safe-conduct for Bishop of St Andrews	XII, 325: Sept. 23, 3 Henry VII	II, 469: Sept. 23, 1 Henry VII
3.	Safe-conduct for Alexander Bruce	XII, 328: Nov. 24, 3 Henry VII	II, 469: Nov. 24, 1 Henry VII
4.	Henry Earl of Northumberland made a commissioner to treat for peace	XII, 334: Jan. 30, 3 Henry VII	II, 471: Jan. 30, 1 Henry VII
5.	Safe-conduct for ambassadors of King of Scots	XII, 334: Feb. 2, 3 Henry VII	II, 471: Feb. 2, 1 Henry VII
*6.	Safe-conduct for Scottish ambassadors	XII, 343: July 7, 3 Henry VII	II, 472: July 7, 1 Henry VII
7.	Richard Salkeld to treat about the Fishgarth	XII, 339: Mar. 26, 3 Henry VII	II, 479: Mar. 26, 2 Henry VII
8.	Ratification of Scottish truce	XII, 345: July 26, 3 Henry VII	II, 473: July 26, 1 Henry VII
9.	Prorogation of Scottish truce	XII, 525: Apr. 23, 8 Henry VII	II, 497: Apr. 23, 6 Henry VII
10.	De tractando cum Rege Scotorum	XII, 532: June 17, 8 Henry VII	II, 500: June 16, 6 Henry VII (the date on the original Scottish Rolls is June 17
11.	Safe-conducts to Alexander Hume, Lundy, etc.	XII, 548: Aug. 4, 8 Henry VII	II, 505–6: Aug. 4, 7 Henry VII
12.	Safe-conduct for Bishop of Orkney	XII, 556: no date. Quotes mem. 10, 9 Henry VII	II, 515: no date

In the original Rotuli Scotiae the entry is on mem. 10, 10 Henry VII, with no date for the month. Bain (IV, 1603) gives April 7, from the Chancery Warrants, with a queried date of 1494 for the year. *Date should be April 7, 1495*.

| 13. | Matrimonial treaty with the King of Scots | XII, 572: June 23, 10 Henry VII | II, 521: June 23, 11 Henry VII |

CORRECTION OF BAIN'S *CALENDAR OF DOCUMENTS RELATING TO SCOTLAND*

Vol. IV, no. 1593. July 28, 1493. This should be **1494**. It is 9 Henry VII on the original Scots Rolls (Rec. Com. II, 514)

[1] Identified by collation with the Rotuli Scotiae, P.R.O. In each case the Record Commission edition of the Rotuli is correct. Hardy's *Syllabus* corrects none of these errors.

[2] Herkless and Hannay (*Archbishops of St Andrews*, I, 159) have pointed out that Rymer's dating must be wrong. Bain gives it correctly.

APPENDIX III

Corrections of the Record Commission edition of the *Rotuli Scotiae*, collated with the original Rotuli Scotiae, P.R.O. from 1485 to 1497

	Subject	*Rot. Scot.* (Record Commission edition)	Original Rot. Scot.
1.	Safe-conducts for ambassadors of France, Castile and Aragon	II, 499: June 14, 6 Henry VII (*Foedera*, XII, 446); June 14, 6 Henry VII	June 17, 6 Henry VII
2.	Safe-conducts for Bothwell and Hailes	II, 495: Feb. 8, 6 Henry VII	Feb. 8, 5 Henry VII
3.	Safe-conduct for Bishop of Glasgow, Argyll, Erroll, Morton, etc.	II, 495: Feb. 8, 6 Henry VII	Feb. 8, 5 Henry VII
4.	Safe-conduct for Hume of Fastcastell	II, 495: Feb. 8, 6 Henry VII	Feb. 8, 5 Henry VII
5.	Safe-conduct for Abbot of Kelso	II, 494: Jan. 29, 6 Henry VII	Jan. 29, 5 Henry VII
6.	Safe-conduct for Bishop of Glasgow, Morton, Prior of St Andrews, etc.	II, 499: May 30, 6 Henry VII	May 30, 5 Henry VII
7.	About Eske fishing	II, 498: May 9, 6 Henry VII	May 9, 5 Henry VII
8.	About Lord Dacre	II, 498: Apr. 25, 6 Henry VII	Apr. 25, 5 Henry VII
9.	Safe-conduct for Bishop of St Andrews	II, 497: Apr. 17, 6 Henry VII	Apr. 17, 5 Henry VII
10.	About the Fishgarth	II, 496: Apr. 4, 6 Henry VII	Apr. 4, 5 Henry VII
11.	About George Edwardson	II, 496: Mar. 28, 6 Henry VII	Mar. 28, 5 Henry VII
12.	About Robert Multon	II, 494: Dec. 24, 6 Henry VII	Dec. 24, 5 Henry VII
13.	To Richard Bishop of Durham, "De metis et limitibus terrarum"	II, 513: May 22, 9 Henry VII	May 22. No year is given, but the entry comes after the last dated membrane of 9 Henry VII and before the first dated membrane of 10 Henry VII, 1495

Richard Fox was appointed Bishop of Durham in December, 1494, so this Commission must belong to May 22, 1495

APPENDIX IV

Letter from Henry VII to Lord Dynham, Sir Reginald Bray and Robert Lytton, July 22, 1493

P.R.O. Ancient Correspondence, LI, 110

[right trusty] a[nd] welbeloved and trusty and right welbeloved We grete you wel And praye you [i]n ou[r] right affectuous wise that with al diligence ye doo vitailles to be arredied at Ippeswiche [for] [t]hose shippes of warre that been [undir the] loding of our *servauntes* Stephin Bul John Clerc and William Wasshe Soo [as] they [maye] be revitailled in oure haven of Orwell without delay [and] theire re-tour[ned] and [theire] newcopired and furthre to be waged for Six *Wekes* We wol also that ye mak d[ue] serche in oure Rivier of the Tem*mes* in oure poort of Sandewiche in Ippeswiche forsaid [a]nd [serche] our poort*es* aboute the same for to undrestande what shippes we [maye] have in thoes p[oort]es [be] [they] estrangiers or othres and of what portage every ship is. [Tell] us redily whi[ch] we shal soo appointe and whedir ye can be assured that if we renforce [ ]ur Armee the same Armee maye be vitailled at the said Ippeswiche Oure mynd is furthremor that ye shulde comÿne and debate whedir we shulde set any of oure grete shippes to the see And to make serche howe soone any of theym maye be set furthe. And whiche of the grete shippes ye thinke most convenable and howe to be vitailled We remembre unto you oure said havon of Orwell because it lyeth metely bitwene the costes of fflanders and of Scotland for oure flete the sonner to be o̅n the see And for the sonner to rancontre our rebelles and their complices in their saillinges to and fro In these premisses We Wol ye have resort to the Moost Reverend fadre in god oure Chanceller of England And as yetoguyder thinke good soo to advertise us withal spede in every behalf as our trust is in ẏou yeven undre our signet at oure Castel of kenelworth the xxii day of July.

(endorsed)

To oure Right trusty and welbeloved the lord dynh̊m oure

Tresourer of England and to our trusty and right welbeloved

Sir Raynold Bray Chaꞷncellr of oure duchie of lancastre

and Robert litton our undretresourer of England, our

counseilles.

NOTE. The letters in square brackets are conjectural.

APPENDIX V

Letter from Sir James Ormond to Thomas, Earl of Ormond, February 20 [1494/5][1]

B.M. Cotton, Titus, B XI, vol. I, fol. 52 (new pagination).
Cal. of Cotton MSS, Article 47

My lord pleas it yo̊r lordshepp it is soo that I wrytt to you off veray good mynd thoo be it I kañe nott peynt my mater but Ipray yo̊r lordshupe to hyr & See what ye will in h̊t & leve the remenaunt. Sir it is soo that ther is aparliam̅[2] kept her which is nott yet endyd my lord ther is añacte off Rcsu̅pcio̅n ffor the kinge in the seid parliam̅ senn kinge Edward þe Second is days.[3] Item the Tresorer[4] her ys nott yo̊r best

[1] From internal evidence.
[2] The Parliament opened by Poynings on December 1, 1494.
[3] Appendix XXIII.
[4] Sir Hugh Conway, Treasurer till April, 1495.

ffrend & he hath mad a serch. & as he hath shevyd me therby therbe
many p*ar*cels that long to yor lordshepp Resumed. & I seyd nay &
caused hym to showe som off them to me. I*tem* he seith the p*r*ice
wyñes[1] Ogg*ter*ard Castell Warnȳg Blakcastell[2] Kilkeny[3] yor Annute in
Waterford[4] & xiii town*es* besyd*es* thes which he wold nott showe þ
names my lord it is good to be ware & looke well about. ffor ye have to
doo both her & ther ye ar leyd att on both the syd*es*. My lord yew nev*er*
yor Right ov*er* ffor nothyng. copper wyll aper wher it is hastely. & all
shalbe well by god*es* g*r*ace. S*ir* & I shall writt any thinge ffor my selffe
I p*ray* you be nott displeased ffor ye may doo therin as hitt shall like
yew thes bind you nott. I*tem* ht is soo that þ kinge hath the two p*ar*tes
off yor land*es* her & ye but the third p*ar*t which is but xl pownd*es*. & the
kinge*s* p*ar*te iiii pownd*es*.[5] I thinke my lord yff ye wold lett me have
yor p*ar*t off the sam her I shold gett the kinge*s* partt & yett shold ye
loos nothinge therby in regard. ffor I wold ffind you suerte In water-
fford in dyvelyn o*þer* in Ēgland to pay you yerly xl m*ar*kes whill ye lett
me have ht my lord I am att grett cost her wayting uppon the deputey[6]
& I thinke he is content w^t me. & as for yor land*es* In the contes off
Kilkeny & Typpare I have rec' nothinge as yett ne*þer* I have non
auctorite off yor lordshepp by wrytting & such land*es* as is nott in yor
hand*es* nother hath ben many yer*es* yor lordshupe myght lett me have
it & yor titill in ht wher ye have no p*r*ofitt no*þer* noo ffrend off yo^rs.
I*tem* my lord it is good ye be p*r*ovyded by the kinge for all man*er*
land*es* & other thing*es*. & send hit hether hastely. ffor ther is on Ric'
nãgle[7] gon fform þ Tresorer to ye king to showe hym all and to cause

---

[1] Prise of wines at Waterford. See Appendix XVI, p. 188.
[2] For the value of these manors to the Crown by Resumption see Appendix XII, note 5.
[3] Two-thirds of the Kilkenny manors may have made up the sum to £80.
[4] The fee-farm of Waterford was £10. See Appendix XVI, p. 188.
[5] For the sum of £80 resumed from the Earl of Ormond as an absentee, see Appendix XVI, p. 188.
[6] Poynings.   [7] Richard Nangle.

hym to have aconetise in ht which Ric' is caus*er* off all yor p*er*te. God Deffend þ ye shold loos þ thing*es* that the frist Erll off Ormond had off Right. as ffor tyding*es* the depute is as good aman as I knowe ffor all Irysh in thes p*ar*ties hath put in ther pledg*es* ffor suerte off the peas & thoo that Refused peas he hath desturyd all þ land*es* þ^t they wer ffayn too put In ther pledg*es* w^t amend*es*.¹ and her he bydyth grett payn. wheroff I take my p*ar*te / my lord I have send by yor s*er*vau*n*t Ric' hay to yor lordshupe an hoby & an hanke² agood hanke I think. my lord ye knowe all. & my mynd and as I begann soo shall I end w^t god*es* gr*a*ce who ev*er* pr*e*serve yor lordsheppe amen wrytten att dyvelyn the xx day off ffebruare

yor owyn Iwiss

James ormond³

To my lord off ormond
Chamb*er*leyn unto the Quenn

APPENDIX VI

The Earl of Desmond's oath of submission to Henry VII, March 18, 1493/4
P.R.O. E 30, 1563

To all Cristen Princes Dukes Erllis Barones and men of honure And worshupp. Be hit knowynge that I maurice Erll of dessemond knyght the xviii day of marche the ixth yere of kynge henry the sevfth my natturall liege lord yn the presence of Richard Salkeld Grome of the Chambre of the forsaid oure sov*er*ayn lord and manny ors⁴ there then beynge presente whose names hier folweth Davyd Archbisshop of Casshell Thomas Bisshoppe of lissemore The mair of youghull w^t his Conseill Maurice Roche of Corke Esquier un to the forsaid oure sov*er*ayne lord and manny moo not requiseth to be named I pr*o*myt and graunte be myn oothe upon the holie Ev*a*ngelist of god be me

---

¹ Loss. Not in *N.E.D.*   ² A rope to hold a horse.
³ Sir James Ormond's handwriting throughout.   ⁴ Others.

solempnelie touched w^t myn right hand that at all tymes fram hensfourthe I shall be feithfull Subict and true liegman un to oure said soverayn lord and to his heires And doo un to his grace true and feithfull service duringe my lif natturall and lyv and dey yn his querell agaynnest all other creatures soo help me god Oone thinge excepted savynge subsequent reformacone I can not promeis to apier before the said oure soverain his depute ne lieutenante of this his land of Irland at anny sesone unlesse I think that sauffelie fram thens agayne I may departe throughe fere leste I should be myssentreted yn semblable wise as my fader have bene wich is reputed and taken for a presedent bothe w^t me and all my wellwillers throughoute this land and ever will as I think unperpetuit Besechinge the kynge his grace as therein to have me excused And I suere be the said oothe that adiectone is leid for nother fraude ne cavelacone but for the fere forwritten All soo I shall at all tymes frohensfourthe be reddie w^t all my power to resist and subdue all rebellis and ennemyses of oure said soverayn lord win all Citteis Townes Burghes and Contreis wherof I have or here after shall have rule or governance under his grace so help me god And all soo if I shall knowe anny confideracies or unleifull conventicles made to the hourte or yn derogacone of the kynge or of his Crowne of England I shall be my power take the persones by whom such confideracies or unleifull conventicles so shall be made or els showe thar names w^t thar demeanoure yn that behalf yn to the kynge is grace or to som of his Conseill such as I shall trust shall shewe hit to the kynge All so I shall never consent to anny thinge that shall be preiudiciall to oure said soverayn lord or to his crowne All so I shall trulie content the kynge for myn enheritaunce yn all pointes as duhelie and as large as myn Auncestries have doone un to his moste nobel progenitoures And shall framhensfourthe extone all suche landes offices or ffees to be graunten unto me be the kynge acordinge to his pleasire and w^t such condicones therto annext All so I shall not mak noone Insurreccons ne gadderinge

of noo poople agaynnest noone of the kynge u̇ͬ true subiett*es* And that

I shall not bren ne waste noone of the said oure souvrain is subiettes

unlesse hit is ẏn the suyt of my right els yn the defence of the same

after the custom of this youre land so help me god And that

I shall send my son and heir un to my Cosyn the Erll of kildare And

that all these articles above reherset shall be well and trulie kept yn

my behalf so that the said oure sov*er*ayne houlde hym contented ẘͭ all

and be gode and gracious lord un to me and all myne And for the

more suerte upon that condicone I the said Erll hath put hier to the

sele of myn Armes the day and yere abovesaid.

APPENDIX VII
Indenture between Henry VII and the Earl of Kildare, May 14, 1494

P.R.O. E 30, 1562

This endenture made at Westm*inster* the xiiii day of may in the yere

of oure lord M̊ͯ CCCCˡiiiixx̊ͯ iiiiᵗʰ bitwene o̊ͬ souv*er*ain lord king henrẏ the

VIIᵗʰ on the oon part, and his Right trusty and right welbeloved

Cousin Gerald Erle of kildare on the othre part witnesseth that the

said Erle byndeth hymself p*ro*mitteth and graunteth by this endenture

that if Therele of desmond whiche hath made his solenne ooth uppon

the holy ev*a*ngelies auctorized and affermed undre the seal of his armes

to p*er*fourme obeye truely kepe and obs*er*ve anempst oure said souv*er*ain

lord all suche thing*es* as be conteyned in certain articles heraftre folowing

doo at any season disobey breke or varye from any of the said Articles

that than the same Erle of kildare whensoever the king shal com*m*aunde

him shal surely sende unto his grace the Son and heire of the said Erle

of desmond he being oones in his hand*es* and keping by suche persone

or persones as the king*es* highnesse shal appointe to receive of the same

Erle of kildare the Son and heire of Therle of desmond forsaid

ffurst the said Erle of desmond promitteth and graunteth by his oeth that he shalbe feithful subgiet and true liegeman unto oure souverain lord forsaid and to his heires and doo unto his grace true and feithful service during his life naturall And live and deẏe in his quarell against al othre creatures

Itm̄ that the said Erle shal at all tẏmes be redy w^t his power to resiste and subdue all rebelles and ennemyes of o^r said souverain lord win all Citees townes Burghes and contreys wherof he hath or heraftre shal have rule or gouvernance undre the king

Itm̄ if he knowe any confederacies or unleful conventicles made to the hurt or in derogacon of the king or of his Corowne of England he shal by his power take the persones by whom suche confederacies or unleful conventicles soo shalbe made orelles shewe theire names w^t their demeanure in that behalve unto the kinges grace or to som of his counseill suche as the said Erle shall truste wol shewe it to the king

Itm̄ he shal never consente to any thing that shalbe preiudicial to oure said souverain lord or to his corowne

Itm̄ he shal truely contente the king for his enheritance in all pointes as duely and as largely as his auncestres have doon unto his noble progenitours

Itm̄ he shall execute all suche landes offices or fees to be graunted unto hym by the king according to his pleasyr and w^t suche condicions therunto annexed

Itm̄ he shal not make noon Insurrections ne gaderinges of noo people against noon of the kinges true subgettes and that he shal not brenne ne waste noon of the kinges subgiettes. onlesse it be in the suytt of his right orelles in the defense of the same after the custom of that the kinges land of Irland

Itm̄ that he shal sende his son and heire unto Therle of kildare

ffinally the said Erle of kildare byndeth hymself estsones by this said endenture that he shal endevoire hym to the best of his power to gete the said Son and heire into his hand*es* and possession with al spede unto hym possible And when he shal have the same Son and heẏre oones in his said hand*es* and possession then aftre not to deliv*er* hym for any man*er* cause w̱^tout the king*es* mynde and pleasyr be furst shewed unto hym by the king*es* especial writing that he shal soo doo ffor these point*es* to be thoroughtely fulfilled in every behalve The said Erle of kildare byndeth hymself by these said endentures at the place day and yere abovesaid signed w̱^t his signe manuell and sealed w̱^t his seal of his armes.

G E of k.

APPENDIX VIII

Inventory of B.M. Royal MSS, 18 C xiv

ACCOUNTS OF WILLIAM HATTECLIFFE
(*Under-Treasurer of Ireland*, 1495–6)

fol. 1. Indenture signed by George Bulkley, Mayor of Westchester, on delivery to Hattecliffe of 12 dozen bills of the King's Ordnance for the King's Wars in Ireland the Monday before Pentecost. 10 Henry VII (June 1, 1495).

fol. 2. Hattecliffe's travelling expenses to Ireland. (Printed in Gairdner, *Letters*, 11, 297–8.)

fol. 3. A small page of accounts. (Hattecliffe's handwriting.)

fol. 4. Receipt for clothes for Hattecliffe's household from Gerrard Danyell by the hand of John Danyell at Drogheda. July 23, 1496. (Hattecliffe's handwriting.) Compare fol. 228.

fol. 5. A note of payments to Garth beginning January 4 (1496). On the back is a note of payments to Walter Nugent, Thomas Cruso, John Porter, Henry O'Neill, John Joseph, etc. (Hattecliffe's handwriting.)

fol. 6. Five lines of accounts, from Trinity Term, 11 Henry VII, to Hilary Term, 12 Henry VII.

fol. 7. Letter from John Brenan, vicar of Donabate (Co. Dublin) to Hattecliffe about the payment of the subsidy of the Deanery of Swords, Co. Dublin.

fol. 8. Certificate by Christopher Fleming, (8th) Baron Slane, that William Telyng of Sidane is his tenant and not the King's.

fol. 9. A list of the taxation of the benefices in the Deanery of Swords. (See fol. 7.)

fol. 10. "*Memorandu*m of all ye paymentes yt y payd to m*a*ster tresurer seynce y laste accultet." (Undated.)

fol. 11. Memoranda for Hattecliffe's household requirements. (Hattecliffe's handwriting.) (Partly printed by Gairdner, *Letters*, 11, 298.)

fol. 12. Hattecliffe's repayments to William Sturton for petty cash for his expenses in Ireland in June and July 1495. (In his handwriting.)

fols. 13–70. *General Register of Irish Receipts and Payments kept by Hattecliffe.*
(Extracts printed by Gairdner, *Letters*, II, 298–314.) The entries are mostly ticked off as entered under their headings in the final compotus. A few signatures of recipients occur in the margin. The receipts and payments are added at the foot of each page, but there are no totals for the terms.

fol. 13. Receipt of £900 from the Treasurer on June 21, 1495, paid by Hattecliffe in instalments to John Pympe and John Mountford.

fol. 13 v. Note of fine of 800 marks owed by Thomas Dovedall. (Compare fol. 121.) Probably June, 1495.

fols. 14–21 v. General Register for Trinity Term, 10 Henry VII (1495), beginning on June 15.

fols. 22–31. General Register for Michaelmas Term, 11 Henry VII (1495).

fols. 31 v.–48 v. General Register for Hilary Term, 11 Henry VII (1496), beginning on January 4.

fols. 49–60. General Register for Easter Term, 11 Henry VII (1496).

fols. 61–70 v. General Register for Trinity Term, 11 Henry VII (1496).

fols. 71–78 v. "*Assignationes.*" Charges on the Irish revenues, received from various collectors, for the payment of salaries to officials. Easter and Trinity Terms, 11 Henry VII; and a fragment for Michaelmas Term, 12 Henry VII (1496). (Hattecliffe's handwriting.)

fols. 79–83 v. "*Denarii mutuati pro domino rege.*" Payments received in kind and changed into money for the King. (Hattecliffe's handwriting.) (A few extracts printed by Gairdner, *Letters*, II, 314.)

fols. 84–89 v. "*Assignationes facte per tallias levatas.*" Michaelmas Term, 11 Henry VII, 1495. (Hattecliffe's handwriting.) Charges on the revenue in the form of annuities paid out of the customs and subsidies levied in various places in Ireland.

fol. 90 v. *Payments to Sir James Ormond* by the Treasurer, Sir Hugh Conway, March 10, 1495, April 11, 1495 (for expenses at the siege of Carlow and for his fee "ex assensu Henrici Wyot"). Total £96. 13s. 4d. (Hattecliffe's handwriting.)

fols. 91 v.–92. "*Mensales pro vadiis guerre solvendis in Hibernia.*" A calendar of the months, each containing 28 days, on which pay is calculated. September 14, 1494–July 19, 1496. (Hattecliffe's handwriting.)

fol. 92 v. Copy of indenture between Bartholomew Ailmer, Sheriff of Co. Kildare, and William Hattecliffe, Under-Treasurer, on behalf of Sir Hugh Conway, concerning estreats of fines, etc. August 9, 1495. (Hattecliffe's handwriting.)

fol. 93. Account of ironmongery bought November 9, 1495. (Hattecliffe's handwriting.)

fol. 93 v. Page of miscellaneous entries, in Hattecliffe's handwriting, ending with a certificate of good conduct given by Hattecliffe to the gunners on their discharge from the army. August 8, 1496.

fols. 94–99 v. *Payment of the King's army in Ireland for each of the 4 months ending January 31, February 28, March 28, April 25, 1496.* (Hattecliffe's handwriting.)

fol. 94. Fragment of account of wages paid to Sir Richard Salkeld and Thomas Garth. (This is the only remaining wage sheet for January, 1496.) See fol. 5.

fols. 94 v.–95 v. Payment of the King's army in Ireland from February 1 to 28, 1496.

fols. 96–97 v. Payment of the King's army in Ireland from February 28 to March 28, 1496. (Extracts printed by Gairdner, *Letters*, II, 315.)

fols. 98–99 v. Payment of the King's army in Ireland from March 28 to April 25, 1496. (Extracts printed by Gairdner, *Letters*, II, 315–16.)

fols. 100–103 *v.* *Miscellaneous expenses in connection with the army in Ireland,* including entries of payments to Sir James Ormond for his galloglasses, March and April, 1496. (Extracts printed by Gairdner, *Letters,* II, 315–17, who has confused them with the army payments for February and March, 1496 (fols. 96–99 v.).) They belong to the same collection as fol. 104, which should precede these four pages and is transposed in the binding. (Hattecliffe's handwriting.)

fols. 104–104 v. "Paymentes necessaryes payed by me Johann Joseph in the name of Mastre Pympe tresaurer of the Kinges warres in Irlond syne the 4th day of Januarye A° XI° unto the XXIIIIth day of Maye there next ensewinge for dyverse expences necessaryes in the kinges warres here which was payed by thadvyse of my lord Chauncellor and al the Kinges Counsayle here." (Hattecliffe's handwriting.) (Extracts printed by Gairdner, *Letters,* II, 317.) (This is the headed page, which should precede fols. 100–103 v.)

fols. 105–109 *v.* *A preliminary estimate of revenue in Counties Meath, Dublin, Louth and Kildare, under the headings of subsidies, manors, wards, marriages, absentees and customs,* 1496. (Hattecliffe's handwriting.)

fols. 105–105 v. A list of places in Counties Meath, Dublin, Louth and Kildare giving the number of ploughlands in each, on which a subsidy is leviable. This draft gives full details for the finished estimate on fol. 148.

fol. 106. A list of royal manors in Meath and Dublin. (This draft is subsidiary to the finished estimate on fol. 148 v.)

fol. 106 v. A list of wards and marriages, subsidiary to the finished estimate on fol. 148 v. A list of absentees and customs, fee-farms, hanaper, coinage, estreats, subsidiary to the finished estimate on fol. 149.

fol. 107. Notes on Counties Kildare and Meath.

fol. 107 v. A list of places in Co. Kildare, giving the number of carucates in each, on which a subsidy is leviable.

fol. 108. Extent of the ancient subsidy (in Leinster) before 1495.

fol. 108 v. Ploughlands in the baronies of Co. Meath from the records of the subsidy to the Earl of March, 1 Henry V. (This is signed "per me Willm Hatteclyff" followed by a monogram and gives the clue for his handwriting throughout the volume.)

fols. 109–109 v. Estimate of ploughlands and subsidies in the Counties of Meath, Louth, Dublin and Kildare. Undated, but probably 1495.

fols. 110–113. *The Actual Receipts from Royal Manors, Wards, Resumptions and Customs* in 1495. (All in Hattecliffe's handwriting.)

fols. 110–111. Moneys received by James Dillon from the issues of the King's manors in Ireland for Easter Term, 10 Henry VII, and those falling due in Michaelmas Term, 11 Henry VII.

fol. 111 v. Receipts from wards in the King's hands. Michaelmas Term, 11 Henry VII (1495).

fol. 112. Receipts from manors and lands in the King's hands by reason of resumptions. Michaelmas Term, 11 Henry VII (1495).

fol. 113. Receipts of customs from ports of Drogheda and Dublin. Undated, probably 1495. Compare estimated receipts of Drogheda Customs for 1496, fol. 149.

fols. 115–120. *Estimates of Receipts in the Exchequer from Fines, Fee-Farms of Cities, Rents and services of Royal Manors, "Petty farms" in the 4 Counties, and services in County Dublin.* (All in the same handwriting, not Hattecliffe's.)

fol. 115. Amount of fines in the Irish Exchequer charged on the Sheriffs of Meath, Louth, Dublin, Kildare and Drogheda. Michaelmas (1494) and Hilary Terms (1495), 10 Henry VII.

fol. 115 v. Annual fee-farm of Dublin and "petty farms" of Dublin. Fee-farm of Drogheda and "petty farms" of Drogheda. (Subsidiary to estimate on fol. 149.)

fol. 116. Annual fee-farms of Waterford, Limerick and Cork. Rents of manors.

fols. 116 v.–119. Annual "petty farms" in the Counties of Dublin, Louth, Kildare and Meath.

fol. 119 v. Services of the King annually rendered in Co. Dublin.

fol. 120. Names of absentees from Ireland without licence. (Subsidiary to Hattecliffe's audit, fol. 149.) Undated.

fol. 121. Copy of release to the executors of Sir Thomas Dovedall (al. Dowdall) upon a recognisance in the Irish Chancery given by him, May 20, 1495, for 500 marks; March 30, 11 Henry VII (1496). Compare fol. 13 v.

fol. 122. A few notes in Hattecliffe's handwriting.

fols. 123–128. *First Report of Sir Hugh Conway as Treasurer of Ireland.* (Hattecliffe's handwriting?)

fol. 123. Summary of Conway's receipts from the King by the hand of Sir Reginald Bray, for the payment of the army in Ireland during the first year of the Poynings administration, according to an indenture of August 12, 10 Henry VII. £7000. (This should be August 12, 9 Henry VII.) (£8000 in the margin is an error for £7000.)

fols. 124–126. Summary of payments made for the wages of soldiers in Ireland from June 24, 1494 to June 24, 1495. Total = £3795, for an army of 653 men, composed of 32 lancers, 46 sub-captains, 449 archers, 90 gunners and 36 soldiers and mariners.

fol. 126 v. Payment to Sir Hugh Conway of £44. 2s. 0d. for wages of 3 sub-captains and 57 archers from June 21 to July 18, 1495.

fols. 127–128. Salaries paid to officials in Ireland from October 13, 1494 to June 1495. Incomplete.

fols. 129–129 v. "*The Nombre and charge of the Kinges armie in Irland apoynted in thabsence of my lord depute begyning the* iiii^th *day of the monyth of Januarie.*" 11 Henry VII (January 4, 1496). (Hattecliffe's handwriting.)
Total = £294. 11s. 1d. a month for 325 men and 100 kerns.

fols. 130–130 v. "*Visus armati domini Regis dimiss' in Hibernia post* xxiiii *diem mensis Maii anno undecimo.*" (May 24, 1496.) "per Johanni Redyng miss' domino Rege." (Hattecliffe's handwriting.)
Total = £123. 7s. 9d. a month for 164 men.

fol. 131. *Fees and Diets of the Lord Chancellor of Ireland.* (Hattecliffe's handwriting.)

	£	s.	d.
Fees for Easter Term, 10 Henry VII (1495) and Michaelmas Term, 11 Henry VII (1495)	40	0	0
Diets from November 10, 1494 (when he received the Great Seal), to Michaelmas, 1495 (323 days)	161	10	0
Diets from Michaelmas (1495) to Easter (1496)–(April 3) 197 days	93	10	0
Diets as locum tenens for the Lord Deputy from January 1 to Easter (1496) at 6s. 8d. a day	31	6	8[1]
Fee for Easter Term, 11 Henry VII (1496)	20	0	0
"Et pro denariis per eundem dominum cancellarium domino Rege mutuatis"	212	4	10

fols. 133–139 v. *Second Account of Sir Hugh Conway, Treasurer of the King in Ireland.* From June 21, 1495, to end of Michaelmas Term, 1495.

fol. 140 v. Six lines in Latin on rules for accounting. (Hattecliffe's handwriting.)

fols. 141–151. *A collection of auditors' reports on Irish finances from 1494 to 1495 and estimates of Receipts and Expenditure for 1496.* (All in the same handwriting. A fair copy. Hattecliffe's handwriting?)

fols. 141–141 v. *Audit on the first Report of Sir Hugh Conway* (fols. 123–128). Signed and sealed by Henry Wyatt and William Hattecliffe alternately.[2]

fols. 142–144. *Audit by Wyatt and Hattecliffe on the second Report of Sir Hugh Conway* (fols. 131–139 v.). Signed and sealed by Henry Wyatt and William Hattecliffe alternately.[2]

fols. 144 v.–145 v. *Declaration by William Hattecliffe of Receipts to Michaelmas 1495.* (June 21–December 1495.)

fols. 146–147 v. *Audit on Hattecliffe's Declaration of Receipts.* (June 21–December 1495.)

fols. 148–149 v. *Estimates of the King's Revenue in Ireland for a year.* Taken at the end of the Michaelmas Term, 1495. (Compare fols. 105–106 v., 113 and 115 v. The two documents, fols. 110–113 and fols. 115–120, served as the foundation for the estimate.)

fols. 150–151. *Estimate of payments of fees and salaries for Officers of the Crown in Ireland for 1496.*

fols. 151 v.–152 v. A repertory of all returns contained in the Great Roll of the Exchequer for 11 Henry VII. (Hattecliffe's writing.)

fol. 153. Fealty of John de Burgh before Gerald Earl of Kildare, Deputy. October 26, 1496. (Printed by Gairdner, *Letters*, II, 326.) (Same handwriting as fol. 154; Hattecliffe?)

fols. 154–154 v. Ordinance for the Irish Exchequer. April 30, 20 Edward I. Extracted from the Red Book of the English Exchequer (ed. Hall, Rolls Series, 1896, 974). Latin. The text supplies a few words now lost in the Red Book.

fols. 154 v., 156, 156 v., 157. Table of weights and measures.

fol. 155. A rough list of receipts for Easter Term, 11 Henry VII (1495). (Hattecliffe's handwriting.)

fol. 157 v. List of unlucky hours in the week. (Hattecliffe's handwriting.)

[1] "non concluditur" in margin.
[2] See Appendix XVIII, A Note on the Declared Account.

fols. 159–165. "*Regale Servicium omnium comit(atu)um Hibernie.*" A computation of Knights' Services for the baronies in Counties Dublin, Kildare, Louth, Wexford, Kilkenny, Limerick, Tipperary, Waterford, Cork and the provinces of Connaught and Ulster. (In the handwriting of fol. 108 v. (?).) The original of this dates from *c*. 1297–8. See Orpen, *Ireland under the Normans*, II, 47 note 1. For other variants of the original see Irish Exchequer Memoranda, *E.H.R.* XVIII, 497; Carew, *Cal. Misc.* I, 232; *Cal. Docs. Ireland*, 1293–1301, nos. 288, 473.

fols. 166–170 v. *A legal treatise in French.* "De Vee de naam", sc. de vetito namii. (Hattecliffe's handwriting.)

fols. 171–177. *Fragment of Hattecliffe's register of Irish Receipts and Payments for Trinity Term*, 11 *Henry VII* (1495). The catalogue of the Royal MSS calls this a continuation of fols. 61–70; but it is a fragment of another copy not quite the same. The first ten entries are common to both; the next is not in fols. 61–70; the next two are the same, differently phrased; the next five are the same; fol. 63 has two entries not in this copy, and fol. 174 v. has three entries not in the other. The next five entries are the same. The next varies in the name; "Philip Manning" as against "Philip Messangere",[1] the next four entries are the same; the next two entries are in different order and again "Philip Manning" occurs instead of "Philip Messangere". There is one entry more on fol. 64 (about Richard White). The next eleven entries are the same. Fols. 61–70 contain more entries.

fols. 178 v.–179 v. "*Assignationes.*" Charges on the Irish revenue received from various collectors. June to August, 1496 (?). (Hattecliffe's handwriting.) The catalogue of Royal MSS calls it a continuation of fols. 71–78; one entry is a duplicate.

fol. 180 v. *Exchequer fines charged on Robert Taff, late Sheriff of County Uriel (Louth)* for Easter and Trinity Terms, 9 Henry VII; Michaelmas and Hilary Terms, 10 Henry VII, etc. (Hattecliffe's handwriting.)

fols. 181–182. *Names of soldiers in Ireland paid three weeks' wages from May 27, 11 Henry VII* (1496). (Hattecliffe's handwriting.)

fol. 183. *View of Hattecliffe's account of Receipts and Payments in Ireland.* Trinity Term, 10 Henry VII (1495), to Trinity Term, 11 Henry VII (1496) inclusive.

These figures for two corresponding terms can be checked by the audit on Hattecliffe's Declaration of Receipts and Payments from June 21 to Michaelmas Term, 1495, fols. 146–147. They vary slightly, and I am inclined to think that this view of Hattecliffe's accounts was a preliminary draft subsidiary to the audit. A comparison with the figures from the General Register of Irish Receipts and Payments, added for the corresponding two terms, also varies slightly.[2] But as the Register is the rough material and not necessarily quite complete, the totals are sufficiently close.

	Receipts			Payments		
	£	s.	d.	£	s.	d.
Audit version, fol. 147	3997	12	6	4220	16	1½[3]
Hattecliffe's View of Accounts, fol. 183	4125	1	8	4206	13	2½
General Register	4008	6	1½	4196	8	5½

fols. 185–215. Inventory of James V of Scotland's wardrobe taken just after his death, 1543. (Nothing to do with the rest of the volume.)

---

[1] Gairdner (*Letters*, II, 307) says that "Manning" was probably the "messenger's" name.
[2] For additions of Receipts and Payments, see p. 74.
[3] Appendix XIV, pp. 182–3.

fol. 216 at bottom. *Note on the joynture of the Countess of Kildare.* (Elizabeth St John, second wife of Gerald Fitzgerald, 8th Earl.) (Hattecliffe's handwriting.)

fols. 216–226 and fol. 236. *Memoranda of wages, chiefly of Hattecliffe's household.* They include the wages and names of all Hattecliffe's servants (fols. 225–226). Henry Wyatt is mentioned in connection with the engagement of John Fitzhughes (fol. 217). The expenses of the "hospice" are mentioned on fols. 221 and 224 v. (Hattecliffe's handwriting.)

fols. 227–228. *Note of clothes from England purchased for Hattecliffe's family.* (Hattecliffe's handwriting.) (Compare fol. 4.)

fol. 229. Table for calculating subsidies for fractions of a ploughland, the ploughland of 120 acres paying 26s. 8d. (Hattecliffe's handwriting.)

fols. 230–230 v. and 236 v. Memoranda of silver delivered for coining in Ireland. 11 Henry VII. (Hattecliffe's handwriting.)

fols. 231–233. *Memoranda for the better regulation of the Irish Exchequer.* (Hattecliffe's handwriting.) Printed in Gairdner (*Letters*, ii, 64) under the heading of "Financial Measures for Ireland". Gairdner calls these "Hattecliffe's instructions from Henry VII".

fols. 233 v.–234 v. Copy of compotus of the executors of Geoffrey de Turville, Bishop of Ossory and Treasurer of Ireland, May 3, 1250–September 29, 1251. Latin. (Hattecliffe's handwriting.)

fols. 235 v. Cloth bought in Kent. (Hattecliffe's handwriting.)

APPENDIX IX

Chronological classification of B.M. Royal MSS, 18 C XIV

HATTECLIFFE'S ACCOUNTS

Including the entries from B.M. Royal MSS, 7 C XVI, fols. 4–4 v.

Accounts extant for 1494

August, 1494. (fol. 123.)	Summary of the King's payments for Irish purposes of £7000 to Sir Hugh Conway by the hand of Sir Reginald Bray.
Mich. Term, 10 Henry VII. (fol. 115.)	Amount of fines in the Irish Exchequer charged on the Sheriffs of Meath, Louth, Dublin, Kildare and Drogheda. Meath, £5. 2s. 10d. Louth, £4. 18s. 6d. Dublin and Kildare, o.
Easter & Trinity Terms. 9 Henry VII. Michaelmas Term, 10 Henry VII. (fol. 180 v.)	Exchequer fines charged on the Sheriff of Louth.

Documents beginning in 1494

June 24, 1494– June, 1495. (fols. 124– 126 v.)	Details of wages of soldiers in Ireland (incomplete). (From Conway's first Report.)
June 24, 1494– June 1495. (fols. 127– 128.)	Details of salaries paid to officials in Ireland. (From Conway's first Report.)
Aug. 1494– June, 1495. (fols. 141– 141 v.)	Audit by Wyatt and Hattecliffe on Conway's first Report.
Nov. 10, 1494– Mich. 1495. (fol. 131.)	Diets of the Lord Chancellor.

Accounts extant for 1495
Hilary Term

(fol. 115.)	Amount of fines in the Irish Exchequer charged on the Sheriffs of Meath, Louth, Dublin, Kildare and Drogheda.
(fol. 180 v.)	Exchequer fines charged on the Sheriff of Louth.
From March 10 onwards. (fol. 90 v.)	Payments to Sir James Ormond.

Easter Term

June 1, 1495. (fol. 1.)	Indenture signed by George Bulkley, Mayor of Westchester, with Hattecliffe.
June. (fol. 2.)	Travelling expenses to Ireland.
Probably June. (fol. 13 v.)	Note of fine owed by Dovedall.
Easter Term. (fol. 131.)	Fees and Diets of the Lord Chancellor.
Easter Term. (fol. 110.)	Receipts of Issues and Rents of the King's Manors.
(fol. 90 v.)	Payments to Sir James Ormond.
Easter Term. (fol. 155.)	A rough list of Receipts.

Trinity Term

August 9, 1495. (fol. 92 v.)	Indenture between Ailmer and Hattecliffe about estreats.
June 21. (fol. 3.)	Hattecliffe's receipt of £900 from Conway.
Trinity Term.	Charges on the Irish revenue received from various collectors.
Trinity Term. (fols. 14– 21 v.)	General Register of Irish Receipts and Payments.
Trinity Term. (fols. 171– 177.)	General Register of Irish Receipts and Payments (a shorter version).
June 21–July 18. (fol. 126 v.)	Payment of soldiers' wages to Sir Hugh Conway.
June–October.	Incomplete summary of payments for wages of soldiers.
Trinity Term. (fol. 183.)	Hattecliffe's report on his Receipts and Payments.
(Trinity Term, 11 Henry VII.	Money received in Ireland for the Baron of Delvin.)[1]

[1] From Royal MSS, 7 C XVI, fol. 4 v.

APPENDICES

Documents beginning in the Trinity Term

June 21–Dec. (fols. 133–139.)	Second Report of Sir Hugh Conway.
June 21–Dec. (fols. 142–144.)	Audit by Wyatt and Hattecliffe on Conway's second Report.
June 21–Dec. (fols. 144 v.–145 v.)	Hattecliffe's Declaration of Receipts.
June 21–Dec. (fols. 146–147 v.)	Audit on Hattecliffe's Declaration of Receipts.

Michaelmas Term

Nov. 9, 1495. (fol. 93.)	Payments for ironmongery.
Mich. Term.	Fees and Diets of the Lord Chancellor.
Mich. Term.	Money received in Ireland for the Lord Chancellor.[1]
Mich. Term. (fols. 84–89 v.)	Charges on the revenue "facte per tallias levatas".
Mich. Term. (fols. 22–31.)	General Register of Irish Receipts and Payments.
Mich. Term. (fol. 183.)	Hattecliffe's Report on Receipts and Payments.
Mich. Term. (fol. 111.)	Rents from the King's Manors.
Mich. Term. (fol. 111 v.)	Rents from the King's Wards.
Mich. Term. (fol. 112.)	Rents from Resumptions.

Documents covering the year 1495

(fols. 109 & 109 v.)	The number of ploughlands and subsidies in the Counties of Meath, Louth, Dublin and Kildare.
(fol. 113.)	Receipts of customs from the ports of Drogheda and Dublin.
(fols. 115–119.)	Annual fee-farms of Dublin, Drogheda, Waterford, Limerick and Cork. Petty ferms of Dublin, Drogheda, Counties Dublin, Louth, Kildare and Meath.
(fol. 119 v.)	Services annually rendered to the King in Co. Dublin.
(fol. 120.)	Names of absentees from Ireland.

Documents covering the year 11 Henry VII
(August 1495–August 1496)

(fols. 151 v.–152)	"Repertorium omnium compotorum prout in magno rotulo Scaccarii de anno XImo Henrici septimi continetur."
(fols. 230–236.)	Memorandum as to the quantity of silver coined in 11 Henry VII.

[1] From Royal MSS, 7 C XVI, fol. 4.

Hilary Term 1496

January, 1496. (fol. 94.)	The last sheet of payments for wages to Salkeld and Garth for the month, giving the total. The earlier pages are missing.
January, 1496. (fol. 5.)	A note of payments to Garth.
Feb. 1–28. (fols. 94 v.– 95 v.)	Payment of the King's army in Ireland.
Feb. 28– March 28. (fols. 96– 97 v.)	Payment of the King's army in Ireland.
Jan. 4–May 24. (fols. 100– 104 v.)	Payments for expenses in the King's wars in the name of Pympe, Treasurer of the Wars, paid by the advice of the Lord Chancellor.
Jan. 4. (fols. 129– 129 v.)	The number and charge of the King's army in Ireland appointed in the absence of the Lord Deputy.
Jan.–Easter (April 3).	Diets of the Lord Chancellor.
Hilary Term. (fols. 31– 48 v.)	General Register of Irish Receipts and Payments.
Hilary Term. (fol. 183.)	Hattecliffe's summary of Receipts and Payments.

Easter Term 1496

March 28– April 25. (fols. 98– 99 v.)	Payment of the King's army in Ireland.
May 27–for 3 weeks. (fols. 181–2.)	Names of soldiers paid 3 weeks' wages.
May 24 onwards. (fols. 130– 130 v.)	A view of the army in Ireland on May 24 sent by John Reding.
Easter Term. (fols. 49–53.)	General Register of Irish Receipts and Payments.
Easter Term. (fols. 54–60.)	General Register of Irish Receipts and Payments.
Easter Term. (fol. 183.)	Hattecliffe's summary of Receipts and Payments.
Easter Term. (fols. 71– 74 v.)	Charges on the revenue received from various collectors.
Easter Term. (fol. 131.)	Diets of the Lord Chancellor.
March 30. (fol. 121.)	Release to the executors of Sir Thomas Dovedall.

Trinity Term 1496

Trinity Term. (fols. 61– 70 v.)	General Register of Irish Receipts and Payments.
Trinity Term. (fol. 183.)	Hattecliffe's summary of Receipts and Payments.
Aug. 8. (fol. 93 v.)	Hattecliffe's draft certificate for good conduct to "A B C Gonner".

APPENDICES

Michaelmas Term, 12 Henry VII (1496)

(fol. 76.)	Two entries of charges on the revenue received from various collectors. (In Hattecliffe's handwriting.)
(fol. 77.)	One entry of General Register of Irish Receipts and Payments.
Oct. 26, 1496. (fol. 153.)	Oath of fealty taken by John de Burgh, before Gerald, 8th Earl of Kildare, Deputy of Ireland. (Printed in Gairdner, *Letters*, II, 326.)

Document covering the year 1496

(fols. 148–151.)	Estimates of Irish revenue and expenditure for a year, following immediately, as part of the same document, after Hattecliffe's declaration of Receipts, June–December, 1495.

APPENDIX X

Sir Hugh Conway's first Report as Treasurer of the Poynings Administration, October 1494–June 1495

B.M. Royal MSS, 18 C xiv, fol. 123

Summary of Receipts

Received from the King at different times, namely,

	£	s.	d.
From Sir Reginald Bray by the hand of William Hungate on separate occasions:			
August 12	340	0	0
August 13 by the hand of John Deonys	526	15	10
August 13 by the hand of William Hungate	243	8	0
August 16 and 18 by the hand of William Hungate	568	5	4
August 29 by the hand of William Hungate	21	10	10

In all, paid for the wages of the army sent by the King to Ireland, and for the fees paid to the Chancellor and other officials, and for other ordinary expenses of the army, according to an indenture made "xiimo die mensis August anno domini Regis xmo"[1] — **1700 0 0**

From the King, received at various times from Sir Reginald Bray by the hand of John Shaw, August 17–29, by indenture — **5300 0 0**

viiim li in margin—an error for £7000.

[1] This must be a mistake for "9 Henry VII".

Summary of wages of soldiers in Ireland. 1494–June 1495

fols. 124–126 v.

Paid to Edward Poynings for wages of:

TOTALS
£ s. d.

5 lancers at 18d. a day each
22 sub-captains at 12d. a day each
400 archers at 6d. a day each
    from October 11, 1494 to November 8, 1494   322 0 0
8 lancers
14 sub-captains
97 archers
    for 8 months from November 9, 1494 to June 20, 1495   716 16 0

Paid to Henry, Bishop of Bangor, Chancellor, for wages of:

12 archers
    for 9 months from September 12, 1494 to June 20, 1495   75 12 0

Total for page   £1114 8 0

Paid to Hugh Conway, Treasurer of Ireland, for wages of:

3 sub-captains at 12d. a day each
57 archers at 6d. a day each
    for the same 9 months   396 18 0

Paid to John Pympe, armiger, Treasurer of the Wars, for wages of:

8 lancers at 18d. a day each
20 archers at 6d. a day each
    for 8 months, beginning November 9, 1494 to June 20, 1495, deducting
    £24. 10s. for 8 lancers for 20 days; 3 archers for 112 days; 7 archers for
    20 days; 3 archers for 28 days   104 6 0

Paid to Thomas Garth, armiger, for wages of:

5 sub-captains at 12d. a day each
95 archers and "gunners" at 6d. a day each
    for 9 months from October 16, 1494 to June 24, 1495, deducting £12 for
    wages of 2 archers for 224 days   650 6 0

Paid to Henry Raynford, armiger, for wages of:

8 lancers at 18d. a day each
42 archers at 6d. a day each
    for 8 months from November 9, 1494 to June 20, deducting £11. 18s.
    for wages of archers, viz. 1 for 112 days; 3 for 84 days; 4 for 28 days   240 2 0

Total for page   £1391 12 0

Paid to John Morton, for wages of:

{ 8 lancers
{ 50 archers
    for 5 months from November 9, 1494 to March 28, deducting £7 for
    archers for 28 days   178 10 0
{ 8 lancers
{ 41 archers
    from March 28 to May 23, 1495   61 12 0
{ 8 lancers
{ 44 archers
    from May 23 to June 20, 1495   32 4 0

Total in margin   £272 6 0

Paid to Antonio Arteright, for his wages:

Antonio Arteright at 18d. a day
8 archers at 6d. a day each
    for 8 months from November 9, 1494 to June 20, 1495, deducting 14s.
    for 8 archers for 28 days   60 18 0

Total for page   £333 4 0

	TOTALS
	£ s. d.

Paid to William Mayho, for wages of:

8 sub-captains at 12*d.* a day each
20 archers at 6*d.* a day each
    for the same 8 months, deducting £35. 14*s.* for 7 archers for 7 months and
    2 archers for 1 month   87 10 0

Paid to John Mountford, for wages of:

8 sub-captains
20 archers
    from November 8 to June 20, deducting 14*s.* for wages of 8 archers for
    1 month   122 10 0

Paid to John Sakfeyld, for wages of:

8 sub-captains
20 archers
    from November 8 to June 20   123 4 0

Paid to Adam v. Edington, for wages of:

Edington at 12*d.* a day
63 "gunners" at 6*d.* a day each
    from November 8 to June 20, deducting £49. 14*s.* for wages of 8 gunners
    for 7 months; 8 for 5 months; 3 for 8 months; 12 for 3 months; 5 for
    2 months; 1 for 1 month   314 6 0

                                Total for page   £647 10 0

Paid to William Warwick, for wages of:

Warwick at 12*d.* a day
27 "gunners" at 6*d.* each
    for 8 months, from November 9 to June 20, deducting £14 for wages of
    2 gunners for 4 months; 5 for 2 months; 4 for 8 months   142 16 0

Paid to John Clerk

John Clerk at 12*d.* a day
36 soldiers and mariners at 6*d.* a day each
    for 6 months from November 9 to April 24, deducting £21 for 6 soldiers
    for 5 months   138 12 0

Paid to John de La Barna and Prigent Meno

John de La Barna at 12*d.* a day
John Prigent at 12*d.* a day
8 archers at 6*d.* a day each
    for 8 months from November 9 to June 19, deducting £4 to John Prigent
    for 3 months   23 16 0

Paid to William Hattecliffe, sub-Treasurer of Ireland, for wages of:

1 sub-captain at 12*d.* a day
7 archers at 6*d.* a day each
    for 14 days beginning June 7 ("quo die arripuit apud Dyvelyn") to
    June 20, 1495   3 3 0

                                Total for page   £308 7 0

                         Total for war wages £3795 0 0[1]

(These wages are correct, the "deductions" having all been paid during
the time.)

Total of Troops

Lancers   8 + 8 + 8 + 8 = 32.
Sub-captains 14 + 3 + 5 + 8 + 8 + 8 = 46.
Archers   97 + 12 + 57 + 20 + 95 + 42 + 50 + 8 + 20 + 20 + 20 + 8 = 449.
Gunners   63 + 27 = 90.
Soldiers and Mariners = 36.

                           Total = 653.

[1] A mistake for £3795. 1*s.* 0*d.*

Salaries paid to officials

fols. 127–128.

October 1494–June 1495

	TOTALS		
	£	s.	d.
Sir Edward Poynings—October 13, 1494			
In addition to £100 received in England	397	10	0
Henry, Bishop of Bangor, Chancellor			
In addition to £40 received as above	60	0	0
Hugh Conway, Treasurer			
In addition to £26. 13s. 4d. received as above	40	0	0
Thomas Bowring, Chief Justice of the King's Bench			
In addition to £26. 13s. 4d. received as above	40	0	0
John Topcliff, Chief Justice of the Common Bench			
In addition to £26. 13s. 4d. received as above	40	0	0
Thomas Garth, for wages of soldiers in Ireland			
From June 24, 1494 to October 15, 1495, viz. 5 sub-captains and 95 archers, by warrant of privy seal	294	0	0
Edmund Pierson, Baron of Dunboyne in Ireland			
For wages of 68 horsemen at 12d. a day each, for 20 days, from April 10 to April 30	80	0	0
For wages of 60 horsemen "ut supra" from May 5 to May 25	60	0	0
For wages of 48 horsemen "ut supra" from May 25 to June 19	77	4	0
Edmund Milles, Constable of Carlow			
For wages of 24 soldiers from March 1 to April 28	44	0	0
John Austyn, servant of the Deputy for the safe custody of the Castle	16	0	0
For the wages of 16 soldiers in the retinue of the Constable of Carlow, who were driven out by James, brother of the Earl of Kildare, at the time of his treason; at 6d. a day each for 4 months, beginning March 2 and ending June 21	44	16	0
Richard Salkeld, Constable of Leixlip			
12d. a day for himself and 7 soldiers at 6d. a day each from October 16, 1494 to June 24, 1495	50	8	0
Henry Wright, Constable of Carrickfergus	14	0	0
William Chetwyn, Constable of Carrickfergus			
For his wages of 12d. a day and 14 archers at 6d. a day from April 26, 1495 to August 21, 1495	44	16	0

(Stops here—unfinished.)

(This should be compared with the audit on the Report, fols. 141–141 v. The receipts and payments correspond with the audit as far as they go, and the Report gives the fullest details.)

APPENDIX

Balance Sheet for the first year of the Poynings

The figures are taken from Sir Hugh Conway's first Report as Treasurer of Ireland made by Henry Wyatt and William Hattecliffe

Receipts

	£	s.	d.
From the King at different times:			
From Sir Reginald Bray by the hand of William Hungate, August 12	340	0	0
August 13. By the hand of John Deonys	526	15	10
August 14. By the hand of William Hungate	243	8	0
August 16 and 18. By the hand of William Hungate	568	5	4
August 29. By the hand of William Hungate	21	10	10
From the King through Reginald Bray on various dates from August 17 to August 29 by the hand of John Shaw	5300	0	0
	£7000	0	0

XI

Administration, October 1494–June 1495

(B.M. Royal MSS, 18 C xiv, fols. 123–128), p. 165 and from the audit on this Report
(B.M. Royal MSS, 18 C xiv, fols. 141–141 v.)

Payments

		£	s.	d.
1.	*Old War Wages* Wages of 100 soldiers with Thomas Garth (from June 24, 1494) till the army came out with Poynings on October 13, 1494	294	0	0
2.	*Deputy's Fee* For a year in addition to £100 already given him in England	397	10	0
3.	*Gifts and Salaries* Given by the King to the Irish Chancellor, Treasurer and two Chief Justices	180	0	0
4.	*War Wages* Wages of the army for 9 months from October 13, 1494 to June 20, 1495	3795	8	0[1]
5.	*Wages of Constables of Castles* for the same period	169	4	0
6.	*Extraordinary Payments* Wages to 16 soldiers in Carlow Castle for 4 months in the retinue of Edmund Milles	45	10	0
7.	*Gifts to Irish Chiefs.* Sir James Ormond, Edmund Pierson, O'Brien and others	427	11	4
8.	*Necessary Expenses*	177	13	0
9.	*"Conductor Navium"* For the Captain and the wages and victuals of the soldiers and sailors conveying the King's treasure and Treasurer, from Waterford to Dublin	25	0	0
10.	*Messengers* conveying letters from the Treasurer to the King in England	77	10	5½
11.	*Purchase of Artillery* by the Treasurer	5	10	7
12.	*Repayment of the Deputy's payments for necessary expenses*	152	8	4½
13.	*Payment to Henry Wyatt and William Hattecliffe,* commissioners in Ireland. (Conway's balance on June 21, 1495)	900	0	0
14.	Balance in the hands of the Treasurer	342	14	3
		£6990	0	0[2]

[1] Given as £3795 on p. 167.
[2] There must be an error of £10 in the original figures.

APPENDIX

Balance Sheet of the Poynings Administra-

The figures are taken from Sir Hugh Conway's second Report as Treasurer (Royal MSS,
Hattecliffe (Royal MSS,

Receipts

	£	s.	d.
Sir Hugh Conway's balance in June 1495	342	14	3
From the Mayor and bailiffs of Dublin in part payment of the fee-farm of the City for Michaelmas and Easter Terms, 10 Henry VII[1]	54	12	9
From Robert Forster in part payment of the customs of the port of Dublin in 10 and 11 Henry VII[2]	150	0	0
From the Mayor and Sheriffs of the town of Drogheda in part payment of the fee-farm for Michaelmas and Easter Terms, 10 Henry VII[3]	24	13	4
From John Porter, collector of customs in the port of Drogheda, in part payment for 10 and 11 Henry VII[4]	110	18	10
From James Dillon, Receiver-General of the King's manors in Counties Dublin and Meath, in part payment for Easter Term, 10 Henry VII, and Michaelmas Term, 11 Henry VII[5]	118	0	0
From John Knight, collector of customs and poundage on many parts of the sea-coast, Fingal and elsewhere	5	14	0
From the issues of the mills of the King's Manors of Chapel Isolda and Newcastle in Co. Dublin	3	6	8
From Thomas Petit, clerk, for various sums received at the Exchequer of Receipt	3	1	6½
	£813	1	4½

[1] Annual farm estimated at 300 marks (fols. 115 v. and 149 r.).
[2] Estimated at £200 a year (fol. 149 r.).
[3] Estimated at 100 marks (£66. 13s. 4d.) a year (fols. 115 v. and 149 r.).
[4] £53. 13s. 4d. was received in 1495 (fol. 113 r.) and £66. 13s. 4d. was the estimated yield for 1496 (fol. 149 r.).
[5] *Actual Receipts. Easter Term* (fol. 110), 10 Henry VII (compare Appendix XVI). Saggard, £6. 7s. 6d. Leixlip, £3. 19s. od. Rathtoath, £1. 14s. 11½d. Moylagh, by resumption, £8. 0s. 4d. Skreen, £6. 1s. 8d. through nonage. Feldiston £3. 10s. 8d. through nonage.

For *Michaelmas Term*, 11 *Henry VII. Rents leviable excluding wastes* (fols. 111, 112, and 116 r.):

		"Today"			"Ex antiquo"		
	Crumlin	£14	0	0	£37	7	6
	Saggard	8	10	0	32	3	4
	Newcastle	29	0	0	120	5	2½
Co. Dublin	Esker	11	13	1	33	6	8
	Leixlip	0			81	4	0½
	Chapelizod	0			26	13	4
	Ballymergy lies waste in default of tenants.						

Meath   Trim, £22. 0s. od. Baskeny and Rathcore, £5. Castlerickard, £2. 13s. 4d. Dervor, £3. 6s. 8d. Ardmulaghan (40 marks), Belgard (20 marks) and Fore (20 marks) all conceded to Sir James Ormond, 0.

			Resumptions			
	Michaelmas Term		Michaelmas Term			
Wards	Baron of Skreen, £18 a term		Moylagh late with Kildare	£16	0	0
	Heir of Feldiston, £5 a term		Portlester late with the Earl and Sir			
	Ward of Bermyngham of Ballydongan		Rowland Fitz Eustace	15	0	0
	conceded to James Ormond, 0		Rathwer, late with William Darcy	13	6	8
			Kyldalke and Dunmow, late with			
			William Darcy	10	0	0
			Blackcastle and Donaghmore	13	6	8
			Castelwaring and Oughterard	5	6	8

XII

tion, June 21, 1495–December 1495

18 C XIV, fols. 133–139) and the audit on this Report by Henry Wyatt and William
18 C XIV, fols. 142–144)

Payments

	£	s.	d.
To the Treasurer for the wages of 3 sub-captains and 57 archers from June 21 to September 12	132	6	0
To William Hattecliffe on July 28, 1495, for his fee	33	13	4
To Thomas Bowring, Chief Justice of the King's Bench, in part payment of his salary for 10 Henry VII	43	6	8
To John Topcliff, Chief Justice, for his fee for the previous year	53	6	8
To Nicholas Turner, Second Justice of the Court of Common Bench for his fee for the same year, in addition to £14 already paid	10	0	0
To Hugh Blagge, Chief Chamberlain of the Exchequer, in part payment of his fee for Michaelmas Term, 10 Henry VII, in addition to £8 assigned him through the Sheriff of Drogheda	2	0	0
To John Bathe, Chief Remembrancer of the Exchequer, in part payment of his fee for Easter and Michaelmas Terms, 10 and 11 Henry VII, in addition to £5 assigned him by Nicholas Holywood	1	13	4
To Sir James Ormond in part payment of his fee from the King	40	0	0
To the Carmelite brothers of Dublin in payment for the year 10 Henry VII of a pension assigned them by the King's ancestors		6	8
To John Lacy and John Larbonce, messengers of the Irish Exchequer, in part payment of their fee for 10 Henry VII		6	8
To Sir Hugh Conway for his fee of £40 a year and wages at 6s. 8d. a day for a whole year, finishing on September 12, 1495	161	13	4
To the same for wages of 6s. a day from September 12, 1495, to November 8, 1495	18	13	4
To the same for wages of £40 for Michaelmas Term, 11 Henry VII	20	0	0
To Richard Nangle, Controller of the Mint at Dublin Castle, for his fee of 10 marks a year for Easter and Michaelmas Terms, 10 and 11 Henry VII	6	13	4
Fees to Macmurrowe and O'Connor, 2 Irish Captains	43	6	8
For several pieces of green cloth embroidered with crowns	2	15	0
Repairs to Carlow Castle done by Thomas Garth	22	0	0
Repairs of the King's Mills at Newcastle de Lions	4	17	8
	£596	18	8

Balance Sheet of the Poynings Administration,

Receipts

	£	s.	d.
Brought forward	813	1	4½

---

¹ Fol. 137:

	£	s.	d.
To Robert Forster for 3 rods of good cloth for O'Brien at 9s. a rod	1	7	0
1 rod of velvet for the wife of O'Brien	1	4	0
5 rods of camelot at 4s. a rod for Bishop O'Brien*	1	0	0
3 rods of good cloth for Tirlagh O'Brien at 9s. a rod	1	7	0
½ a rod of velvet for the wife of Tirlagh		12	0
½ a rod of velvet for Gilduff O'Brien		12	0
3 rods of good cloth for McWilliam at 9s. a rod	1	7	0
2½ rods of good cloth for the wife of McWilliam at 9s. a rod	1	2	6
1 rod of velvet for the aforesaid wife	1	4	0
	£9	**15**	**0**

* Maurice O'Brien, Bp of Kilfenora (Gairdner, *Letters*, II, 316).

June 21, 1495–December 1495—*contd*

Payments

	£	s.	d.
Brought forward	596	18	8
For presents of cloth, etc., made by the Lord Deputy to the Irish, the O'Brien's, McWilliam, etc. (for details see fol. 137)[1]	9	15	0
For the necessary expenses of the Deputy and 30 horsemen riding to superintend the royal manors in Counties Meath, Dublin and Kildare for 12 days	4	0	0
To Thomas Bowring, Chief Justice, for assessing plough-lands for the King's subsidy in Counties Meath and Dublin, at 18*d.* a day for himself, and 8*d.* a day for 8 horsemen for 9 days	3	1	6
To Walter Houthe, the King's attorney, for his expenses and those of 2 servants riding with him, on the same errand		13	4
To the Treasurer riding with 16 horsemen during the same time at 6*s.* 8*d.* a day	3	0	0
To Nicholas White, one of the Barons of the King's Exchequer, and to Hugh Blagge and James Dullyn, sub-commissioners of the King in the aforesaid counties, for writing the books and rolls of the assessment for 13 days; viz. to the Baron for himself and 2 servants for 4 days 9*s.* 4*d.*; to Hugh for 13 days, 13*s.*; and to James for himself and 1 servant at 20*d.* a day, £1. 1*s.* 8*d.* Total for necessary expenses	2	4	0
To John Knight for his work and expenses in scrutinising the sea-coast for the King's customs	3	6	8
To Richard Nangle for his work in scrutinising the King's records and in the writing of books and rolls for his profit	6	13	4
To James Dullyn for his work in scrutinising and writing books and rolls	3	6	8
To the Treasurer for his expenses in connection with the King's subsidy and for visiting royal manors with 24 horsemen for 30 days, from September 25 to October 24, 1495 (see fol. 138 v.)	10	0	0
To James Dullyn 40*s.* and to 2 horsemen on the same errand 13*s.* 4*d.*	2	13	4
To divers others	5	0	0
To the Treasurer for the wages of 3 sub-captains at 12*d.* a day and 57 archers at 6*d.* a day, with 2*d.* a day allotted to 3 archers for their horses for a month ending November 7	44	16	0
For the wages of 3 sub-captains and 51 archers for half a month ending on November 21	17	17	0
To Owenne Eton sent from Waterford to the King in England with letters about the rumours of the Earl of Desmond's and Perkin Warbeck's journey in August	5	0	10
To Philip Messenger sent on various errands for the King's profit in Ireland at the cost of the Treasurer for 4 months	2	0	0
For petty expenses, paper, parchment, ink, etc.	1	0	0
For artillery, to Jacob Corde, merchant of Dublin, for 8 bows		12	4
	£721	18	8
Surplus	91	0	0

"pro quibus var" £100

"In cuius Rei testimonium tam idem thesurarius quam Henricus Wyot et Willelmus Hattecliff commissarii in supervidendo dicto compoto huic repertorio sua nomina cum sigillis suis alternatim apposuerunt."

APPENDIX

Hattecliffe's Declaration of Receipts in

B.M. Royal MSS, 18 C xiv,

(These receipts and payments are additional to the money spent by Conway during

Receipts for the Army

	£	s.	d.
1. From Sir Hugh Conway, Treasurer of Ireland[1]	900	0	0
2. From the King by the hand of Geoffrey Elys, Chaplain[2]	420	0	0
3. From the King by the hand of Robert Sotell, armiger	420	0	0
4. From the King by the hand of Robert Sotell, armiger	500	0	0
5. From the King by the hand of Robert Sotell, armiger	11	19	4
Total	£2251	19	4

Receipts for the Retinue of John Morton[3]

	£	s.	d.
From the King by the hand of Geoffrey Elys	446	12	8
From the King by the hand of Robert Sotell	210	0	0
Total	£656	12	8

	£	s.	d.
Total Receipts	2908	12	0
Balance in hands of Hattecliffe	137	17	9

[1] This was the surplus of the first year's income paid over to Wyatt and Hattecliffe on June 13, 1495.
[2] On June 14, 1495, Geoffrey Elys was paid £200 out of the Chamber Account "for waging of men unto Irelande". He received a payment of £42. 17s. 4d. for his costs, presumably in going to Ireland, on July 23 (Bentley, *Excerpta Historica*, pp. 103–4).
[3] He commanded 10 sub-captains and 289 archers at the siege of Waterford and afterwards.

XIII

Ireland, June 1495–December 1495

fols. 144 v.–145 v.

(the same period set out in Appendix XII. The extra sum was spent on the army)

Payments for the Army

	£	s.	d.
By William Hattecliffe to John Pympe, Treasurer of the Wars, for the expenses of the army from June 20, 1495	2362	13	4
Surplus held by Pympe above what the King had sent	110	14	0

Payments to John Morton

To John Morton in reward in addition to £6. 13s. 4d. paid him in England	13	6	8
Other payments to John Morton for himself, 10 sub-captains and 289 archers in August, September and October 1495 (at Waterford) (elaborate details given)	394	14	3
	£408	0	11

Total Payments (excluding Pympe's surplus of £110. 14s. 0d.)	2770	14	3

Hattecliffe's Declaration of Receipts in Ireland,

Receipts at the Irish Exchequer

	£	s.	d.
1. From Robert Forster, collector of the customs at the port of Dublin[1]	102	5	4
2. From Henry Wyatt for the *Kekeout* captured from Perkin at Waterford and bought by him from the Lord Deputy	26	13	4
3. From John Clerk on the part of the Council for ships bought by the Council	66	13	4
4. From Richard Whyte, chief of the Mint in the Castle of Dublin[2]	16	18	5
5. From the Treasurer (Sir Hugh Conway) by the hand of John Pympe at Waterford	30	0	0
6. From Captain Orch at Le Naas	1	0	0
7. From Gerrard Cavanagh, Constable of Carlow, for repairs	2	13	4
Total	246	3	9
Balance from the Army Receipts	137	17	9
Total Receipts	384	1	6

	£	s.	d.
Balance over in money for payment of salaries of the Chancellor, Justices, etc., till Michaelmas. In addition to which £40 is in woollen cloth, making a total balance of	116	8	6
	156	8	6

[1] See previous payment of £150 to Conway (p. 172).
[2] In Hattecliffe's audit on the declaration the Mint yielded £43. 12s. 5d. (p. 182). The estimated annual yield was £100 (fol. 149 r.).

June 1495–December 1495—*contd.*

Payments from the Irish Exchequer

	£	s.	d.
Payments to the Irish by command of the Deputy	83	6	4
Payments to Henry Wyatt for loans made by him together with £20 paid him by the King's command (details given on fol. 18 v.)	44	6	8
Payments to the Mayor and citizens of Waterford in return for payments made by them while the Deputies' army was there	100	0	0
	£227	13	0

12-2

APPENDIX

Audit on Hattecliffe's Declaration of

B.M. Royal MSS, 18 C xiv,

(The audit includes more revenue than Hattecliffe's Declaration of Receipts, from figures of his receipts for Trinity and Michaelmas Terms on fol.

Receipts from the Treasurer

	£	s.	d.
From Sir Hugh Conway	900	0	0
From Sir Hugh Conway	30	0	0
From Captain Ordh at Le Naas	1	0	0
From Gerrard Cavanagh	2	13	4
	£933	13	4

Receipts from the King

	£	s.	d.
From Geoffrey Elys	420	0	0
From Robert Sotell	420	0	0
From Robert Sotell	111	19	4
From Geoffrey Elys	446	12	8
From Robert Sotell	220[1]	0	0
From John Reding, clerk of the spices	600	0	0
	£2608	12	0[2]

Receipts from the Irish Exchequer of Receipt

From Robert Forster, collector of the Dublin Customs[3]	139	5	4
From John Porter, councillor, collector of the Customs of Drogheda[4]	10	0	0

[1] This is a mistake for £210; see fol. 144 v.
[2] In the original MS (fol. 146 r.) the first three items are made to total £1351. 19s. 4d. A £400 item must have been omitted in the text.
[3] With the previous payment of £150 to Conway, in the same year (p. 172) the Dublin Customs yielded £289. 5s. 4d. from October, 1494, to December, 1495. The annual estimated revenue was £200.
[4] With the previous payment of £110. 18s. 10d. to Conway (p. 172) the estimated revenue for 1496 was reached.

XIV

Receipts, June 1495–December 1495

fols. 146–147 v.

Irish sources as well as £600 from England by the hand of John Reding. Hattecliffe's 183 is £4125. 1s 8d. and was probably a preliminary statement)

Payments

	£	s.	d.
To John Pympe for the wages of the army, etc.	3349	0	11½
To John Morton, captain, for his salary and the wages of his captains and bowmen	408	0	11
To John Legh at 12d. a day			
To Humphery Bowtok at 9d. a day and 36 bowmen at 6d. a day, for their wages for 3 weeks at Waterford after the departure of John Morton	20	14	9
To Sir James Ormond in payment of his fee for a year; to Macmurowe, O'Neill, and other Irish chiefs; and in part payment of various salaries for officers of the Crown	224	6	8
	£4002	3	3½

Audit on Hattecliffe's Declaration of Accounts,

	£	s.	d.
Brought forward	149	5	4
From Henry Wyatt for the *Kekeout* captured from Perkin at Waterford and bought by him from the Lord Deputy	26	13	4
From John Clerk for ships bought by the Council	66	13	4
From Richard White of the Dublin Mint	43	12	5
From John Forster, late clerk of the Hanaper, for his profits [1]	10	0	6
From fines, reliefs, services, etc. [2]	27	18	0
From the fee-farms of Dublin and Drogheda [3]	17	9	9½
From the revenues of the King's lands and manors [4] from the hand of James Dillon, Receiver-General	122	5	4
From the subsidy from the King's lands by the hand of the Abbot of St Thomas outside the new gate of Dublin and from the collector of the Barony of Moishall	18	13	4
For the price of 1¼ pieces of unseasoned timber sold by Henry Wyatt		10	1
	£483	1	5½

Receipts from the King's wines [5]

	£	s.	d.
For the price of 1 cask of Gascon wine	5	0	0
For the price of 1 butte of Romney	5	6	8
	£10 · 6		8

Receipts

	£	s.	d.
Total (from the Treasurer, the King, the Irish Exchequer and the King's wines)	4035	13	5½
Whence there remains in kind (woollen cloth) in the Treasury, the equivalent of	38	0	11
Total in ready money	£3997	12	6

[1] The annual yield of the hanaper was estimated at £40. (p. 188.)
[2] The fines in Michaelmas and Hilary Terms, 10 Henry VII, charged on the Sheriffs, amounted to £75. 10s. 8d. (fol. 115 r.).

Michaelmas Term				Hilary Term			
Meath	£5	2	10	Meath	£9	13	8
Louth	4	18	6	Louth	3	15	4
Dublin		0		Dublin	1	15	4
Kildare		0		Kildare	49	15	8
				Drogheda		9	4

[3] Conway had already received £79. 6s. 1d. in part payment of Dublin and Drogheda farms, which were estimated at £133. 6s. 8d. and £66. 13s. 4d. respectively. (p. 172.)
[4] Conway had already received £118 from the revenue of the Royal Manors in Dublin and Meath. The total of £240. 5s. 4d. exceeds the estimated yield from Dublin and Meath for the Easter and Michaelmas Terms by £3. 9s. 10½d. Hattecliffe's estimate of the yield from Leixlip (Co. Kildare) for 1496 was £34 and he made no estimate for Louth. (p. 188.)
[5] The annual prise of wines was estimated at £66. 13s. 4d. (p. 188.) £50 from wines was assigned direct to Henry Fagan.

June 1495—December 1495—*contd.*

	£	s.	d.
Brought forward	4002	3	3½

To Henry Fagan of Waterford in payment of £100 from the Mayor and citizens there, above the payment of £50 from wines, assigned him by the King by 3 tallies[1]	50	0	0
To Henry Wyatt and John Pirrigent (Prigent Meno) for loans made by them at various times to messengers carrying the King's letters about Ireland, and sent on journeys by the King's Council	60	0	0
For loans to other Councillors	2	9	2
To Richard Nangle for loans for building the Treasury of Receipt at the King's Exchequer and for repairs at Dublin Castle and the Custom House at the Port	64	1	3
For the expenses and wages of William MacMahon at Dublin for a month, for the purchase of several "byrthes"[2] of weapons, for payments to the Irish, and for various holdings of horsemen in Ireland	38	5	8
For 4 virgates of unseasoned timber paid to the Lord Chancellor for a Council Table, and for parchment, paper, ink, etc.	3	16	9
	£4220	16	1½

Deficit	£223	3	7½

---

[1] See p. 182, note 5.
[2] "Byrthe" is derived from an Irish word "beart", meaning a "stack, heap or cluster". The expression "barth" of rushes, is used to-day.

APPENDIX XV

Letter from William White of Waterford to Thomas Earl of Ormond, April 12, 1495

B.M. Cotton, Titus, B xi, vol. i, new pagination, fol. 54

Right honoᵘable and my Right especiall goode lorde I recomaunde me unto yoᵘ lordshup. And howe be it that mẏ lord deputie of this land at his departur from yoᵘ lordshup at Saint Augustyns of Bristowe promysed you to Be goode lord unto all your servauntes here and to suffer your Recevers and all othr your officers here to enioy their Revenues whiche your lordshup have sett theim ¹ⁿ / he entendeth to doo othre wise in somoche as he will have the possession and receit of your prese wynes in the portes of Limeryke and waterford and to make recevers of his owin uppon the same. and the saide Recevers to deliver unto you yᵉ thride part reteignyng the twoo partes in their owin handes to the use and behouf of the deputie. and not only thus but also he will have the possession of yoᵘ manours in the Countie of Kilkenny in likewise paing you the thride parte of the Revenuez of the same Therfor my lord it were goode for you to send writing herupon aswele from the kinges grace as from yourself. or elles to laboᵘ for aluence of absentie. whiche the veray statute of absentie yeveth yoᵘ lordshup if ye had right for all men being in the kinges service be except. And also my lorde deputie will not allow yoᵘ fermes. whiche ye have graunte to John Comyn and to me uppon yoᵘ prise wynes whiche is contrarie to the pᵘport of the saide statute. for it will that the kinge shulde receve the twoo partes of asmoche revenuez as the lord absent recevith. Wherfor ẏ pray yoᵘ good lordshup that it maẏ like you to send me awriting under yoᵘ seale uppon suche covenauntes and price of yoᵘ prise wynes here as I have theim. for my lord deputie woll take theim in to his owin handes. wᵗout ẏ may shewe for me by writing. I have send by sir william garvey in abill of the price and covenauntes. And my lord sir william is greatlẏ wronged by the bishop of Kylkenny¹ and his kynnesmen as y understande and as he can showe yoᵘ lordshup at leynth And god preserve yoᵘ lordshup. ffrom Waterford the xiiᵗʰ day of April

By yoᵘ servᵃnt williã white pp

(dorso) To the right honoᵘable and my Right especiall goode lord
therll of Ormond.   W. White.²

¹ Bishop of Ossory.
² His own signature. He was Recorder of Waterford in 1499. Charles Smith, *State of the County and City of Waterford*, p. 138.

APPENDIX

A. Hattecliffe's estimate of Receipts and Payments from Ireland

B.M. Royal MSS, 18 C xiv,

Receipts

Subsidies   £ s. d.

Co. Meath[1] (figures from fol. 105 r.)

Earldom of March. Baronies of Delvin, Farbill, Moycashel, Mullingar, Fore, Moygoish, 6 carucates each. Corkaree, 4 carucates. Baronies of Navan (32), Kells (24), Skreen (32), Deece (24), Moyfenrath (12), Dunboyne (10), Lune (16), Ratoath (18), Slane (16), Morgallion (22), Duleek (30)

		£	s.	d.
Total: 276 carucates		368	0	0
Clerical grant		89	6	8
Total Subsidy, Lay and Cleric		£457	6	8

Co. Dublin[2] (fol. 105 v.)

From baronies of Balrothery (44), Coolock (35), Castleknock (28), Newcastle (40), Rathdown (12)

	£	s.	d.
Total: 154 carucates[3]	205	6	8
Clerical grant	23	6	8
Subsidy of Dean and Chapter of St Patrick's	23	6	8
Subsidy from the Cross-lands[4]	102	13	4
Total Subsidy, Lay and Cleric	£354	13	4

Co. Louth[5] (fol. 148 r.)

	£	s.	d.
Lay Subsidy from 240 carucates	320	0	0
Clerical grant	44	0	0
Total Subsidy, Lay and Cleric	£364	0	0

Co. Kildare[6] (fol. 107 v.)

From baronies of Leixlip (20), Naas (20), Otymy (7½), Ikethy (6), Oughterany (7), Conall (6), Offaly (9), Kilcullen (4), Norragh (8), Lyons (6), Kilkea (6), Dunleckny (7), Reban (5), Carbury (7)

	£	s.	d.
Total: 118½ carucates	£99	11	0
Total	£1275	11	0

[1] In a survey of 1 Henry V, copied by Hattecliffe (fol. 108 v.) the carucage was: Delvin (21), Farbill (6), Moycashel (6), Fore (6), Navan (40), Kells (32), Skreen (33), Moyfenrath (21), Dunboyne (13), Lune (30), Ratoath (20), Slane (21), Morgallion (24), Duleek (36).
In Hattecliffe's estimate (fol. 109 r.) Meath was reckoned as containing 360 carucates, amounting at 26s. 8d. to £480.
[2] Hattecliffe previously reckoned Co. Dublin as 200 carucates, amounting to £266. 13s. 4d.; the clerical grant at £58. 7s. 8d.; the Dean and Chapter of St Patrick's at £58. 7s. 8d.; and the "Cross" at £58. 7s. 8d. (fol. 109 r.).
[3] The numbers add up to 159, but the sum is right for 154.
[4] The ecclesiastical area of Co. Dublin: "Crocea".
[5] Hattecliffe previously reckoned Louth as 360 carucates, assessable at £480; the clerical grant at £44 and the "primate and the cross" at £44 (fol. 109 r.).
[6] Hattecliffe previously reckoned Kildare as assessable at £160 (fol. 109 v.). Under this earlier reckoning the total receipts from subsidies would have amounted to £1739. 3s. 0d.

XVI

for 1496, made at the end of 1495. Excluding the Army

fols. 148–151

Payments

	£	s.	d.
Fees and Offices of the Crown in Ireland			
Lord Deputy	500	0	0
The Lord Chancellor for his fee for a year	40	0	0
His diet of 10s. a day for a year	182	10	0
To the Treasurer of the Wars for 6 months	33	6	8
To the Master of the Rolls for a year	20	0	0
To the Clerk of the Hanaper[1] for a year	6	13	4
To the Clerk of the Council for a year	6	13	4
To the Clerk of the Crown if there is one £6. 13s. 4d. (this year)	0	0	0
Total	£789	3	4
Court of King's Bench			
To the Chief Justice for a year	40	0	0
For his diet of 3s. 4d. a day for a year	60	13	4
To the Chief Clerk and Clerk of the Crown and Common Pleas for a year	5	0	0
Total	£105	13	4
Court of Common Bench			
To the Chief Justice for a year	66	13	4
To the Second Justice for a year	40	0	0
Total	£106	13	4
The King's Exchequer			
To the Treasurer of Ireland	40	0	0
Diet at 6s. 8d. a day	121	13	4
To the Under-Treasurer for 6 months	33	6	8
To the Chief Baron of the Exchequer if there is one (this year)	0	0	0
To the Second Baron of the Exchequer for a year	13	6	8
For expenses	4	0	0
To the Chancellor of the Green Wax[2] if there is one £10. 0s. 0d. (this year)	0	0	0
To the Chief Chamberlain for his fee	10	0	0
For expenses	4	0	0
To the Chief Remembrancer and second Remembrancer for their fee between them	5	0	0
For expenses	4	0	0
To the Chief Grossar for his fee for a year	6	13	4
For expenses	4	0	0
To the "aperto" (usher?) of the Exchequer, 5d. a day, £4. 8s. 4d. (this year)	0	0	0

---

[1] William Shraggar appointed, September 1, 1495. *Irish Patent and Close Rolls*, Record Commission.
[2] Edward Bernewall was appointed Chancellor of the Exchequer and of the Green Wax, December 16, 1495. *Irish Patent and Close Rolls*, Record Commission.

A. Hattecliffe's estimate of Receipts and Payments

Receipts

	£	s.	d.
Brought Forward	1275	11[1]	0

Royal Manors

Co. Dublin (Details from fol. 148 v.)

Crumlin, £26. 13s. 4d. Chapelizod, £5. Saggard, £17. Newcastle, £57. Esker, £23	128	13	4

Co. Kildare

Leixlip	34	0	0

Co. Meath

Trim, £46. Rathcore and Baskeny, £10. Castlerickard, £3. 6s. 8d. Moylagh, £32. Portlester, £25. Moymet, £3. 6s. 8d. Ratoath, £20. Blackcastle, £40	179	13	4
Total	£342	6	8

Wards and Marriages. (Details from fol. 148 v.)

Baron of Skreen; married and under age, £32. Heir of John Felde of Feldiston, £8. Heir of James Eustace of Dublin, £3. 6s. 8d. Heir of Baron of Galtrim, £13. 6s. 8d. Heir of John Tute, £13. 6s. 8d. Heir of Patrick Birmingham, £40, conceded to Sir James Ormond	70	0	0

Absentees (fol. 149 r.)

Earl of Ormond, £80. Abbot of Ferns, £20	100	0	0

Customs and Poundage (fol. 149 r.)

Port of Dublin, £200. Drogheda, £66. 13s. 4d. Waterford, 0	266	13	4

Prise of Wines (fol. 149 r.)

Dublin, Drogheda and Waterford	66	13	4

Fee Farms[2] (fol. 149 r.)

Dublin, £133. 6s. 8d. Drogheda, £66. 13s. 4d. Waterford, £10 (of old belonging to the Earl of Ormond: now by resumption in the hands of the King)	210	0	0

Hanaper (fol. 149 r.)

	40	0	0

Coinage (fol. 149 r.)

	100	0	0

Estreats (fol. 149 r.)

	220	0	0
Total	£2691	4	4[3]

---

[1] This eleven shillings is omitted in the total on p. 149 r.
[2] The fee-farms) f Limerick and Cork were estimated on fol. 116 r. as respectively £73. 6s. 8d. and £53. 6s. 8d. Waterford in the same estimate was £66. 13s. 4d.
[3] On fol. 149 r. this sum is mistakenly written as £2791. 4s. 2d.

from Ireland for 1496, made at the end of 1495—*contd.*

Payments

		£	s.	d.
Brought Forward		1001	10	0
The King's Exchequer (continued)				
Brought Forward		246	0	0
To the "summamsterus"[1] for a year, £6. 13s. 4d.	(this year)	0	0	0
For expenses		4	0	0
To the Clerk of the Common Pleas for a year, £3. 6s. 8d.	(this year)	0	0	0
For expenses		2	13	4
To the 2nd grossar for a year, 5 marks	(this year)	0	0	0
For expenses		2	13	4
To the King's attorney for a year		5	0	0
To Robert Lyme the second Remembrancer for a year		4	0	0
To the Marshall for a year		2	5	1½
To the proclamator for a year		2	5	1½
To the 2nd Chamberlain of the Exchequer for a year		4	0	0
Total		£272	16	11

	£	s.	d.
For the expenses of the 2nd Chamberlain	1	6	8
Two cursors at 1½d. a day a year	4	10	4
"Capitalis[2] Scaccarii" for a year	5	0	0
Clerk of the King's works for a year	5	0	0
To 4 sheriffs at £10 a year each for expenses	40	0	0
To the Controller of "the Mint" for a year	6	13	4
To the Controller of Customs and Poundage at Dublin	29	3	4
To the Constable of Trim Castle[3]	6	13	4
To the Constable of Dublin and Master of the Mint[4]	66	13	4
To James Ormond for his fee for a year	100	0	0
To Macmurrowe for a year	53	6	8
Total	£318	7	0

	£	s.	d.
Total of all the fees and offices of the King in Ireland	1592	13	11
Paid	1189	13	4
Remainder to be paid	403	0	7
(written as ΘΘΘΘLX⁸ VII^d = 400. 60. 7)			

[1] The summamster was the man who compiled the sum.
[2] A second word must be omitted.
[3] John Brown appointed Constable of Trim, August 28, 1495. *Irish Patent and Close Rolls*, Record Commission, p. 271.
[4] Thomas Garth was appointed Constable of Dublin Castle with £20 a year out of the profits of the coinage and £46. 13s. 4d. yearly "of further grace" out of the coinage of Ireland; March 20, 1494. *Cal. Pat. Rolls, 1485–94*, p. 461.

Estimate of Receipts payable at the end of the Hilary Term, 1495–96

B.M. Royal MSS, 18 C xiv, fol. 149 v.

	£	s.	d.
From *Subsidies*	1275	11	0
From Revenues of Royal Manors, Wards, Marriages, Absentees, payable from the "arrears" of the Receiver, James Dillon from Michaelmas Term last (1495)	268	18	0
From Customs and Poundage in Dublin and Drogheda	60	0	0
From prise of wines	20	0	0
From fee-farms before Easter	0	0	0
From the Hanaper	10	0	0
From the Mint	25	0	0
From Estreats of the Courts	60	0	0
From other revenues from lands before Easter	0	0	0
Total	£1719	9	0

Debts owing from this sum

	£	s.	d.
For payments in kind, changed into money	223	3	7½
Fees owing to the Chancellor, two Chief Justices, the Barons of the Exchequer and their substitutes in the King's Courts in the year ending Michaelmas last (1495)	399	13	11
Total	£622	17	6½
Remainder unassigned	£1096	11	5½

B. Hattecliffe's actual Receipts and Payments for Hilary,

B.M. Royal MSS,

Receipts	£	s.	d.
Hilary Term, 1496	644	14	3
Easter Term	442	15	9¼
Trinity Term	196	5	4
Total	£1283	15	4¼

Easter and Trinity Terms, 1496[1]. Including the Army

18 C xiv, fol. 183

Payments

	£	s.	d.
Hilary Term, 1496	1022	12	0¼
Easter Term	532	4	0½
Trinity Term	187	11	9¼
Total	£1742	7	10

APPENDIX XVII

Payment of the Army in Ireland, January 1496–June 1496

A. *Payment of the King's Army in Ireland from January 4–June 22, 1496*

B.M. Royal MSS, 18 C xiv, fols. 94–99 and 130 r.–130 v.

(These figures are taken out of the Register and classified under the names of officers. The remaining items which would not admit of this classification are collected in "B" on pp. 194–5.)

		£	s.	d.
fol. 94.	Total Army wage-bill for *January*, 1496	262	10	0
fol. 94 v.	*February*. To *Thomas Garth* for wages of 2 men at 12*d.* a day, for 20 archers on horseback at 8*d.* a day, for 28 on foot and a "tabret" at 6*d.* a day	41	15	4
fol. 95 v.	To Thomas Garth for 8 spears on horseback at 12*d.* a day	11	4	0
fol. 96.	*March*. To Thomas Garth for wages of 1 man at 12*d.* a day, 20 archers, etc. (the same numbers as in February)	40	7	4
	To Thomas Garth for wages of 8 basnetts at 12*d.* a day	11	4	0
fol. 98.	*April*. To Thomas Garth. (Same as March)	40	7	4
	To Thomas Garth for 8 horsemen at 12*d.* a day	11	4	0
	April 25–*May* 24. Missing			
fol. 130.	*May* 24–*June* 22. To Thomas Garth for wages of 1 horseman and 1 gunner at 12*d.* each, 38 horsemen at 8*d.* each and 26 footmen at 6*d.* a day each (Names of four of his footmen are given on fol. 181)	57	3	4
fol. 94 v.	*February*. To *William Hattecliffe*, Under-Treasurer, for 8 men in his retinue at 6*d.* a day	5	12	0
fol. 96.	*March*. Ditto	5	12	0
fol. 99.	*April*. Ditto	5	12	0
	April 25–*May* 24. Missing			
fol. 130 v.	*May* 24–*June* 28th. To William Hattecliffe, Under-Treasurer, for 8 men in his retinue at 6*d.* a day	5	12	0
fol. 94 v.	*February*. To *William Gerald*, servant to the Lord Deputy for 25 men keeping Dublin Castle, 2 at 9*d.* a day and 23 at 6*d.* a day	18	4	0
fol. 96.	*March*. To William Gerald for 2 men at 9*d.* a day and 22 at 6*d.* a day each	17	10	0
fol. 98.	*April*. Ditto	17	10	0
	(The names of all 25 men are given on fol. 182)			
		£551	7	4

		£	s.	d.
	Brought forward	551	7	4
fol. 94 v.	*February.* To *Edward Raynfford* for himself at 12*d.* a day, for 6 archers on horseback at 8*d.* a day, for 17 on foot at 6*d.* a day	18	18	0
fol. 96.	*March.* To Edward Raynfford. Ditto	18	18	0
fol. 98.	*April.* To Edward Raynfford for himself at 12*d.* a day, for 7 archers on horseback at 8*d.*, and 16 on foot at 6*d.* a day	19	2	8
	(The names of 5 horsemen and 16 footmen given on fol. 101 v.)			
fol. 94 v.	*February.* To *Anthony Outright* for himself at 18*d.* a day, for 13 archers on horseback at 8*d.* a day, for 13 on foot at 6*d.* a day and one tabret at 6*d.* a day	24	0	8[1]
fol. 96.	*March.* To Anthony Outright. Ditto	24	0	8
fol. 98.	*April.* Ditto	24	0	8
	(Names of 11 horsemen and 14 footmen given on fol. 181)			
fol. 95.	*February.* To *John Crosby* for himself at 18*d.* a day, 1 trumpet at 10*d.* a day, 17 archers on horseback at 8*d.* a day, and 11 on foot at 6*d.* a day	26	16	8
fol. 96 v.	*March.* To John Crosby for 24 archers on horseback at 8*d.* a day, for 4 footmen at 6*d.* a day; the rest like February	28	9	4
fol. 98 v.	*April.* Ditto	28	9	4
	April 25–*May* 24. Missing			
fol. 130.	*May* 24–*June* 22. For himself at 18*d.* a day, and 16 equestrians at 8*d.* a day	17	0	8
fol. 95.	*February.* To *John Hattecliffe* for himself at 12*d.* a day, for 2 archers on horseback at 8*d.* a day, and for 8 on foot at 6*d.*	8	17	4
fol. 96 v.	*March.* Ditto	8	17	4
fol. 98 v.	*April.* Ditto	8	17	4
fol. 130.	*April* 25–*May* 24. Missing			
fol. 130.	*May* 24–*June* 22. To John Hattecliffe for himself at 12*d.* a day, 4 equestrians at 8*d.* a day and 10 footmen at 6*d.* a day	12	2	8
	(Names of 1 horseman and 3 footmen given on fol. 181)			
fol. 95.	*February.* To the *Captain of the Gunners* for himself at 12*d.* a day and 24 gunners at 6*d.* a day	18	4	0
fol. 96 v.	*March.* To the Captain of the Gunners for himself at 12*d.* a day and 23 gunners at 6*d.*	17	10	0
fol. 98 v.	*April.* For himself at 12*d.* a day and 22 gunners at 6*d.*	16	16	0
	(Names of 9 gunners given on fol. 101 v.)			
		£872	8	8

[1] The sum is torn off on fol. 94 v.

			£	s.	d.
	Brought forward		872	8	8
fol. 95.	*February*. To the *Clerk of the Signet*, 12d. a day		1	8	0
fol. 97.	*March*. Ditto		1	8	0
fol. 98 v.	*April*. Ditto		1	8	0
	April 25–May 24. Missing				
fol. 130 v.	*May 24–June 22*. To the Clerk of the Signet, 12d. a day, and clerks		2	16	0
fol. 95.	*February*. To *Hans Gunner*, 12d. a day		1	8	0
fol. 95.	*February*. To *Richard Salkeld*, Constable of Leixlip, for himself at 12d. a day and 6 others at 6d. a day		5	12	0
fol. 96 v.	*March*. Ditto		5	12	0
fol. 99.	*April*. Ditto		5	12	0
	April 25–May 24. Missing				
fol. 130 v.	*May 24–June 22*. To Richard Salkeld, Constable of Leixlip, for himself at 12d. a day and 6 others at 6d. a day		5	12	0
fol. 95 v.	*February*. To *Sir James Ormond* for 40 horsemen or basnetts at 12d. a day		56	0	0
fol. 97 v.	*March*. Ditto		56	0	0
fol. 99.	*April*. Ditto		56	0	0
fol. 95 v.	*February*. The *Chancellor* for 12 men on foot at 6d. a day		8	8	0[1]
fol. 96.	*March*. Ditto		8	8	0[1]
fol. 99.	*April*. Ditto		8	8	0[1]
	April 25–May 24. Missing				
fol. 130 v.	*May 24–June 22*. The Chancellor for 12 men on foot at 6d. a day		8	8	0
	Total		£1096	8	8

B. *Additional payments for the Army, covering various months*

B.M. Royal MSS, 18 C xiv, fols. 94–99 and 130 r.–130 v.

	£	s.	d.
William Warwick for himself at 12d. a day	3	0	8
1 man at 8d. and for another at 6d. during March (fol. 97) and April (fol. 98 v.)	3	0	8
Ditto. May 24–June 22 (fol. 130)	2	16	0
William MacMahon for 3 months from January 8 to April 3 (fol. 97), for himself and 3 horsemen at 12d. a day each, and £3. 12s. 0d. paid him by assignment	13	4	0
Delvin pursuivant for himself at 12d. a day for 3 months from January 4 to March 27 (fol. 97)	4	4	0
Nicholas Gallon for himself at 6d. a day, during March (fol. 97)		14	0
Ditto. April (fol. 98 v.)		14	0
	£27	13	4

[1] All these items are marked "Cred" in the margin. The February payment is not included in the February totals, or in the grand total.

	£	s.	d.
Brought forward	27	13	4

Tybot Walsh for 20 horsemen "with him in holdinge" for
2 months, from January 4 at 6s. 8d. a month (fol. 97 v.) — 13 6 8
And for 20 for 6 weeks at 6s. 8d. each (fol. 99 v.)—April — 6 13 4
And for 20 pedestrian marchmen each getting for 6 weeks
6s. 8d. paid for a month (fol. 130 v.) — 4 7 9[1]

William Chatwyn, Constable of Carrickfergus, for himself at
12d. a day, for 6 men at 6d. a day for 4 months, from
December 6 to March 27 (fol. 97 v.) — 22 8 0

£74 9 1

Richard Salkeld when he went to Carrickfergus, for himself at
12d. a day and for 12 men at 6d. for 2 months from the last of
February (fol. 99) — 19 12 0

For *Nicholas Butler* and 7 equestrians "de marchiis" in the
retinue of Thomas Garth at 8d. a day (May–June) — 7 9 4

£101 10 5
Appendix XVII. A. Army Payments — 1096 8 8

£1197 19 1

C. *Payments by John Joseph*[2] *in the name of Pympe*

Treasurer of the Wars from January 4 to May 24, 1496

B.M. Royal MSS, 18 C xiv, fols. 100–104 v.

(Fol. 104 is the first page. The items are summarised)

		£	s.	d.
fol. 104.	To Sir Edmund Pierson on February 1 in reward for diligent service to the King's Government from the departure of Poynings to February 1	10	0	0
	To John Hattecliffe on March 17 for the costs of the King's ordnance from Dublin to Lyons at that time	1	10	0
	On March 19 in reward to 3 soldiers, 6s. 8d. each	1	0	0
	Paid to Sir James Ormond's galloglasses on March 19 at Dublin	2	13	4
	On the last day of March for 15 dozen of bread carried to the Castle of Maynooth for victualling James Ormond's galloglasses		15	0
	Paid to Sir James Ormond's galloglasses at Dublin for their costs for 2 nights on their first arrival there	4	0	0

£19 18 4

[1] Wrong sum in MSS.
[2] John Joseph was Pympe's Deputy. Royal MSS, 18 C xiv, fol. 5.

		£	s.	d.
	Brought forward	19	18	4
fol. 100.	To 9 soldiers out of wage, for a reward, 6s. 8d. each	3	0	0
	In reward to 5 soldiers out of wage, who were sent to the Castle of Maynooth the last day of March	1	13	4
	To Sir James Ormond for his galloglasses when they came from Naas to Dublin	3	6	8
	To Sir James Ormond on April 6 for the finding of the same galloglasses	6	13	4
	For the costs of Bishop O'Brien (Bishop of Kilfenora) for 2 nights and 2 days	2	13	4
	For the costs of Bishop O'Brien for 3 days and 3 nights in Dublin paid on April 19	4	0	2
fol. 100 v.	For horsemeat and men's meat at Newcastle for Shane Butler and his horsemen with O'Brien's son and the galloglasses for 2 nights	3	15	8
	For food for the same horsemen and galloglasses at Naas; for 24 basnets each with 3 horses, and 18 score galloglasses, for 4 nights	6	7	5
	To 3 horsemen of Welseleys to scour the country for news between the King's host and their enemies		3	4
	To a messenger to fetch Harold and Tybot Walsh to the King's host with their company at that time (sum torn off)			
	Paid to Garrard Cloysh, Thomas Garth's captain, for 6 meals for himself and 60 kerns in Dublin, at 2d. a meal	3	1	0[1]
	(sum torn off)			
fol. 101.	To the said Garrard for the wages of the 60 kerns for 6 weeks at 3s. 4d. each, for the 6 weeks	10	0	0
	To Richard Salkeld in part payment of his journey to Carrickfergus and back		8	0
	To Howe Roo, a Captain of Sir James Ormond's galloglasses, in reward, on March 18		6	8
	To Thomas Russell, servant to O'Brien, in reward, for his horsemeat and for himself for 2 days		2	6
	To Sir James Cantewell, Marshall of Sir James Ormond's galloglasses, in reward, on March 9		1	8
fol. 101 v.	To a messenger of the Earl of Desmond, on March 9, in reward for bringing letters to the King's Council		3	4
	To a messenger of Sir James Ormond, who went for his horsemen, in reward, on March 9		6	8
	To the Captain of O'Brien's and Tybot Walshes horsemen, for his expenses in Dublin on March 21		3	4
		£66	4	9

[1] Calculated from totals at foot of page.

	£	s.	d.
Brought forward	66	4	9

To a servant of Sir James Ormond, riding from Trim to Newcastle, to Garth, being with the King's army, on March 21 — 1 10[1]

To James Harold for his costs at Newcastle on March 22 — 6 8[1]

fol. 102. On March 22, to a messenger of the Bishop of Dublin, who went with letters from the King's Council at Dublin to Sir James Ormond at Trim — 1 8

On March 23 to Tybot Walsh for the costs of himself and 20 horsemen for 2 days — 1 0 0

On March 23 to a messenger of MacMahon's carrying letters from the King's Council to his master, for horsemen to do the King service in his wars against his enemies — 1 8

On March 23 to the Captain of Sir James Ormond's galloglasses in reward — 3 4

Paid in reward to divers soldiers who were [with] [the] [P]rymet[2] of Armagh and at Drogheda — 3 4

fol. 102 v. On March 23 for saffron given in reward to MacMahon — 13 4

On March 23 to Tybot Walsh for the costs of himself and his horsemen for a day and night — 10 0

On March 24 to a White Friar sent with letters from the King's Council at Dublin to Sir James Ormond at Newcastle in reward — 1 8

On March 24 in reward to John Furber for carrying letters from the King's Council in Dublin to Tybot Walsh — 1 8[1]

In reward to 4 gunners who were out of wage for their diligence in the King's service — 1 9 4[1]

fol. 103. To a messenger of Wa[lsh] who brought letters from thence to the King's Council in Dublin — 1 8

On March 29 to a messenger of Bartholomew Gylemers in reward for divers messages at divers times brought by him to the King's Council — 3 4

On March 30 to Tybot Walsh for the costs of himself and his horsemen for 2 days — 1 6 8

On March 30 in reward to a horseman of Sir James Ormond for messages brought to the King's Council — 6 8

£72 17 7[1]

[1] Calculated from totals at foot of pages, the sums being torn off.
[2] Primate? The MS is torn.

197

	£	s.	d.
Brought forward	72	17	7

fol. 103 v. On March 30 to the Captain of Sir James Ormond's
galloglasses in reward — 1 8

On St Patrick's Day to a horseman of Sir James
Ormond in reward for messages brought to the
King's Council — 2 0

On the same day in reward to divers soldiers out of
wage who came from Drogheda to Dublin to do
the King service, in his war — 2 0

On the same day to a messenger of MacMahon in
reward for letters from MacMahon to the King's
Council — 1 4[1]

£73 4 7[2]

Totals for the payment of the Army in Ireland from January to June, 1496 (A, B and C)

B.M. Royal MSS, 18 C xiv

	£	s.	d.
Wages for Army, January 1496 (fol. 94, p. 192)	262	10	0
Wages for Army, February 1496 (fol. 95 v.)	238	0	0
Wages for Army, March 1496 (fol. 97 v.)	300	14	0
Wages for Army, April 1496 (fol. 99 v.)	273	7	4[3]
	£1074	11	4
May 24–June 22 (fol. 130 v.)	123	7	9
	£1197	19	1[4]
April 25–May 24. No figures exist			
Payments made by John Joseph (pp. 195–198)	73	4	7
	£1271	3	8

[1] Sum torn off, but calculated from totals at the foot of each page.
[2] These accounts are incomplete, as no payments figure for May.
[3] On fol. 99 v. the total is mistakenly given as £273. 7s. 8d.
[4] See total of A, p. 194, and B, p. 195.

APPENDIX XVIII

Note on the Declared Account

I have not made a transcript of Wyatt and Hattecliffe's audits of Sir Hugh Conway's first and second Reports as Treasurer,[1] because a combination of the figures in the Reports and the Audits gives fuller information about the administration.[2] From the point of view of the development of the Declared Account this might be worth doing. Dietz[3] defines "Declared Accounts" as those made up by the King's auditors from the accountants' original books; written on paper; and declared before the King. The earliest was that rendered by Sir John Turbervile, Treasurer of Calais in 1493–4,[4] and is a perfect balance sheet, written on paper, arranged in parallel columns of receipts and payments, and summarised at the end. It was made up from a more detailed account, beautifully written in a book, but with no additions or totals.[5] Turbervile's account for the previous year, 1492–3,[6] was merely a "compotus" consisting of a long list of receipts and payments from which a balance sheet might be compiled.

The formal Declared Account was drawn up in three copies by special auditors. A signed and sealed copy was given to the accountant as his acquittance and two other copies were preserved by the auditors.[7] The audits of Wyatt and Hattecliffe on Conway's first and second Reports correspond with Dietz's definition. They are beautifully written on paper, in parallel columns of receipts and payments, balanced at the end. Conway, Hattecliffe and Wyatt signed and sealed the documents, and each, no doubt, kept a copy. The surviving specimens are the copies declared before the King, together with the rough day-book, which was the best voucher for the accuracy of the completed statements.[8] They may be considered the earliest examples known at present of the Declared Account with the exception of that of Sir John Turbervile. This form of account was adopted by the Court of Augmentations and introduced into the Exchequer by Elizabeth.[9]

[1] Royal MSS, 18 C xiv, fols. 141, 141 v. and 142–144.
[2] Appendices xi and xii.
[3] Dietz, *English Government Finance*, p. 76.
[4] P.R.O. E 101, 201/10.
[5] P.R.O. D.L. 28, 2/2, 9–10 Henry VII.
[6] P.R.O. E 101, 201/2.
[7] Dietz, *English Government Finance*, p. 77.
[8] Gairdner, *Letters*, ii, p. xlviii.
[9] Notes on the origin of the Declared Account. Mrs Eric George, *E.H.R.* xxxi, 41–58.

APPENDIX XIX

Henry VII's instructions to Richmond Herald, December 30, 1494

B.M. Cotton, Caligula, D vi, fol. 20

H R   Instructions a Richemōt Roy darmes de clarenceaulx de ce quil aura adire et Remonstrer depar le Roy n̄r̄e souverain *seigneur* a son bon frere etcousin le Roy Charles de france.

Extract from the middle of fol. 20 v.:

Lesquelles sont telles / Que graces adieu le Roy *nostre*dit souverain *seigneur*/est en bonne sante et prosper[e]¹ de sa personne / aussi bien ayme et obey en son Royaulme / que fu[t] Jamais Roy en angleterre / et que les affaires de son pais dirlande von[t] avant tout ainsi quil les sauroit ou vouldroit demander / Et pour to[ut] certain. Les notables prelatz. gens deglise / grans seigneurs / gens dom[   ] et de facon / et tous autres dud*it* pais dirlande / aussi bien ceulx dela[ngue] saulvarge / que celle de la langue angloisse / se sont tous venuz Rend[   ] lieutenant general du Roy *nostre*dit souverain *seigneur* / estant deput ond*it* pa[is] dirlande / en faisant les foy et hommage au Roy *nostre*dit souverain *seigneur* [   ] Reste tant seullement / fors de mettre Icelluy pais en bonne Justice or[dre] et police / Et que le Roy *nostre*dit souverain *seigneur* espoire. sera fait de brief [sans] aucune difficulte / a son tres grant honne*ur* et prouffit / desquelles [   ] Il a bien voulu advertir son d*it* bon frere et cousin / parce quil scait quil en sera Joyeulx ainsi que le Roy *nostre*dit souverain *seigneur* est de sa [   ] et felicite /.

Extract from the middle of fol. 21 r.:

Et si daventure led*it* bon frere et cousin du Roy *nostre*dit souverain *seigneur* luy dema[nd] ou touchoit aucunement de la paix et amytie. dentre le Roy *nostre*dit souvera[in] *seigneur* / et le Roy descosse / Led*it* Richemont pouvra Respondre sur ce que a son departement le Roy *nostre*dit souverain *seigneur* / avoit nouvelles certaine[s] dud*it* Roy descosse dune grande et notable ambassade quil envoyoit deve[nt] luy pour conclure lad*it* paix et amytie dentre eulx / et la faire plus forte que Jamais. /

[fait et expedit au manoir de grenewiche le penultisme Jour A⁰ iiiiˣˣ xiiii.]

---

¹ The ends of the lines are rubbed and the letters within square brackets conjectural.

APPENDIX XX

List of Chapters of the Poynings Parliament assembled from the *Irish Statutes at Large* and

P.R.O. E 30, 1548, and Lambeth, Carew MSS, 608, fols. 113–116

Chapter I P.R.O. E 30, 1548, fol. 1 (French).
    II   ,,   ,,   ,,   fol. 1 (French).
   III   ,,   ,,   ,,   fol. 1 (French).
   IV   ,,   ,,   ,,   fol. 1.
    V *Irish Statutes at Large*, Act 1.
   VI ,,   ,,   ,,   ,, II.
  VII ,,   ,,   ,,   ,, III.
 VIII P.R.O. E 30, 1548, fol. 4.
   IX *Irish Statutes at Large*, Act IV.
    X ,,   ,,   ,,   ,, V.
   XI P.R.O. E 30, 1548, fol. 5–8.
  XII *Irish Statutes at Large*, Act VI.
 XIII ,,   ,,   ,,   ,, VII.
 XIV Lambeth, Carew MSS, 608, fol. 115 (Summary).
  XV P.R.O. E 30, 1548, fol. 11.
 XVI ,,   ,,   ,,   fol. 11.
XVII ,,   ,,   ,,   fol. 11.
XVIII ,,   ,,   ,,   fol. 12.
 XIX *Irish Statutes at Large*, Act VIII.
  XX ,,   ,,   ,,   ,, IX.
 XXI ,,   ,,   ,,   ,, XI.
 XXII ,,   ,,   ,,   ,, X.
XXIII ,,   ,,   ,,   ,, XII.
XXIV Lambeth, Carew MSS, 608, fol. 115 (Summary).
 XXV *Irish Statutes at Large*, Act XIII.
XXVI P.R.O. E 30, 1548, fol. 10.
XXVII ,,   ,,   ,,   fol. 14.
XXVIII *Irish Statutes at Large*, Act XIV.
XXIX ,,   ,,   ,,   ,, XV.
XXX   ,,   ,,   ,,   ,, XVI.
XXXI P.R.O. E 30, 1548 (Heading).
XXXII *Irish Statutes at Large*, Act XVII.
XXXIII Lambeth, Carew MSS, 608, fol. 115 v. (Summary).
XXXIV P.R.O. E 30, 1548, fol. 18.
XXXV *Irish Statutes at Large*, Act XVIII.
XXXVI ,,   ,,   ,,   ,, XIX.
XXXVII ,,   ,,   ,,   ,, XXI.

APPENDIX XXI

Poynings' Parliament. Chapter IV. "For extortion of coyne, livery and pay"

P.R.O. E 30, 1548, fol. 1

ffor Extorcōn of coẏgne lyv*ere* & paẏe

Itm at the Request & Supplicatōn of the Comẏns of this lande of Irelande that where of long tyme ther hathe bẏn usid & yet is by the lord*es* and Gentyllmen of that lande manye & dyv*erse* dampnable Customes & usage whiche byn Callid Coẏne and lyv*ere* and paẏe / That is for to saẏe horsemete & mannes mete for ther ffindeing of ther horssemen & ffotemen & ov*er* that *IIII∂* or *VI∂* daẏlẏe to ev*ery* of them to be hadde & p*er*ceẏvid[1] of the poore trewe Erthe Tillers & Tennt*es* a Inhibytunt*es* of the said lande w*t*oute anẏthing doing or paẏing therfor besides dyv*erse* & manẏ murders opp*ress*ions Robories Ravisheing*es* of Maẏdens & wẏfes and manẏfolde Extortōns & Inconvenyenc*es* bẏ the saide horssemen and ffotemen daẏlẏ & nẏghtlẏ comm*y*tteid and don whiche byn the principall causeis of the desolacōn & destruc̄con of the said lande etc. Therfor beit Enacteid ordeyned & Establysid bẏ

[1] collected.

thauctorite of this present parlyamᵗ bẏ thassent of the lordes spu̅all and
Temporall procters & the saide Comens of this lande in this present
parlyamᵗ assemblidt hat oʳ Soveraigne lorde the king have yerely of
every of v̇ı̇ Acres of Errable lande of Temporall possession and In-
heritaunces wᵗin this saide lande of Ireland occupied manured or
hereafter occupied manured wᵗin this saide lande of Ireland from the
tẏme of the manurunce ᵃ xxvıs vıııꝺ of good and laufull moneẏ of
Irlande to be levied as it hathe bẏn custumably usid in tymes past to
be dyschargeid of Coẏne Lyvere and paẏe / and of other unlefull
Imposicōns / And of the landes of the Churche callid the Crosselandes
for every vı̇. xxvıs vıııꝺ and the clergie and chaptours to be chargeid
with lyk Subsydie as hathe heretofore ben ᵃgrunteid by the clergẏe there
and in especiall in the tyme of William late bisshop of methe to be had
and perceyved from the ffeast of Ester in the yere of oʳ lorde god
Mˡˡ cccc lxxxxv unto the full end and terme of fyve yeres then next
ensuing / And that every ploweland wᵗin thesaid land so as is afore
discharged of coygne lyverey and paye and other Imposicions / And
that almaner other landes at any tyme heretofore plowed or occupied
in tyllage be rated and charged after the same price so it be not waste /
be in nomaner wise excepted or exempted of thesaid yerely xxvıs vıııꝺ
durying the said five yeres / Any estatute acte or ordynnᵘce hertofore
made or had therof to the contrary notwᵗstandyng / And that every
suche v̇ı̇ acres lande be trewly & egally rated apporcyoned and measured
by trewe and indifferent persones elected & sworne indifferently / That
for to doo soo that every suche v̇ı̇ Acres lande be like charged yerely
wᵗ thesaid xxvıs vıııꝺ during the said five yeres /

Provyded alwaies that the lieutenunte and deputie of this lande and
the kinges counsaill of thesame for the tyme being / at all tymes
necessarie & requesite have full power and auctoritie after their discrecyon to adde and enlarge more Acres of lande unto every v̇ı̇ Acres of

erable lande not being fertyll as other acres be Wherof every Acre excede

not II^d or under that Some that the value of the nombre of suche Acres

of erable lande being of small value / be made and extended egall and

according in value unto vi Acres of erable lande being good and fertyle

APPENDIX XXII

Poynings' Parliament. Chapter VIII. A grant of 12d. to the King on every pound of merchandise

P.R.O. E 30, 1548, fol. 4

A gªunte of *XIIᵭ* of every pounde of merchauntes duryng v yeres to the kynge

Item one Acte that the kynge in mayntennce of his warres & other costes shall have yerely *XIIᵭ* of every pounde duryng v hole yeres next ensuing the daye of the begynnyng of this present parliament of every suche merchaunt straunger & denyzen for all suche merchaundizes[1] commyng into that lande & goyng out of that lande / Excepte of the fremen of the cities of Dublyn & Waterford & the towne of Drgheda.

APPENDIX XXIII

Poynings' Parliament. Chapter XI. Act of Resumption

P.R.O. E 30, 1548, fols. 5–8

Resumpsions of lande into the kinges handes from the last day of kynge E the Second with previso for divers persones

Item prayne the commons in the consideracyon of the great & divers Roberies murders brennyng Ravisshing of wifes & maydens / the univer & dampnable extorcyon of coygn lyverey & paye / hadde usid & Continued wᵗin the power lande of Ireland wᵗ manẏ other Intollerable

---

[1] Carew MSS, 608, fol. 114, adds: "hides & wyne excepted". The summary ends with "a repeale of all graunt to all persons of any poundage to this tyme".

Oppressions and Extorcōns of the poore Innocentes and trewe Subiectes the whiche cannot be Reformid & punysheid w*out the kinges greate & Royall provȳsion for the Represseing of the same wch cannot be don w*oute greate costes & Charge / And forasmuche as his noble grace entendeith bȳ the grace of Allmygtie godde tordre and Reduce the saide lande to his hoole & perfȳt obeysūnce & the greate parte of his Revenus of the saide lande be dymynysheid and Graunteid unto diverse persons suche as for the moste parte doo ffully litill service for the Comen wealle for lack of the saide Revenus the lande coulde not be defendeid for the destruccōn of the Irishe Enȳmis / Therfor be it ordeined Enacteid and Establissheid bȳ Auctoritie of this present parlyam* that ther be Resumyd Seasid & Taken into the king o^r Soveraigne lorde handes all maner honoures maners lordshippes Castelles Garrisons ffortresseis Advousons of Churcheis ffrechaples Measeis¹ landes Tentes Rentes services mores medowes pastures woodes Rivers waters milnes dove-cottes parkes forestes warennes Custums Cockettes Fees fefermes Exempcons and all other maner profittes Inheritūnces and Commodities whereof o^r saide Soveraigne lord or any of his noble progenitors kinges of England was at any tȳme Seasid in Fee Simplle or Fee Taȳlle from the last daye of the Raigne of king Edwarde the II^de to this present Acte /

And by the same Auctorite Allmaner of feffem^tes Guȳftes in Taill Gruntes leaseis for terme of lyffe for terme of yeres Releaseis confirmacōns Annuyties ffees pensions Eschetes wreckes wayffes Revercōns of all and every of the foresaid honoures maners lordshippes and of all other as before it is specified or of any parcell of them aswell by Auctorite of parlyam* as by any lr̄es patentes made under the greate Seall of England or of Irland to any person or persons by what soever Name or Names theȳ be Namid Jointlȳ or Severallȳ from the saide daȳe be Resumid Revoked Adnulleid and demȳd voide & of none

¹ messuages.

205

Effect in the lawe / provideid allwaies that this Acte of Resumpcōn or any other Acte or Actes made or to be made or hadde in this present parliam[t] extende not nor in any wise be hurtfull and preiudiciall to the prior and convent of the house or monasterie of the hollie of[1] Dublin nor unto ther Successors as twicheing anny Graunte or Gruntes made bẏ oure Soveraigne lorde the King that nowe is or bẏ any of his progenitors late kinges of Englande unto the saide nowe prẏor and Convent or unto any of his predicessors late priors of the saide place and to ther Successer of any yerely Somes of moneẏ not being above the Some of XL merkes bẏ the yere to be hadde and perceẏveid to them & to ther Successors accordeing unto ther Severall Tenures of the same but onlẏ to be in Suspense at the kinges pleasir for & by the space of V yeres next Insuing to be Accompteid from the fyrste daẏe of the begynneing of the saide parliam[t] forewarde and after the saide V yeres finisheid the saide lr̄es patentes to stande goode and Effectuos in the lawe And that fromthensforthe the same prior & Convent perceive all suche yerelẏ Somes of moneẏ accordeing to the saide lr̄es patentes anẏ Acte or Actes made to the contrarẏe notwstanding

provideid allwaẏe that this Acte of Resumpcōn ne anẏ other Acte made in this present parliam[t] extende not ne in anẏ wise be preiudiciall or hurtfull unto the Reverend Father in godde Henrẏ Bisshoppe of Banger and prior of the house of o[r] lady of lantony in England for any of his possessions spūalls or Temporalls being in this lande of Ireland or any parte of them nor of the profites therof comeing nor for anẏ Grunt or Gruntes made unto hẏm or his predecessors by o[r] Soveraigne lorde the king or anẏ of his progenitors or predecessors kinges of England but that theẏ & every of them be as goode profiteable and Availleable to him as this Acte hadde not byn made /

[1] "of" scratched out. Carew MSS, 608, fol. 114 v., gives "prior and convent of Christchurch".

Provideid allwaẏe that the saide Acte of Resumpcon̄ extende not unto sir Jamẏs Ormounde knight of one Anuytie of XLli to be paide yerelẏ unto him bẏ ffrẏer Jamis Keteing late prior of Seint Johns Jhr̄m in Ireland and by his brother & under ther chapter Sealle /

It[1] like proviso made unto the saide sir James Ormounde of the custodie & wardship of the bodie & landes of Richard Birmẏngham Sonne & heẏre unto patrick Bermyngham & of all Lordshippes maners castelles landes Tēntes advousons of churcheis Rentes Anuyties knight-fees in the counties of meathe / kilkennẏ & Typparrie / and also of the kinges grunt made unto the saide sir James of thoffice of Constableship of the Castell of Lymeryk of his waẏes & Fees to be perceyved of anẏ of the kinges lands for thexcerciseing of the saide Office

A proviso that the saide Acte of Resumpcon̄ extende not unto sir peter Talbote of malahide knight and his heẏres of any graunte made by the king or any of his progenitors in tyme paste /

provideid also that the saide Acte of Resumptōn extende not to the Suffrain portreffeis[2] Burgessis and Commins of the Towne of kenleſ[3] in the countie of meathe for anẏ gruntes liberties ffrunchiseis Ratẏfi-cacōns privilegeis or confirmacōns geven or grunteid by the king or his progenitors

provideid also that the saide Acte be not preiudiciall unto Walter Archebisshoppe of dublin for his dygnitie of Archebisshopriche /

provideid also that the saide acte be not preiudiciall unto John Archebolde marcheall of the kinges courtes in Irlande in or for the same Office /

provideid also that the saide Acte Extende not unto Thoms Erlle of Ormounde ne unto his heyres Erlles of Ormounde for anẏ grunte made of ther Creacon[4] name stẏlle or dignitie of Erlle of Ormounde

---

[1] Item.   [2] portreeves.
[3] Kells.   [4] Creation.

provideid also that the saide Acte extende not to any gruntᵃes & l͞res
patentes bẏ the king or his progenitors unto sir Rouland Fitzewstace
knight lorde of portlestre or to anẏ of his Auncesters of anẏ heredytamᵗᵉˢ
grunteid to them and ther heires males or to ther heẏres for ever /

Provideid also that the saide Acte extende not unto the chorall vicars
of the cathedrall churche of Seint patrẏk in Irlande being of the kinges
fundac͞on nor to ther Successors as twicheing anẏ gruntᵃes or Con-
firmac͞ons made bẏ the king or his progenitors /

Provideid also that the saide Acte Extende not to the Baylifes Jures
and Comens of the Towne of dundalk for anẏ Gruntᵃes made unto
them or to anẏ of ther predecessoʳs by the king or his predecessors /

provideid that the saide Acte be not preiudicial to Edmunde piers
Sonne Lorde of dublin /¹

provideid that the saide Acte be not preiudiciall unto x͞rofer Bernewell and Elis his wiffe for the fferme of the lordship or manor of Ratouthe /

provideid that the saide Acte be not preiudiciall to any Gruntᵃes or
l͞res patentes made unto Geraʳde Fitzgerarde Erlle of kyldare /

provideid also that the saide Acte be not preiudiciall unto anẏ
gruntᵃe or gruntᵃes made by oʳ Soveraigne lorde the king to sẏr Edwarde
poyninges knight deputie to oʳ soveraigne lorde henrẏ Bysshȯp of
Banger / hughe Conwaye knight Tresaurer / Thoᵃms dourẏ² chief
Justice and dyverse others for any office ffee Rewaᵈ͞e /

provideid also that the saide Acte be not preiudiciall to anẏ gruntᵃe
or Gruntᵃes made bẏ the king or his progenitors unto the maẏre and
Comens of oʳ Citie of dublin of the Some of *LXIX li VIs VIIIð* of the
Feferme of the saide citie /

provideid that the saide Acte Extende not unto Thoᵃms Bouring
Chieff Justice of the kinges Benche for thes leasse of the manoʳ of
Clantarf whiche John Beket late helde /

¹ Error for "Dunboyne".   ² "Bowring."

provideid that the saide be not p*r*eiudiciall unto Thoᵐs Garthe for any grunt or grunt*es* made unto him bẏ the king under his greate Sealle /

provideid that the saide Acte be not p*r*eiudiciall unto the dean and Chaptre of the Cathedrall Churche of the blessed Trinite wᵗin the Citie of Wat*er*forde for a Grunte made unto them of one Annuẏtie of *XVIᵗi XIIJs IIIJd* to be p*er*ceiveid yerelẏ of the feferm of the saide Citie /

provideid that the said Acte Extende not unto the maẏre Baẏliffes and Citizens of the Citie of Wat*er*forde nor to ther Successors but that theẏ maẏe have and Inẏoie Allmaner ther lib*er*ties hereditamᵗᵉˢ and possessions /

provideid that the saide Acte Extende not unto william darcẏe of Rathewer Gentillmayne to his heẏres males of anẏ graunte made bẏ king Edwarde the IIJᵈᵉ at Noteingham the ixᵗʰ yere of his Raigne / To Joħn Darcẏe le cousẏn & Johan his wiffe and to ther heẏres malis of the manoʳ of Rathewere and Kyldalke and in the Grange of Rathewere /

provideid that the saide Acte Extende not unto wiłłiam darcẏe by king henry the IIIJᵗʰ to John darcie Esquier and to his heẏres males in & of the man*er*s of ¹ welston & Staunton / The manor of phillipiston Raynoldeston IJ measeis & viii ˣˣ acres of lande in balleregan Rathoplẏn & of other land*es* & Teñt*es* in Dundalke and loueth /

provideid that the saide Acte Extende not unto anẏ grunt*es* or l̄res patent*es* made bẏ oʳ Sov*er*aigne lorde the king or his p*r*ogenitors unto the monast*er*ie of oʳ Blessed² of Trẏm of anẏ land*es* grunteid unto the same for ever /

provideid that the saide Acte Extende not to anẏ l̄res patent*es* heretofore made unto the maẏre Sherif*es* Alderman & Comens of the Towne of drogheda of the Some of *XXXIII ᵗi VJs VIIJ ∂* yerely of the Feferm of the Same Towne /³

¹ The name of a manor is omited.　　　² "Lady" omitted.
³ Carew MSS, 608, adds: "the Lo of Dunboyne".

APPENDIX XXIV

Poynings' Parliament. Chapter XIV. An act for the cancelling of records done in the name of Edward VI (Lambert Simnel)

Lambeth, Carew MSS, 608, fol. 115

An act for the Cancellinge and revocation of all recordes, processe, pardons, or any such, done in the name of the pretenced kinge, Latlie Crowned in Irland. whosoever the be do receave the abovenamed ordinance Conceale or keepe the same they so doinge after the proclemation, shalbe adjudged traytors attaynted.

APPENDIX XXV

Poynings' Parliament. Chapters XV–XVIII. Concerning the Priory of St John of Jerusalem

P.R.O. E 30, 1548, fols. 11, 12

CHAPTER XV

No *person* to be lorde of Seint Johns Jhr̄m but of thenglyshe bloade.

Itm at the Supplicatòn of the Comens of the lande of Irlande that where as the hedde house & priorate of Seint John̄s Jhr̄m w⁴in the same lande hathe bẏn above all other houseis of Religion and foundeid & Endueid wᵗ possessions wherof agreate *parte* lẏe desolate & ben Alẏoned bẏ Evill dysposed priours ther etc Wherfor be it ordeynid and Enacteid that fromhensforthe_ he that shalle be made prior of the saide pryoratie of Seint John̄s Jhr̄m in Irlande bẏ the lorde mʳ of the Rodes shalbe a man of the englẏshe blode and haveing lyvelod bẏ the Religion wᵗin the Reallme of Englande /

CHAPTER XVI

ffor the lorde of Killmaẏne.

Itm̄ at the Supplication of *sir* John Kendall prior of Seint John̄s Jhr̄m w⁴in the Reallme of Englande in the Name of the lorde greate mʳ of the Rodes that where the same Religion w⁴in the lande of Irelande is Indueyd wᵗ manẏe & dyverse greate Lordshippes & other heredytam^{tes}

& possessions whiche have bẏn partelẏ Alyoned and Grunteid in ffees Anñuẏties & leaseis for terme of yeres terme of lyffe and some for ever / nothing Reserveing theruppon by sir Jamys Keteing[1] Intrused prẏor of Seint Joħns Jhr̄m̄ and one sir Thomas Talbot his predicessor to the utter dystrucc̄on of the same Religion /

It is ordeined and Enacteid that all suche Alẏenac̄ons shalbe voide whatsomever theẏ be and of none Effect. And that it shalbe lefull to the prior of the priorite in Irlande to Entre into the saide possessions and all other possessions wrongfullẏ wᵗholden by other persons and them to Inẏoine to the use of the saide Religion anẏthing to the Contrerye notwᵗstandeing

CHAPTER XVII

ffor the lorde of Seint Joħns.

Itm̄ at the lẏke Supplicac̄on of the saide sir John Kendall that where the sayde sir Jamẏs Keteing and other his predecessours have bẏ ther mysgovernaunce solde and layde to pledge a precious Relẏque a pece of the hollẏ Crosse and dyverse other Relyques & Juelles / yt is ordeyned that the same Relẏques & Juelles shalbe delyverid unto him that shalbe made prior by the grete mʳ of Rodis paẏing suche Somes of moneẏ wherfore the Same Juelles were solde and leide to pledge. /

CHAPTER XVIII

ffor the lorde of Kyllmaẏne.

Itm at the Supplicac̄on of the saide sir John Kendall for that that the saide sir Jamys Keteing dyverse tẏmes hathe presumẏd wᵗoute Thauctoritie of the greate mʳ of the Rodes wrongfullẏ to make and professe of the saide Religion dyverse persons of the saide lande and hathe gẏven unto them com̄aundymᵗᵉˢ belonging to the saide Religion to the greate hurt & damage of the saide Religion

It is Enacteid that he whiche shalbe made prior of the said prẏorite bẏ the greate mʳ of the Rodes and thassent of the king and his heyres shalle Compell all suche persons bereing thabbite of the saide Relẏgion tappere before them to shewe bẏ what Auctorytie theẏ be professed and made of the saide Religion and kepe the com̄maunders apperteyneing to the saide Religion / And if theẏ have noo Sufficient Tytlle to the pmisseis then to medill no further wᵗ thoccupat̄on therof uppon certen paẏn unto the tyme theẏ be lawfullẏ made / And that the deputie shalle ayde the prẏor duelẏ elect to the Reformac̄on of the premysseis /

[1] Sir James Keating was one of the few unpardoned supporters of Lambert Simnel.

APPENDIX XXVI

Poynings' Parliament. Chapter xxiv. Acquittance for Kildare and Sir James Ormond (Summary)

Lambeth, Carew MSS, 608, fol. 115

that the Erle of Kildare, Sr James of Ormond knight, & all persons adherant to them w^{t}hin this Land, shalbe Cleerlie acquited, of any action, sute, vexation or troble of any person, for murder, Roberie, or any offence, done in these querters.

APPENDIX XXVII

Poynings' Parliament. Chapter xxvi. The Treasurer to be Governor in the absence of the Deputy

P.R.O. E 30, 1548, fol. 10

That the Tresorer shalbe Gove*r*ner In thabsence of the deputie.

Itm the King o^r Sove*r*aigne Lorde considerith how is lande of Irland hathe bẏn oftentẏmes at ffẏnall destruccōn bẏ his Enẏmẏes and Rebelles for lacke of a Sufficient Gove*r*noure as when the lieutenunt or his deputie have dyed or Surrendered ther l̄res patent*es* of ther Auctorite and or that anẏ provẏsion coulde be hadde oute of this Reallme of Inglande considering that is a lande sepe*r*ate from Englande the saide lande hathe ben manẏ tymes in greate Juberdẏ / Wherfor o^r saide Sove*r*aigne lorde bẏ thassent of his lordes Spūall or Temp*or*all and the Comens in this p*r*esent p*ar*lyament Assemblyd and by thauctoritie of the same have ordeẏned enactid and Establẏsheid that whensoeve*r* at anẏ tẏme hereafter his said lande fortune to be voide for anẏ of the saide Causeis or for anẏ other cause That then The Tresorer of the saide lande for the tẏme being be Justice & Gove*r*noure of the saide lande at *every* suche Avoydaunce unto suche tẏme as the king sende his Auctorytie That is to saẏe the lieuten̄nt or deputẏe of his saide lande / And the saide Tresorer to defende the saide lande from Enẏmẏes or Rebelles surelẏ and See the kinges lawes duelẏ mẏnistred And that all other lr̄es patentes prescriptons & usage of theleccōn of Justice at every suche Avoydaunce be clerelẏ dampned Repelid and of none Effect /

APPENDIX XXVIII

Poynings' Parliament. Chapter XXVII. For discharge of annuities, coyne and livery granted by compulsion out of the marchlands

P.R.O. E 30, 1548, fol. 14

ffor discharge of annyties coygne & lyverey gunted[a] by compulsyon out of the marchelandes

Item thatt where the kynges Subiectes of this lande have been of longe tyme mysordered in defalte of Justice not onely by extorcyon called coygne or lyverey dayly exercysed aswell by suche persones as had the great auctoritie of the said lande / As by lordes & gentylmen of great power marchors & Rebelles of the same etc / And likewise where the coen[1] weale of the said lande was abused by extirpable custume that the kinges Subiectes having landes and Rentes within the marches & borders of the same / kould never enioye enẏ proffit therof / without so be that the said marchers shuld have the fferme of the said lande bering therfore suche Rente as shuld like them / Orels the said lande shuld be brente robbed and destroyed / by the fals & subtyll meanes of the said marchers / And so thesaid Subiectes disherẏted / wherby they be not able to kepe hospitalitie neither mayntaigne the kinges warres as their Auncettos[r] were wonte to doo / Wherfore the premisses consydered and forasmoche as all the forsaid Annuities fees rentes & leases were graunted at suche tyme as no ordre nor Justice was had within thesaid

[1] common.

213

lande / That it be ordeyned enacted and established by thauctoritie of this present parliament / that all and every suche Annuities ffees pensions and leases aswell for terme of lif / as for yeres / or otherwise graunted or yeven by any monastery had or made or compulsyon of any person to whom any suche gr^aunte was made or had afore this by any of thesaid Subiectes spūall or temporall to eny maner suche persone w^tin thesaid lande / be revoked repealed before or from the first yere of kinge Edward the IIIIth to this present tyme adnulled and demed voyde and of noon effecte in the lawe And by thesame auctoritie whatsoever persone will dystreyne or make any clayme or tytle to any suche title to any suche annuȳtie ffee pension or lease by reason wherof any persone spūall or temporall of the kinges subiectes shalbe troubled vexed hurte or disturbed in his persone goodes or landes / that they he or they that so shall offende this present Acte / and as often to forfaite / *xx li* / half therof to the kinge and the other half to the partie that will sue therfore by writ or bill in eny co^rte that the kinge hath in thesaid lande / Provyded alwaye that all the proffites whiche shall growe of the premisses by one hole yere next comyng by reason of the advoyding of any of thesaid grauntes or of eny of the premisses be paied within II monethes next after thesame yere to the kinges thresaurer of Ireland to the use of o^r Soveraign lorde the kinge towarde his charge borne for the common weale of the said lande /

APPENDIX XXIX

Poynings' Parliament. Chapter XXXI. A confirmation of an Act against Lollards and heretics. (Heading only)

P.R.O. E 30, 1548, fol. 17

Item that the Acte agaynst lollardes & heretikes be auctoryzed by this present parliament /

Poynings' Parliament. Chapter XXXIII. The Chancellor to have authority to continue and dissolve Parliament in the absence of the Deputy. (Heading only)

Lambeth, Carew MSS, 608, fol. 115 v.

That the chancellor shall have authoritie to Continew, adiourne, prorogue & dissolve this parlement, in the absence of the Lo. Deputie, & shall have Like authoritie for all things to be done therein, as if the Lo. Deputie were present.

APPENDIX XXX

Poynings' Parliament. Chapter XXXIV. Ditches to be made about the English Pale

P.R.O. E 30, 1548, fol. 18

diches to be made aboute the Inglishe pale /

Item prayn the commons that in consideracyon the marches of the iiii Shires be open & not fesible[1] in ffastnes of diches and castels / wher through Irishemen doo great hurtes by their oft Skulles[2] & making of prayes in the same / It be enacted by auctoritie of this present parliament that every Inhitaunt erthtyller & occupier in thesaid marches / that is to saye in the counties of dublyn from the watter of Anliffy to the Mountaign In Kyldare from the watter of Anliffy to Trym & soforthe into meth & Urill as the said marches been made & lymitted by one Acte of parliam[t] holden before the Reverend ffather in god William Bisshop of meth[3] doo buylde & make a double diche of vi foote of herth above the grounde at thende syde or parte of thesaid lande that he doth so occupie / which Juneth next unto Irishemen bitwixt this lammas next comyng / And the said diches so buylded & made / be kepte up & repayred aslonge as they shall occupie thesame lande upon payne of XLs by hym that shalbe fonde fawty in the premisses / And the lorde of thesaid lande / doo Allowe the olde Rent of the saide lande to the saide buylder and maker of the saide dicheis for one yere uppon the saide paynes / And that the Archebysshop of dublyn and Sheryf of the Countie of dublyn to be commissioners wardens Overseers and

---

[1] fencible.
[2] "skull" = iron helmet. Symbolical of "forays".
[3] William Sherwood, Deputy for George Duke of Clarence. Parliament of July 1475 or December 1476 to November 1477.

Executors of the premẏsses wᵗin the same Shẏre / et Alii comīssionarii Aliis Assignantʳ com /¹

And that aswell of this Ordynᵃunce as of the statute of musters for fencible waẏpẏn² and of wacheis before this ordeyned to be put in due Execucon bẏ Inquisicon or otherwẏse as ofte as theẏ or anẏ of them can thinke it expedient for the comen wealle & to make levie of the saide paẏnes so loste to be Imployẏed uppon the saide fastnes / And

over that the said commissioners to cause everẏ of theinhibytuntes of the said IIIIᵒʳ Sheres to make dycheis in the wastes or fasaghe landes wᵗoute the saide marcheis at suche tẏme and placeis as it shalbe thoughte moste expedient by the saide comīssioners etc.

APPENDIX XXXI

Poynings' Parliament. Chapter XLI. The Attainder of Gerald, Earl of Kildare

Lambeth, Carew MSS, 603, fol. 177

Decimo aᵒ R꜀ H VIIᵐˡ Edwardo Poyning milite Deputato apud Droheda.

Attayndor of yᵉ Erle of kyldare for tresene 41.

Item praying the Comyns of this land assembled in this present parlement that forasmuch as *Gerot fitz Thomas Erle of Kildare* for his greate and manifold tresens, Rebellions, confederacies, conceale-mentes & conspiracy late by him commytted and don, as pryvely to send messengers, and lettres missyves unto dyverse of the kinges Irish enemyes and English Rebellyons of this land to cause and provoke them to levye and mak warre and rebellyon against oʳ soveraigne Lord the King and Sʳ *Edward Poyninges knight the* kinges deputye of this Land of Irland, and over that faulsely and trayterously, in pryvye and secrete manner conveyed and sent his men and servantes, to conforte ayde and assist *O'Hanlan* the kinges Irishe Enemy, and to fight against the said Deputye, and over that conspired wᵗ the kinges Irish enemyes to have murdered and slayne the said Deputye in the said *O'Hanlons* countrey at the tyme of his being there, and also caused his brother *James* and other Rebelles to take by treson the kinges castell of Carlaugh, arrering and setting uppe apon the same his connysaunce and Standerds, wᶜʰ Castell was kepte and fortefyed wᵗ men and victualles in the name and by the commandement of the said Erle, untill such tyme as it was gotton by the greate wisdome and manhood of the said Deputye after his long and paynefull lying at the seige of the same. And over that contynually used and kepte openly *Quoyne and lyvery* in dyverse and many places of the Sheres grownde of this Land of Irland since his last arryving into this said land contrary to the

¹ comitatibus.   ² weapon.

estatutes[1] made and provided in that behalf w[t]in the said land, and
over that faulsely and trayteresly assented and agreed w̄ the kinges
great enemy the king of Scottes, to send to this Land a great Army of
Scottes, to ayde and fortefye the said Erle, and therle of Desmound to
destroy the said Deputye and the kinges true subiectes of this land, to
the utter subvercon and desolac̄on of the same. All w[c2] w[t3] dyverse and
many greate and horrible tresons, Rebellyons conceylementes and con-
spiraces by him don & commytted contrary to his faith and allegeance
be notoryously and openly knowne by due examynacon, and perfectly
understanden to all the Lordes of this land and comynes of the same.
wheresoever it be ordened and enacted by aucthoritye of this present
parlement by thole assent and agreeidment of the Lordes and com-
menes of the same that the said Erle of Kldare be adiudged and
demed traytor atteynted of highe treson, and doe forfeyte unto o[r] said
soveraigne Lord the king his life and all his castells, Lordshippes,
manies[4] landes, tenmentes rentes, services, and heredytamentes and
possessyons w̄ all the appertenaunces, whereof he or any other person
or persons to his use or behwe was seased the xth day of November.
the xth yer of o[r] soveraign Lord king Henry the VIIth. Provyded alway
that this Acte extend not, ne in anywise be preiudiciall unto any person
or persons, as touching any right tytle or interest that they or any of
them have in the said Castells, Lordshippes, manes,[4] londes tenntes, and
other premesses, whereof the said erle or any other to his use or behwe
was seased the said tenth day but that it shalbe lawfulle unto every
suche person or persons having right title and interest in any of the
said Castelles, Lordshippis, manes, landes, tenmentes, rentes, services
and other premisses to have ther entry in the same this present Acte
notw[t]standing.

APPENDIX XXXII

Poynings' Parliament. Chapter XLII. Attainder of James Fitzgerald and others. (Heading only)

P.R.O. E 30, 1548, fol. 22

coigne and lyverey

    Item one othere Acte of the Attayndre of James ffitz Thomas Gerald
& many other for divers Treasons ffelonies murdres Roberies In-
surreccions extorcyons coygnes lyvereys & other manyfold mysgovernaunce and Rebellyons committed & doon within this lande /

---

[1] Poynings' Parliament at Drogheda, chapters IV and XXXV.
[2] which.   [3] with.   [4] manors.

APPENDIX XXXIII

Poynings' Parliament. Chapter XLIII. Authority given to the Deputy and Council to examine allegations made by spiritual persons

P.R.O. E 30, 1548, fol. 22

Auctoritie given to the deputie & councell to examyn alyenacyons made by spūall persones

Item one Acte giving auctoritie unto the lieuten⁰nt or deputie & to the kinges counsaill to examyn all alienacyons guntes leases & all other writtinges made by divers prelates heddes & Rulers aswell Religious as other seculers of the churche of their possessions and livelode / And to give their fynall iudgement & determinacyon theron / Except of the Abbot of the monastery of oʳ lady beside dublyn /

APPENDIX XXXIV

Poynings' Parliament. Chapter XLIV. Authority given to the Chancellor for the ordering of annuities granted of spiritual possessions

P.R.O. E 30, 1548, fol. 22

Auctoritie given unto the chauncelloʳ for ordering of Annuyties gunted of Spūall possessions /

Item where it was late enacted ordeyned & establisshed by auctoritie of this present parliament that almaner of pensions & annuities late graunted by any man of the churche unto any persone or persones by compulsyon fere or manace shuld be utterly voyde & of noon effecte And to thentent to amplefye & enlarge thesaid Acte / Be it Ordeyned enacted & established by auctoritie of this present parliament that the chauncellor of this lande of Ireland for the tyme being / have full power & auctoritie as often as the case shall require at the sute of any persone to have advntage of the said estatute to awarde writte or writtes after his discrecyon agaynst suche as have the dede of any suche pension or annuities as is aforsaid / graunted and to have due examynacyon of thesame in the kinges chauncery And in the chauncery there to be cancelled and dampned /

APPENDIX XXXV

Poynings' Parliament. Chapter XLV. Restitution of spiritual possessions to the Church

P.R.O. E 30, 1548, fol. 22

Restytucyon of spūall possessions to the churche

Item one Acte of Restytucyon made to all Religious houses of suche possessions as been taken from them and yerely myscharged extorcyonously / by mighty men of this land of Ireland /

Item dyvers perticler actes at the petycyon of sundry persones

APPENDIX XXXVI

Poynings' Parliament. Chapters XLVI–XLIX

Lambeth, Carew MSS, 608, fol. 116

CHAPTER XLVI

An order for payment of 454[ll] to Tho: Garthe Esquier, for Certayne soldiers retayned by him, for the defence of the kings subiects.[1]

CHAPTER XLVII

A repeale of pensions, fees, graunts, and Leases, made by the Bishoppes of Ardmagh and Dublin, and the Archdeacon of Methe, to the Erle of kildare & others, named in the bill.

CHAPTER XLVIII

A resumption & revocation of all alienations, feofements, graunts, Leases, and Confirmations, made of any Lands, tenements, or hereditam[ts], belonginge to the house of st Johns beside waterford, frō the 9: yeare of kinge Hen. 6.

CHAPTER XLIX

An order for Richard Arnold of Dublin to have a quare impedit for a disturbance made to him, in a presentation made to the vickeradge of st Davids in the Naas, by reason of a graunte in the next avoydance made to him by the house of st Johns Jerusalem, in Irland, & that in the same quare impedit the incumbent or other defendant shall not aver that the church was full six months before the writt sued.

---

[1] Extract from Gilbert's *Viceroys*, p. 610: "Poynings' Parliament voted a benevolence, for the contribution of £454 to Captain Thomas Garth, for the service of his soldiers, as, during a year, he had kept them together for the defence of the country when they were about to disband and go to England. Rot. Stat. Hib. 10 Henry VII, no. 46".

APPENDIX XXXVII

Instructions to Richmond Herald, March 5, 1494/5

B.M. Cotton, Caligula, D vi, fols. 26–26 v.

H R

Advertissement a Richemont de ce quil Remonstrera oultre ses Instructions au cardinal de Sainct Malo / de par le Roy.

Luy dira come le Roy[1] a este aucunement adverti que le Roy descosse entend se mettre endevoir de faire ceste annee quelque destourbice au Roy.[1] si bonnement faire le peult. Mais le Roy enRicus ne le crainct ne doubte.

Toutesfoiz pource que aucune ouverture aeste faicte pardela par aucuns gentlizhommes de france: a messire charles Sommerset. lequel le Roy[1] avoit puisnaguaires envoye en ambassade pardevers le Roy son bon frere et cousin[2] / que si ledit Roy descosse vouloit monnoir guerre alencontre du Roy[1] / et le Roy[2] leur maistre leur vouloir donn[er][3] congie. Ilz ameneroient au Roy[1] / le filz du duc dalbanye qui est pardela / pour sen servir alencontre dudit Roy descosse. /

Surquoy le Roy nostre seigneur adonne commandement audit Richemont den parler audit cardinal de sainct malo. et pareillement a mons[ire] dorleans[4]. pourtant quil en a porte parolles aux messire charles. /

Et dira comme le Roy[1] leur prye bien affectuesement. veu et consider[e] que ledit Roy descosse se delibere de donner et faire ennmy au Roy[1] n[re sr] quilz veullent estre moiens. envers le Roy.[2] sondit bon frere etcousin[ ] ledit jeune filz[5] luy[1] puisse estre envoye / et en ce faisant le Roy[ ] etcousin luy fera ung tres grant plaisir / et se tiendroit gran[ ] atenu aluy / Car comme lesdits sires bien lentendent. Il nya au[cun] prince venant. qui luy[5] puisse mieulx aider. a Recouvrer ce qu[e par] droit luy appartient en escosse / que seroit le Roy nostre dit seigneur [ ] faulte le Roy. le traictera bien et favourablement comme [ ] a son estat / et tellement que le Roy[2] sondit bon frere etcou[sin] qui seront causes de lenvoyer / se tiendront pour conten[tez]

[ ] ledit Richemont saura dudit cardinal de sainct [malo] [ ] quil parle de ceste matiere audit bon fr[ere le] Roy.[2] delapart du Roy nostredit seigneur. et selon son advis etconse[il] Richemont se gouvernera. / Et dela Response que luy [en] sera faicte tant du Roy que desdits sires et comme Il les tr[ouvera] disposez en ce / en advertera le Roy nostre dit seigneur en toute dillig[ence] a luy possible.

H R
de Meautis

[1] Henry VII.   [2] Charles VIII.
[3] The right bottom corner of the page is torn off and the letters in square brackets are conjectural.
[4] Louis, Duke of Orleans.   [5] The Duke of Albany.

APPENDIX XXXVIII

Indenture between Dr Richard Hatton, Maurice, Earl of Desmond, and the Mayor, Bailiffs and Council of Cork, March 12, 1495/6

P.R.O. E 101, 248/19

Thes endent^{r}e trypartid mad atte yoghylle the xii^t daye of Marce the yer of our lorde M iiii^c Lxxxxv betwen maister Richard hatton the ryghte worshipfulle and reverente clerke and Doctoure yn the bede^1 lawes Comissary depute and true attorney un to the moste excellent and dredfull prynce henrye the VII^t be the grace of god kynge of Englande and of fraunce and lorde of Irlande the tryw and feithfull Subiets and s*irvau*nte to our said sove*r*ayn lorde Moryce Erle of dessemond the mayr Ballyf^9 and Consaylle of hise cite of Corke yne Irland wittenessethe thate the said Erle haw delyverede his sone and heir James fytzmoryce of the Geraldynes to the handes of the said mayr and Ballyf^9 and Consayll nowe and hieraftere beynge w^t thus condyc$\overline{\text{on}}$e that yf our said Soverayne lorde kynge henr the VII^t withyne ii yer nexte folowenge graunte une to the saide Moryce Erle of dessemond atte his humble desyr and requeste iiii petic$\overline{\text{on}}$es ase hier folowethe The furst petic$\overline{\text{on}}$e is that hit shalle please our said Soverayn lorde of hise grete and bountewes grace to send home therle of kyldar to his inherytaunce The second petic$\overline{\text{on}}$e is that our said Soverayn lorde shalbe as good and as gracyouxe lord to graunte and to yewe *every* thynge un to the said Erle of dessemond and all hise as kyng Edward the IIII^t and othere kyng*es* of Englande progenitor*es* to thus our said Soverayne lorde haw bene yne tymes paste to the said Erle and his Auncestrese and all hise The tird petic$\overline{\text{on}}$ is thate the said Erle of dessemond shall note be compelled to come to noe parlemente nethere gr*au*nd Consaille in Irlande but ate his pleasur^t The iiii

---

^{1} "both" laws, Canon and Civil. "bede" is an old High German form, said in the *N.E.D.* not to occur in English.

peticon̄ is that hite shalle please our said Soverayne lord of his noble grace to graunte the said Erle that his offices of deputacon̄e nor lieutenaunship be note grauntene to none of the said Erle is ennemyese nethere to the frendes of his ennemyes bute toe indefferent officerse these peticon̄es obteyned thate thene the Mayr ballyf⁹ and Consaylle of Cork for the tyme beynge shalle kype the said sone of the said Erle surlye sauffullye and feythfully to our said Soverayne lord the kynge ise behouff fore terme of iii yer nexte folowenge the date of thus present wrytenge without hit shalle please the kynge is good grace withyn the meane tyme toe commaunde hyme to be delyvered to the said Erle of kyldar the whiche thynge the said mayr ballyf and Consaylle fore the tym beynge shall doe withoute dissimulacon̄ or dylaye yf they shalbe soe commaundethe and yf our said Soverayne lorde graunte note the aforsaid peticon̄es be the ii yer abowlymited next folowenge aftere the date of thus present wrytenge to the said Erle of dessemond thate then aftere the terme of the said ii yer and note afore hite be lafulle to the said mayr ballyf⁹ and Conseylle of the said Cite of Corke for the tyme beynge And aswelle theye byndeth them to delyver his said sone and heir un to thesaide Erle of dessemonde without dissimulacon̄e dylaẏe condicon̄e or contradiccon̄e the promiss notwistandenge In testemon of the same the said parties to thus present endentʳes hath leyd their Sealles yewene the daye yer and place aforsaide &c⁹ And overe thus the said mayre ballyf⁹ and conseyll now beyng present and hir subscribed for the performacon̄ of the promiss to their peer hath mad their solempn̄ otte be the holy sacrament and the holy evangelist hir present be them and every of them bodly touchede

John Lawallyn mayr off cork¹   Jhn Cyragh balyff   Gorrad Cowllys
    ballyff¹   Edmōd goulld

¹ Seal appended.

[On the back]

Providet alweys that yf the second & the tred withynvrytene peticōnes be not graunten be oure Soverayn said lorde wᵗ his *lett*res patentes withene twelf moneth aftere the date of thus *pr*esent wryteng to the said Erle of dessemond that thene hit be lafull to the said mayr ballyf & Consaylle of the Cite of Corke for the tyme beynge to delyv*er* his said sone & heir to the said Erle of dessemond Also yf the kyng is good grace Depute lieuten*au*nt other anye of them other anye other yn their name or comaundemente be their agreament trouble other vexe wᵗ werre notoriouslye the saide Erle of dessemond withyne the III yer after the date of thus *pr*esent writenge that then the said mair ballyf⁹ & Consaylle for the tyme beynge shalle delyv*er* the said sone un to the said Erle Also & when therle of kyldarr shall recew the said sone of the forsaid Erle of dessemond that then he shall fynde sufficyent surte to the said Erle of dessemond to delyv*er* hym his said sone aftere III yer as it is withynwrytene without the said Erle of dessemond notoriously contrary to his allegeaunce Asswell the said mayr of Corke ballyff⁹ & consayll fore the tyme beynge after III yer as abowwrytene shall delyv*er* the said sone to the said Erle of dessemond and there be none other lyv*er*e of the said sone unles the said Erle of dessemond notoriously rebell contrary to his allegeaunce &c⁹

APPENDIX XXXIX

Oath of allegiance of Maurice, Earl of Desmond, to Henry VII, March 15, 1495/6

P.R.O. E 30, 1667

To all tho to whom this *pr*esent writinge connth¹ Morice ffiz Thom*as* of the Geraldines Erle of Desmond sendith gretinge in oʳ lord god *ev*erlastinge. And wher as the moost dradfull and Excellent prince and my sov*er*ainge lord henri the VIIth by the grace of god kinge of

¹ "concerneth" with the abbreviation mark omitted.

England & of ffraunce and lord of Irland of his gret bontwius & superhabundant pite and moost spāll grace have withsauf to send me his gracioux *lett*res paten*tes* of *per*don for all man*er* offen*ces* com*m*itted agains his grace for this tym in to the dat⁹ of this *present* writinge to be deliv*er*it by the hand*es* of the full wise and worshipfull clerke Maist*er* Richard hatton Docture of the both lawes and Chaplian unto my said soverayn lord & his true and ondoubted Comissari proct*er* and spāll messag*ere* to thus pourpos made constitut ordeined and deputted with that furst to make mȳn othe of alegiaunce trowth feaute & due obesiaunce in the fo*r*m that folowith. know ye me the forsaid morice Erle afor the said maist*er* Richard hatton Comissari of my said moost dradfull soverayn lord. And afor all other withnissh her to subscribite.¹ to have made my feaunte & due alegia*u*nce for ev*er*more in this fo*r*me that folowith. I thesaid Morice shalbe feithfull and true liegeman feith & trowth shall ber to the kinge my sov*er*ayn lord henry by the grace of god kinge of England and of ffrau*n*ce and lord of Irland of this nam the VIIth. And to the heiris of his body lawfulle begotten king*es* of England Item I shall not do ne attempt nor as fer as shall ley in my poware suffre to be dōn or attemptted any thinge that in any man*er* of wise may be dishono*r*able hurthfull or *pre*iudiciall unto my said soverayn lord*es* *per*son his said heires lieutena*u*nt or depute of Irland. And if I shall here see other know any sich thinge be any man*er* *per*son or *per*sons of what condiciōn soev*er* he or they be / don ymagened or attempted to be dōn to the dishono*r* hurte or *pre*iudice of my said soverayn lord*es* persoñ his said heiris lieutena*u*nt or depute I shall let it to my power. And if I may not conveniently so do I shall in all hast posseble shew it to them or to oon of them not sparinge so to do for iop*er*tie of my *per*son lost*es* of my good*es* fav*ere* or affecciōn otthe or promes made to the oontrary or any other cause what soev*er* it be.

Item I shall well and truly to my powere convenient in werre & in peace s*er*ve my said soverayn lord his said heires his said lieutena*u*nt and depute agains all erthly creat*ers* making rebelliōn werre or *partie* agains them or any of them. Itm I shall not recew nor to my knolegh & power suffer to be recewed nor to abyd w^tin any Town² or place beinge undre my power rule auctorite or jurisdiccon any of my said soverayn lord*es* Rebell*es* traiters³ or Ennemieis of what estat nacōn or condiciōn soev*er* ther be nor unto them or any of them yew myn Aid favo*re* succor conseill comerike⁴ licence pasport or saufcondith and if any sich heraft*er* come w^t in any lordship Town Cite Contrei or place beinge undre my rule auctorite or jurisdiccon. I shall at all tymes be redy w^t my power to resist & subdue all sich Rebell*es* & Ennemies of o^r said soverayn lord. Item I shall not make non ensurrecciōns ne gadringe of no people agains non of the king*es* subiect*es* ne I shall not brent ne wast onles it be in the sut of my right or in the deffence of the same aft*er* the Costum of this the king*es* land of Irland. Item I shall execut all sich land*es* & fees or offic*es* to be grantten to me by my said soverayn

¹ " know me " omitted.   ² Written " Cown ".   ³ Written "craiters ".
⁴ Irish word, meaning " assistance in fighting ".

lord accordinge to his pleasure and w^t sich condiciōns therintto anexth. Itm I shall truly content my said sove*r*ain lord for myn anheritau*n*ce as duly & as largle as myn Auncesteris hav don unto his noble p*r*e-genito*r*s. Ite*m* wher I have delive*r*it my soon and heire James fiz morice of the Geraldines in to the hand*es* of John Lawalȳn now maire of the Cite of Corke John Crewagh & Gerald Gould*es* Baliff*es* and the Conseill of the said Cite now beinge & he*r*after accordinge to the teno^r & effect of the endent^r try-pa*r*tted made betwen thesaid maist*er* Richard hatton Comissarie & depute to my said sove*r*ayn lord the said maire Baliff*es* and Conseill of Corke & me. And I shall not withdraw him by any craft subtilltie or engen directly or indirectle oppenly other p*r*ivele or cause h*i*m to be w^t drawen out of the same Cite duringe thesaid tym as is in the sam endent^r comprisshed. And if my said soon he*r*after be w^t drawen out of thesaid Cite or kepinge be it be means of himself or any other p*er*sons. I shall in all hast possible upon notice & knolegh had of the same cause him to be restored unto the said Cite and kepinge therto abyd accordinge to the teno^r & effect of the forsaid Endent^{r}es all which p*r*omisses & eve*r*y of them I shall well & truly do & kep so help me god & all Saint*es* and by the holy Sacrament of thaut*er* here beinge p*r*esent thes holy Euangiliste*s* the Canon of the masse & thes holy releke*s* be me bodly tuchit sumittinge me my land*es* and lord-shipis to ent*er*dictō*n* and to all other pañis and censurs of holy Church in case be I obse*r*ve not the p*r*omisses. In withnissh whereof I have made my name to be subsc*r*ibit to this p*r*esent*es* And to it set my seale of Armes. In the presence of theise witness her sbsc*r*ibed w^t ther owne hand*es* yewene at Yoghull in the quier of the fre*r*es minor*es* of ob-se*r*vau*n*te the xv day of marte the XI yer of oure sayd sove*r*ayn lord

Morr Erll of dessond Joħn fyzgyrod^1 Wllm̄s onellayn gar^9 fra m^{9}or^2 dryscll^3 Donat^9 arcm̄t mc^{ne} doctor^4 Morr the lorde Roche^5 John Lawallyn mayr off Corke^6 Johñ Whythe mayr of yoghull Moîyc Roche m̄ philipp^9 Ronan officialis epi^9 Cork et Clonens^7

---

^{1} Master John Fitz-Gerard of Desmond. Pardoned on August 26, 1496. (*Cal. Pat. Rolls*, 1494–1509, p. 76.)

^{2} William Onellan, Guardian of Youghall Friary where the document was signed.

^{3} O'Driscoll of Baltimore in the south part of Cork. ("State of Ireland", *State Papers, Henry VIII*, II, pt III, p. 3.)

^{4} Donatus? doctor of medicine. "arcm̄t" uncertain.

^{5} Son-in-law of Desmond. He was Sheriff of Cork in 1488 (*Cal. Pat. Rolls*, 1485–94, p. 232), pardoned on August 26, 1496 (*ibid.* 1494–1509, p. 76).

^{6} Mentioned in Perkin's confession.

^{7} Magister Philippus Ronan, Chancellor of the Bishop of Cork and Cloyne·

APPENDIX XL

Indenture between the Earl of Kildare, Walter, Archbishop of Dublin, Thomas, Earl of Ormond, and Sir James Ormond, made in the presence of the King and Council, August 6, 1496

P.R.O. E 101, 248/18

This indenture tripartit made at Sar*um* the VIth day of August the XIth yer of the Reigne: of o^r souv*er*ain lord King henrẏ the VIIth king of England and of ffraunce and Lord of Irland wittenesseth that it is aggreed and assuredly promysed and also solempnely sworn upon the holy Ev*an*gelyes afor and in the pr*e*sence of o^r said souv*er*ain lord and his honorable Counsaill by Waltur Archebisshop of Develyn Thomas Erle of Ormond and s*ir* James Ormond his nevoo. on that oon p*ar*tie. / And Gerald fitz Gerald Erle of kyldare on that othre p*ar*tie. That where of long tyme by the great and haynoux discord discencion and variaunce. that have be bitwix thies ii noble blod*es* of the land of Irland called Botellers and Geraldynes / hath ensued aswele great hurt. and damag*es* to the weale publique of that land as to theim self for thappesing thereof / And for a p*er*petuell and a more assured amytye concorde and love to be had and contynued betwix thesaid blod*es* that they and ev*er*y of theim for theim self shall remytte and frelẏ forgeve and by thies pr*e*sent*es* remytteth and frely forgeveth to the othre p*ar*tie his frend*es* allyes serv*an*t*es* adherentes and p*ar*ty takers being the king*es* obeissaunt subgiett*es* and also Irisshmen which take p*ar*te w^t thesaid s*ir* James in the king*es* service without thesaid Irysshmen gyve occasion from hensforth to be werred upon alle man*er* of Ranco^re malic*es* slaunders evill will*es* discord*es* discencions robbories brennyng*es* Iniuries maymes manslaught*er*s and alman*er* offenses doon by theim or anẏ of theim before the date of thies pr*e*sent*es* for any man*er* of cause or occasion happened betwix theim or anẏ of theim / Action of dett and plee of land alway except / And ov*er* that thesaid p*ar*ties and eithre of theim shall induce procure cause and endevo^r asmoche as in theim and ev*er*y of theim is. without fraude or dissimulac*on* to thuttermost of theire powers that theire kynnesmen. frend*es* alyes serv*an*tes adherent*es* and p*ar*ty takrs shall remytte and frely forgeve. to the othr p*ar*tie his frend*es* alyes serv*an*tes adherent*es* and p*ar*tytakrs as above reherced alman*er* Ranco^rs malic*es* slawnders evil willes discord*es* discencions robboryes brennyng*es* maymes manslaughters and alman*er* offenses d*oo*n by theim or any of theim before the date of thies present*es* for any man*er* of cause. or occasion happened betwene theim or any of theim. And ov*er* that thesaid Archebisshop Therle of kyldare and s*ir* James Ormond have promysed and by thies pr*e*sent*es* promytte that they and

226

every of theim shalbe faithfull true and obedient subgiettes to the said most drad souverain Lord the king and his heires. kinges of England. And also true and obedient to his lieutenantes depudie or other his officers in their Rowmes and degrees for the tyme being in his said land of Irland And his highnesse his lawes truely obeye serve and execute according to the duetie of theire alligeaunce fully and holly to the best of theire powers for the defense of that his land and good rule of thesame. / And also the said Archebisshop Therle of kildare and sir James Ormond and every of theim have faithfully promysed and by thies presentes promytten that they and every of theim to thuttermost of their power withoute fraude or dissimulacion shall induce and procure theire kynnesmen frendes alyes servauntes adherentes and party takrs to be true and obedient subgiettes to the said most drad soverain lord the king and his heires kinges of England And to be obedient to his lieutenant deputie. and other his officers in their Rowmes and degrees for the tyme being in his said land of Irland & his highnesse his lawes truely obeye and serve according to the duetye of their alligeaunces fully and holly to the best of every of theire powers. for the defense of that his land and good rule of thesame. And also eithre of the said parties have faithfully promysed and by thies presentes promytten that they shalbe within theim self loving amyable frendly and concordable. eithre of theim to othre and pursue the cause and norisshing of love by amyable and familier conversacion and good company as in commonyng Counsailling aiding and assisting eithre to othre for the defense of theire said souverain lordes right. mayntenyng of his lawes. and encreas of the Comon weale. of his true subgiettes within his said land of Irland without any fraude colour or dissimulacion and to the repressing of his Englisshe and Irisshe Rebelles and othr disobeisaunt subgiettes abiding commyng and going to fro or wᵗin the said land of Irland. Item where oure said souverain lord the king by thadvise of his most honorable Counsaill hath made and ordeyned thesaid Erle of kildar to be deputie / and to have the rule and gouvernaunce of his land of Irland undernethe his derebeloved Son henry duc of york and lieutenant of the said land And where also divers of oure said souverain lordes subgiettes dwelling within thesaid land of Irland have alwaie been true and faithfull unto his highnes and alwaies taken his parte and quarell according to their duetie and ligeaunce. aswele in tymes of trouble as in tymes of peax whoes faithfull and true service the kinges highnesse thankfully remembreth. and bereth in mynde / Thesaid Erle of kyldare faithfully promyseth to oᵗ said souverain lord the king that he shall bere and owe his love and lawefull favoᵗ to every of thesaid kinges subgiettes whiche before this tyme have so taken his parte and quarell. And over that the same Erle frely remytteth and forgyveth and also to the best of his power without any fraude or dissimulacion shall induce and procure his frendes allyes servauntes and partetakrs to releasse and forgyve to every of oure said souverain lord the kinges subgiettes which befor this tyme have take his parte and quarell almaner Rancoᵗs malices. slaunders evill willes

discordes discencions Robbories brennynges Iniuryes maymes manslaughters and offenses. doon by theim or any of theim before the date
of thies presentes. Dette and title of land alway except And over that the
same Erle of kyldar faithfully hath promysed and by thies presentes
promytteth befor oure said souverain lord the king and his said Counsaill
that he shall never trouble vexe ne inquiete ne cause to be troubled
vexed ne inquieted by colo* of his office or otherwise any of oure said
souverain lordes subgiettes. which afore this tyme have taken his parte
and quarell ne the frendes alyes servauntes adherentes ne partetakrs of
the said Erle shal in any wise trouble. vex ne inquiete. ne cause to be
troubled vexed ne inquieted any of the said kinges subgiettes within
the said land of Irland. if the said Erle in any wise may lette it. for any
robbory brennẏng of houses Iniuries slaunders maymes manslaughters
or any other offenses doon by any of the kinges said subgettes to the
said Erle his frendes alyes servauntes and partetakers. befor the date of
thies presentes / Dette and title of land alwaies except / Item the said
Erle promiseth not oonly to remytte and forgeve to suche the king o*
souverain lordes subgiettes as have served hym truely and taken his
parte and quarell according to their duetie but also remytteth and
forgyveth to alle his true and obeisaunt subgiettes within his said land
of Irland and other as above / and also to the best of his power w*out
fraude or dissimulacion shall induce procure and cause his frendes
alyes servantes adherentes and partetakrs to release and forgyve to
every of the said subgiettes and othr as above / alle maner of Ranco*s.
malices. slaunders evill willes discordes discencions. robbories. brennynges. Iniuries. maymes manslaughters and almaner offenses doon by
theim or eny of theim before the date of thies presentes / Dette and title
of land alwayes except / Item that for no light or sinistre report made
by any of their oervauntes or other sounding to any debate displeasir
or dishono* of the said Archebisshop Erles. sir James. or any of theim
they ne noon of theim shalbe light to gif credence nor hasty to
revenge their cause or quarell. but furst frendly to commen of the
same report within theim silf / and endevo* theim for the appeasing
thereof / And if thei can not aggre and determyne the matier then to
shewe it to the kinges grace / And they to procede no further in the
said matier to the revenging of their causes and debates. unto the tyme
they knowe the kinges pleasure in the same. In wittenesse whereof to
the oon partie of thies indentures tripartited with oure said souverain
lord the king remayning aswele Tharchebisshop Therle of Ormond
and sir James Ormond as the said Erle of kildare severally have putte
theire seales and signe manuelles. And to the other parte thereof with
thesaid archebisshop Therle of Ormond and sir James Ormond re-
maynyng thesaid Erle of kyldare hath sette his seal and signe manuell.
And to the thirde parte thereof with the said Erle of kyldare re-
maynyng Thesaid archebisshop Therle of Ormond and sir James
Ormond severally have sette theire seales and signe manuelles Yeven
the day and yere abovesaid In the presence of the kinges honorable
Counsaill. In wittenesse whereof also every of the said kinges Coun-

saill then being present to every partie of thies indentures severally
have sette their signe manuelles.

Walterus dublin̄   T. Ormond   G E of K   Sr James Ormond kᵣ
Archēpiūs

Thomas Roffen henrͦ Bangorensis giles daubney   Robt Wylughby
   Reynold Bray Thomᵃs Lovell Robtus Middleton Hatton Johnes
   kyngesmyll

APPENDIX XLI

A Note on the composition of Henry VII's Council

The previous tripartite indenture is the only document known to me
attested by members of Henry VII's Council in meeting assembled.
The form of attestation is unusual, although two instances have been
noted in the reign of Henry VI, and the whole Council signed the
secret articles devised as a basis for the marriage treaty between
Queen Mary and Philip of Spain.[2]

The records of Council meetings in the nine surviving manuscripts[3] consisting of copies of extracts from the lost Book of Entries
of Henry VII's Council, deal with 107 Council meetings for the
reign. The personnel is recorded in the case of 46 of these, and
averaged from 6 to 10 councillors at each meeting.

I have collected the names of 172 of Henry VII's councillors,
chiefly from these nine manuscripts[3] and from the Calendar of Patent
Rolls. Twelve of them are the names of councillors, said to have sat
in the Court of Requests, who are not mentioned as attending
meetings of the Council. Fourteen other non-recurring names are
given as councillors by Polydore Vergil. The remaining 146 names all
occur among the recorded attendances at one or more of the 46
Council meetings.

Savage, Bishop of Rochester, Sir Reginald Bray and Sir Thomas
Lovell, the King's most trusted advisers in all affairs of state (whom
he chose to figure with himself, his Queen and the Prince of Wales,
in the stained glass window erected by him at Malvern Abbey in 1502),
appear to have attended a large proportion of all the meetings held in
their respective life-times. The fluctuating membership consisted

---

[1] This signature, though peculiar in form, was Sir James Ormond's own.
It can be compared with that in Cotton, Titus, B XI, vol. 1, fol. 52. See
Appendix V. The seals of the Archbishop, Kildare and James Ormond are
appended. That of the Earl of Ormond has disappeared.

[2] Laboree and Moody, "The Seal of the Privy Council", *E.H.R.* XLIII, 192.

[3] B.M. Harl. MS, 297, art. 1; 305, art. 2; 6811, art. 2; 980, art. 137.
B.M. Add. MSS, 4521, art. 9. B.M. Hargrave, 216, art. 23. B.M. Lansdowne,
160, art. 92; 160, p. 307; 83, art. 72. See Scofield, *Star Chamber*.

partly of councillors called in for special knowledge of the business of the meeting, as, in this instance, Henry Deane, the Bishop of Bangor, ex-Deputy of Ireland, and Richard Hatton, Henry VII's envoy to the Earl of Desmond. Giles Daubeney, the Chamberlain, and Robert Willoughby de Broke, the Lord Steward, were mentioned by Polydore Vergil as of the inner ring of councillors. Robert Middleton and Kingsmill were eminent representatives of the law, only occasionally mentioned at meetings of the Council, although they frequently sat in the Court of Requests.

APPENDIX XLII

Articles sworn to by the Earl of Kildare in the presence of the King and Council before his return to Ireland as Deputy, August 1496

P.R.O. E 101, 248/20

H R Here foloweth. tharticules Whiche Therle of Kyldare in the presence of his moste drad souverain lord the King. and his Counsaill. faithefully hath promysed / and also solemplye sworn uppon the holy Evangelies to observe kepe and execute Within the kinges land of Irland.

First the said Erle of Kyldar shal not somon eny parliament to be holden and kepte. or eny suche hold and kepe w'in the said land of Irland befor that same Erle have shewed unto the kinges highnesse. or to his heires kinges of England the cauoeo and consideracons of the kepyng and holding of the same parliament. and the kinges speciall licence or of his heires undr writing and grete Seall of England befor the holding and keping therof be had and obteyned by the said Erle.

Itm the said Erle shal not cause any Acte to be made in any parliament to bee holden w'in the said land of Irland. but suche Actes as the kinges highnes shal licence. undr his said Seal. to bee med in the same parliament.

Itm the said Erle. hath also feithfully promysed. that yf any of the kinges subgettes contrarie to his naturall alligeaunce. offende in treason or rebellion. and soo advoided this his lande of England or othr parties into his lande of Irland. and that so to the said Erle knowen and understande. he shal endevoir hym to the best of his power. to take hym or theim. and to comitte to warde. ther to remaigne w'out baille or maynprise till the kinges pleasyr bee knowen.

Itm the said Erle hath also feithefully promised that yf the kinges highnesse sende for eny Rebell or Traitour being w'in the said lande of Irland to appere or come into this his land of England or to any othr place undr the kinges obeyssaunce. the same Erle of kyldar shal endevoir hym self to the uttermoste of his power. to take eny of the same Rebelles and Traito^rs so sende fore and to sende theim according to the king*es* com*m*aundement. Any statute or pretensed Custume in the said land of Irland notw^tstanding. And in caas that Therle of Desmont or any man*er* of man w^tin the said land of Irland of whate estate or condicō̄ he bee Rebell or offende his grace contrarie to his trouth duetie and liegeaunce ther. that then setting aparte alle consanguinitie. alle affinitie. and alle othr favours and pnalities he shal put hẏm in his uttremoste devoir w^tout any man*er* of colo^r or dissymulacō̄ to subdue and represse theim. be he of the Englishe Irysshe or of the wilde Irysshe or com̄en theder out of any othr place or countrey. And yf any Estraungiers Scott*es* ffrenshemen or othres wold invade the said lande. he shall defende the same against theim to the best of his powr and kepe the said land alwaies in due obeissaunce of the king and of his said heires Soo helpe hẏm god and halydome and by the holy Ev*a*ngelies.

Itm yf the king*es* highnesse for eny man*er* of cause or consideracō̄ by his writte or l*ett*res. com*m*aunde eny man*er* personne being w^tin the said lande of Irland. to come and appere aftor his grace in England or in eny othr place of his obeyssaunce. the same personnes shal not excuse theim self of their noon apparaunce by cause they bee born or dwelling w^tin the said land of Irland. but the same personnes notw^tstanding any Acte statute or custume had or made w^tin the said land of Irland shal come and appere according to the king*es* com*m*aundement. And yf the said personnes refuse soo to do w^tout lawfull Impediment. as sykenes or othr Jeoperdies of life. The said Erle of kyldare feithefully pro*m*yseth that he shal endevoir hym self. to the uttremoste of his pour. to take the same personnes soo disoubeẏing and send theim to the king according to his com*m*aundement.

Itm the said Erle of kyldare now deputie shall endevoir hym self to the best of his powr. that the statut*es* of and against proviso^rs by auctoritie of p*ar*liament & allowed in Irland bee duely put in execucō̄ And that he bare lawfull favo^rs and maẏnteyne the univ*er*sall Churche. of the same land of Irland & the lib*er*ties of the same in the best wise that he can to the pleasyr of god repressyng of vices encreasyng of vertue. and the com*m*en wele of that lande

G E of K

Itm wher as our said souv*er*ain lord the king hath made the said Erle of kyldare deputie of his land of Irland. and also caused the ladẏ Elizabeth saint John his nighe kynnesvom̄ā and of his noble blodde to be maryed to the said Erle. and w^t her mariage among*es* othr thing*es* hath geven to the said Erle land*es* and t̄ent̄es to the yerely valo^r of cc marc^9 above alle charg*es*. Wherof land*es* and tenement*es* to the yerely value of c marc^9 bee assigned and appointed w^tin his Realme of England and the residue w^tin his lande of Irland. and wher his good grace hath also geven & paied to the said Erle of kyldare for the said mariage. v c marc^9 sterling. the said Erle of kyldare for the performaunce and in consideracon of the pro*m*isses graunteth. pro*m*yseth &

a

convenntteth to & with oʳ said souverain lord the king that the same Erle his heires or feoffees befor the fest of Nativitie of saint John Bapte next ensuying shal make or cause to bee made a sure sufficient & lawfull estate of landes & tentes to the yerely value of ccli above alle charges wᵗin the said land of Irland. to the said Elizabeth. to have & to hold to hir & hir assignes for terme of hir lyfe in full recompence of Joynctour and dower. that to hir in any wise nowe perteigne or belong of the landes tentes or enẏ inhereditamentes of the same Erle. And when the said estate in forme forsaid be made to the said ladẏ Elizabeth. then the Archiebisshop of Develyn John Toplief chief Justice of the commen place of Irland. and William Attclief or two of theim befor the fest of Saint Michell tharchaungel then next folowing shal certyfie our said souverain lord the king of the certaintie. & maner & forme of the making of the said estates and the yerely value & the names of the lordshippes maners landes & tentes. Wherof a state as is forsaid shalbe made to the said ladẏ Elyzabeth.

G E of K

Seal appended; half broken.

APPENDIX XLIII

Letter of Sir Ralph Verney to Sir Reginald Bray from Dublin, October 31, 1496

P.R.O. S.C.I. LVIII, 70

Sir aftor al deue recomendacion lykithe it you to understond that the xvɪj day of september my lorde of kyldare my lady his wyfe & all his company landid in Irland at houthe thankyd be god in safte houbeit we had a trubelous & longe passayge durynge the space of xxɪ days. And the xxɪ day of the same moithe we come to drodaugh & ther was my lord & my lady ryght honorably resseyved And ther wer all the lordis assembled at councell & aftor the councell at scte peters churche before the highe aulter. All the lordis & commyns beinge present my lorde depute toke his othe. And the same day All the great Iryshemen of the northe partys of Irland had ther messengers redy attendynge ther on my lorde depute to treat of peace & a day was assygnyd them for all the Gentilmen of the northe & the iiii Comptes of Ulster to mete wᵗ my sayd lord in the northe marche at the towne of dondalke on michas day last passid on whiche day ther met wᵗ us. one of the Onelys¹ thelder Brodir callyd donylonell.² Bothe the mcmahonnys³ the owlde & the newe. / mcgenesse.⁴ Orayle.⁵ & Ohanlone.⁶ All thes ben sworne & hafe put in for pleggis ther Eldyste sonnys⁷ to be the kynges trew servauntes renounsinge all maner fees⁸ which they

¹ O'Neills.	² Donal O'Neill.
³ MacMahons.	⁴ Magennis.
⁵ O'Reilly.	⁶ O'Hanlon.
⁷ Appendix XLIV.	⁸ Black-rents.

wer wont to hafe of the kynge & to do him service aftor the tenore of certeyn Indentours[1] mad betwene my lorde depute & them the copy whereof is enclosed herin w^t the namys of the plegges. harr^9 Onell[2] sent also to my lorde & promysid to met him at the forsaid day apoyntid but he came not wherfor my lord puttithe of donylonell & will not Indent w^t him to suche tyme as he knouthe what harr^9 Onell will do for whiche of them may & will do the kynge Best servyce his parte entendithe my lorde to take for they stryve whiche of them shalbe O'nell this harr^9 Onell kyllyd his eldyste brodir by treason to thentent to have the rewle him selfe as they say here but as yet my lorde herithe no mor^9 frome the sayd harr^9 Onell notwithestondinge he hathe takyn donylonelis othe & plegges in the meane season. moreovyr Sir Odonell & mcboye tuoo the gretteste Iryshemen of the northe whiche marchen uppon scotlond & the oute yeles & on the kastell of knokfergous they sent lettres to my lorde to dondalke desyringe him of peace & pro-mittinge him by ther sayd lettres to come to him at ony place he will assigne them w^{t}in Irland & be rewlyd as he will hafe them & he hathe answord them in asmoche as they wer w^t the scottishe kinge & ayded perkyn warbeke agense the kinge our soverayne lorde thay shulde hafe no peace nor lofe of him but yefe they wil be sworne to the kynge & sew for ther pardone[3] Takynge the kynges parte aynste al men. And nowe of late. Jhon of the oute Iles[4] is come in to mboyes contrey & m^l scottes & keterykes w^t him nye to the kastell of knokefergus what he meanythe we cane not tell as yete he saythe he commethe to restowe his sone wiche was takyn prisoner w^t a stronge Irisheman in thes partys & hathe recowed him in dede as they say not withestondinge he tarithe styll in the contrey & many of the scottes inhabitethe ther nye upon savagis contrey wiche is a sherwde presompcon / my lorde hathe sent secretly to him entendinge yef he may to drawe him frome the kynge of scottes & to take the kyng parte for my lord thinkethe yef he may gete him & the kynge hafe warr w^t the scottes they tuoo shall do the kynge good service but as yet we haffe no answer frome him. Also sir soche direccon & appoyntimentes as is aforsayd takyn w^t them of the northe, semblable peace & directions is takyn w^t All the Irishemen of the Southe & West partys of the land so that nowe thanked be god the kynge hathe peace in all the lande w^{t}out strake or ony great charge or coste to him & all men ben glade to submit them selfe to the kyng grace of ther owne fre wille w^{t}out compulcon excepte m^{c}morwe & O Conore for they wolde not deliver the kastell of karlowe on whon we made tuoo Jurneys & so hafe the kastell delivered & ther plegges w^t ther othis & indenters as is bifor rehersid of whiche mater I will enforme the kynges grace mor playnly at my commynge. And as touchinge the Erle of desmonde he hathe sent divers lettres to my lorde promysinge to performe all promyses that he hathe made to the kynges grace but I se as yet no hasty spede ther in whiche causithe me to tary

---

[1] Appendix XLIV.   [2] Henry O'Neill.   [3] Fol. I v.
[4] Sir John Mor MacDonald of Isla. See p. 96.

so longe here. for I propose to hafe some certente to enforme the kynges grace in that mater er I depart hens. Therle of desmonde hathe promysed to mete w^t my lorde at waterford the weke nexst aftor alhalowetyde & ther to conclude all maters touchinge his promys to the kynge. Also here is a grete Irishemane of the west contray whiche rewlithe all the contray aboute galway whos name is Shane Borke he was the grettest secour that perkyn hade while he was in the londe safe only therle of desmonde he is come & submittyd him selfe to the kynges grace besechinge my lorde to sewe for his pardone & offrethe to come w^t my wyfe to^1 In to Inglonde undir her proteccon to put him selfe on the kynges grace And in lyke wyse dothe di[vers]^2 odir that in lyke forme have offended whiche is deffereyd to suche tyme we may know forther the kinges mynd in that behalfe. not w^{t}stondinge my lorde hathe takyn the sayd Shane Borkes othe before all the lordis to be trew to the kynge & take his parte agenst all men. sir I wolde hafe writ to you or this tyme but I had the certente of no mater of substaunce till now wherfor I beseche you excuse me to the kynges grace to whom I dare not preseume to wryte I trow his grace coude hafe put no mane in auctorite here that in so short space & w^t so little coste coude hafe set this land in so good order as it is now but this mane onlye I trust the kynge shall hafe a great tresor of him. Sir the^3 Erle of desmond hathe brokyn oone appoyntment that he made w^t my lorde gode send grace he kepe this appoyntment he hathe made now yef not I thinke but litle substaunce in him his wordis bene goode & his dedis prove therafter & Jhu kepe you writen at Devolyn the last day of october.

Your servaunt
R. Verney.

Dorso

To my Worshipfull Master Sir Reynold Bray knyght.

APPENDIX XLIV

Oath of allegiance of John O'Reilly taken before the Earl of Kildare; and a list of the pledges of eleven Irish Chiefs to the oath of allegiance of Bernard MacMahon, October 1496

P.R.O. E 30, 1542^4

fforma Iuramenti fidelitatis omnium Hibernicorum.

Ego Johannes Oraylie mee nacionis capitaneus cui competit ex more hibernicorum de Brenya prestare ducatum. Amodo inantea pacem et

---

^{1} Fol. 2 r.　　　　　　　　　　^{2} End of line torn.

^{3} The ink and pen change at this point and the addition was certainly made later.

^{4} This was enclosed in the letter forming Appendix XLIII.

fidelitatem illusstrissimo domino meo henrico Regi anglie heredibus et successoribus suis illibatam retinere curabo. omnia et singula capitula Bernhardina prefato domino meo Regi juramento vallata iuxta ipsorum tenorem vim formam et effectum fraternali modo erga dictum Regem et suos fideles vita mihi comite obligo me servaturum et sic juro per haec sacra dei evangelia et has sanctorum Reliquias.

The form of the oath taken by Bernard MacMahon before Gerald Earl of Kildare on October 2, 1496, follows ($2\frac{1}{2}$ pages). Then come the names of the pledges:

The namys of the plegges.

plege for donyl onell	Shan Onell
	Bren Onell
ffor ould m^{c}mahonne	Ev^{9}[1] m^{c}mahonne
ffor m^{c}mahonne	patrike m^{c}mahonne
ffor m^{c}genesse	Edmod^2 m^{c}genesse
ffor Orayle	kayre Orayle.
ffor Ohanlon̄	phelyme Ohanlon̄.
for m^{c}morwe	kayre m^{c}morowe
for Omore^3	patrike Omore.
ffor Odymsy^4	Ev^{9} Odymsy.
ffor Obryn^5	Edmod Obryn
ffor Oconor	Ev^{9} Oconor

[1] Ever. [2] Edmund.

[3] O'More of Leix, which became part of Queen's County ("State of Ireland", 2).

[4] O'Dempsy of Clanmaliere (Clann-maelughra) in the modern Queen's and King's County.

[5] O'Byrne in County Wicklow (*ibid*.). For the others see p. 95.

APPENDIX XLV

Letter from Henry Wyatt to Henry VII from Carlisle, June 4, 1496

Wyatt MSS (in possession of the Earl of Romney), No. 13

"A letter from Sr Henery Wyate Vnto the Kinge."

beginninge wantinge. "And bothe theye shalbe the safegarde of yor sayde place¹. and theye to attende uppon my sayd lorde² or at his commandemente, and for the defence of the cuntry at all tymes, as any of the sayde crewe; for lyke yt yor grace, in my poore minde, in so muche as this castle is the keye of these part*es* yt forses not, thoughte yt be in the hand*es*, and governaunce of the sayde Sr Rycharde³ as yet, remembringe his age, and service, excepte he woulde by his suite parte therefro, notw^thstandinge he be not so able thearfore as he hathe bene, and yf his strengthe showlde be of my sayde lord*es* chosinge, he mighte not doo but what he woulde, therfore as yor grace seem*es* beste to order yt.

"The other sute ys for a c mark*es*⁴ as he hathe hadd, trouthe yt is,

---

Paraphrase

And they (the new garrison) shall be both the safeguard of your said place ¹ (Carlisle) and in attendance upon my said Lord ² (Dacre) or at his command and for the defence of the country at all times, like any of the said (former) garrison; for it seems to me, your Grace, to my poor mind, that in as much as this Castle (Carlisle) is the key of these parts, it does not matter if it do remain in the hands and under the command of the said Sir Richard³ (Salkeld), taking into consideration his age and service; unless he suggests parting with it of his own accord, notwithstanding the fact that he is not so capable of the work as he has been; and if his garrison were of my said Lord's (Dacre's) choosing, then he (Sir Richard) could not do what he would; therefore let it be arranged as it seems best to your Grace.

My other suit is for 100 marks⁴ as he (Sir Richard Salkeld) used to

¹ Carlisle.

² Thomas, Lord Dacre of Gilsland. Appointed Lieutenant of the West Marches on May 3, 1486, and acted as Deputy Warden and Warden; made "locum tenens" for the Duke of York, and Warden General, on December 10, 1495. *Rot. Scot.* II, 518. See *G.E.C.*

³ Sir Richard Salkeld. Appointed Constable of Carlisle Castle in 1485. Given a grant in 1467 for capturing James, Earl of Wiltshire, seizing the city and castle of Carlisle and defending them against the rebels. Died in 1505.

⁴ For annual grant of 100 marks to Sir Richard Salkeld see P.R.O. E 403, 2558, Easter Term, 9 Henry VII, f. 46: "Ricardo Salkeld militi constabulario sive custod' ville et castri de Carlile pro salva custodia ejusdem ville sive castri per unum annum integrum videlicet a primo die Maii anno IX Regis nunc usque ultimam diem Aprilis extunc proxime sequent' 100 marcas".

that theare ys an acte of parlament[1] yt yo[r] charges of Carlill showlde moste be borne of yo[r] revennewes, but this monney is taken of other men, that will not nowe be hadd, nor shall at any tyme come to his hande*s* as I perceave untyll that yo[r] highnes maye have leasure to have suche matters before yo[r] grace, and yo[r] counsell, and set an orther thearein w[ch] (maye be k[ep]te, and in the meane tyme, he hath no [ai]d*es* he f[in]d*es*)[2] hys owne and all, yo[r] grace hathe not a truer subiecte to his power in myne opinione.

"Johan Mosgrave[3] is nowe wth yo[r] grace, and or he departe, well maye yo[r] grace shewe him that ye have not hearde of any service done by him and the Scot*es* under his rule that hathe[4] farr more hurte yo[r] grace, and dwell well to doe harme daylye, but he maye well saye that theye doe harme in Tyvidall, but yt is little, and the harme theye showlde doe, I woulde theye showlde doe yt uppon youre enymyes; Amonkste them selves theye dwell peasably w[th]oute harme, I am sure he woulde promise largelye, but I woulde he did halfe so myckle, and yf yo[r] grace touche him w[th]e the kepinge of Bewcastle yt shall doe but

have. It is true that there is an Act of Parliament[1] that your revenues should bear the charges of Carlisle; but this money has to be collected from men not now within reach, nor likely at any time to be available for him, until your Highness shall have time to bring these matters before yourself and your Council and make an Order about it which may be kept, and in the meantime he has no help. He keeps himself and finds his own expenses. In my opinion your Grace has no truer subject to the limits of his power.

John Musgrave[3] is now with your Grace, and before he goes it would be well for your Grace to show him that you have not heard of any service done by him and the Scots under his rule that has (not)[4] far more hurt your Grace and continues to do harm daily; but he may well say that they do harm in Teviotdale; but it is little and I wish that what they do could be done against your enemies. Amongst themselves they abide peaceably without fighting. I am sure he (John Musgrave) would promise largely, but I wish he performed half as much, and if your Grace were to call him to book over the custody of Bewcastle, it

[1] Statutes of the Realm, 11 Henry VII, c. 61 (Oct. 14, 1495): The revenues of the Castle and manors of "Penrethe, Soureby, Quenshames, Gamlesby, the Forest of Inglewood and the Park of Plumton" to be paid to the officers of the town and castle of Carlisle. They were crown manors, under Sir Richard Cholmley, Receiver General.

[2] The bottom line of the letter is rubbed and the letters in square brackets are gone.

[3] Sir John Musgrave, keeper of Bewcastle. Statutes of the Realm, 11 Henry VII, c. 61. In 1491 he was owed £150 for the custody of the King's castle, called Bewcastle (Tellers Rolls, E 405, 78, Michaelmas Term, 7 Henry VII, Stokes mem. 2). In 1517 the castle was "removed" (*L. and P. Henry VIII*, 11, pt 11, no. 3383).

[4] The transcriber may have omitted "not". In no other way can I make sense of the passage.

well; this bearer[1] shall shewe yo[r] grace in Jupertye yt is by this, whome I cause to come to yo[r] highnes, to shewe yo[r] grace all at lengh suche thing*es* as he knowethe, and verely of suche whearein he dothe yo[r] grace good service, and I trowe he will not fayle yo[r] highnes, and ofte tymes his playne speache dothe good, to whome yt will lyke yo[r] grace to geve credence, I have wrytten o[r] act*es* heere at lenght to yo[r] Captayne of Barwyke,[2] and liuetenaunt of the cuntry, and the order of the Cuntrey to assye yf yt will amende them, and quicken theyme; for I here not of any greate act*es* theye doe, and soe I writt to theyme.

"Also moste humbly I besche yo[r] noble grace to give yo[r] thank*es* to my Ladye Clyfforde[3] w[ch] shee hathe rithe well deserved for she sente S[r] Rychard Bellingham,[4] and Mr Layton,[5] and owlde Hene'ry Lorde Dacre,[6] w[th] a good company of my Lorde Clyfford*es* tenaunt*es*[7] she rode aboute in Westm[r]lande her selfe to sett them foorthe, truly theare hathe not bene seene suche a company come so shortly oute of this Shire; my sayde Lorde Clyfforde was then in Cro:[8] not wheare he showlde be when we have neede, Sory I am to see him ledd, and guided by simple and undiscreete *persons*, and to his greate hurte. The Cuntrye lovethe muche my sayde Ladye, and speake muche good of her,

---

could only do good. The bearer[1] of this letter shall show your Grace the danger of this state of affairs. I send him to your Highness to tell your Grace at length all the things he knows, and verily, those matters also wherein he, himself, does good service to your Grace; and I trust that he will not fail your Highness, and often his plain speech does good; to whom it will please your Grace to give credence. I have written about our acts here and the state of the country at length to your captain at Berwick[2] and the Lieutenant of the County, to try whether it will mend their ways and put life into them; for I do not hear of any great acts they do and I wrote to them in that sense.[9]

---

[1] Windell, see p. 239, note 1.   [2] Sir *William Tyler.*

[3] Lady Clifford was Anne, daughter of Sir John St John of Bletsoe, Beds., and granddaughter of Margaret Beauchamp, the mother of Margaret Beaufort. See *G.E.C.*; Allen, *Letters of Richard Fox*, no. 10; and the genealogy on p. 95.

[4] Is "*Richard*" a mistake of the transcriber for "*Roger*" or "*Robert*"? Sir *Roger* Bellingham was knighted at Stoke in 1487 and made Knight Banneret in 1497. Sir *Robert* Bellingham was made a Knight by the Earl of Surrey in 1497. No Sir Richard Bellingham is mentioned at the time.

[5] William Layton of Dalmane, Cumberland, was a free tenant of the Barony of Graystoke in 2 Henry VII. (Inquisition Post Mortem on Ralph Graystok de Graystok, Kt.)

[6] There was no such person. Humphrey, Lord Dacre, died in 1485 and was succeeded by Thomas. It may be "old Henry (to) Lord Dacre", as he was evidently subordinate to the sheriff's wife.

[7] Henry, Lord Clifford. Hereditary Sheriff of Westmorland. See *G.E.C.*
[8] "Crewe"?
[9] The remainder of the letter needs no paraphrase.

and yf he woulde be sumwhat ruled by her advise, yt woulde be better for him. A note of a simple Sclander theye have brouthe upp of her, I thinke rather of malyce then otherwyse, for all the com̄on people excuse her bothe poore and riche.

" Itm that wyndell[1] departed towardes the kinge on Satturdaye the iiiith of June,[2] wthe the letters before, and thease instructions, by him I wrot to Mr Lovell[3] and divers others."

APPENDIX XLVI

Thomas, Earl of Ormond, to Gerald, Earl of Kildare.[4] London, May 16, 1497

P.R.O. S.C.I. LI, 140

To etc. therl of kildare xvi° May A° xiimo

Right worshipfull lord and cousin I recommaunde me unto you thanking you in my moost herty maner for the kinde and loving lettres that ye have sent me at diverse seasons And cousin where as in yor seid lettres ye assigne certeyn mysdemeanure to be in sir James / certeynly like as I have hertofore written unto you I am right sory for it / for al god knowt my mynde is that he shulde accompplisshe and performe all suche thinges as he promessed unto or souverain lord and in his presence[5] / neverthelesse the kinges grace hath nowe at this tyme written unto him in suche thinges as concerneth his high pleasir // And also I have written unto him like as Develyn[6] can shewe you. // Also where as ye write to have my landes there in fferme / I shall sende unto you right hastely my servaunte John a Devinshire: whiche shall shewe you my full mynde in þat behalf. And in certayn oþer thinges concernyng my selfe. wherein I pray you that I may have yor good wille & feithfull unstandige // written at lond etc.

[1] Windell received 2od. "for his quarters wage" from the King on March 22, 1499 (P.R.O. E 101, 414/16), and must have been a royal messenger.
[2] Saturday, June 4, 1496. This letter must be later than the Act of Parliament of October, 1495, about the fortifications of Carlisle, referred to in it; and earlier than the Truce at Ayton of September 30, 1497. Henry Wyatt fought at the Battle of Blackheath on June 17, 1497, which rules out June 4 of that year. June 4 fell on a Saturday in 1496, which clinches the only possible date.
[3] Sir Thomas Lovell, Treasurer of the Chamber. Henry Wyatt was Clerk of the Jewels, a subordinate Officer of the Chamber.
[4] A corrected draft on paper on which three lines of Latin are scribbled upside down at the bottom of the page.
[5] Appendix XL.
[6] Gilbert Nugent, Baron of Delvin, made Captain of the Army in 1496.

APPENDIX XLVII

Thomas, Earl of Ormond, to the Countess of Kildare.[1]
London, May 16, 1497

P.R.O. S.C.I. LI, 140

To etc. the Countasse of kildare.

My verey good lady I recommaunde me hertely unto you thanking y[ou][2] for youre good and gentell letter. praying to god madame to sende yo[u] some good ffruete: soo that my lord and Cousin yoʳ husbondes blood and myn: may thereby be encreased: for by verey right of cousinage I must espec[ial] will and desire it and praye for it. And madame if there be any pleasir that lie[th] in me to doo for you in thiese parties / I shalbe as gladde to perfoʳme it [as] eny gentilman in Englande /. As knowᵗ oʳ lord. who preserve you in moche honoʳ longe to contynue.

APPENDIX XLVIII

Gerald, Earl of Kildare, to Thomas, Earl of Ormond, from Carlow, January 28, 1497/8

P.R.O. S.C.I. LI, 163

"Right honnoʳable Loɪd and Cousin in my ful herty maner I recomaund me unto you Certifying you that your Cousin my son in Lawe sir piers Butler hath had Comynycacion wᵗ me concernyng you And hath shewed me that he is veray desirous to bee towardes you And wol gladly bee Ruled by you and ensue your resonable advise in every thing / wherof he hath desired me to Certify you And to desire you to bee good and loving lord and Cousin unto him wherfor I hertily pray you soo to bee / the Rather at this myn instaunce And that ye wold doo for him in his peticions And whatesoever promise he shall make unto you I have very confidence that he wol not faille to perfourme the same in every behalf And whatsoever thing ye wol yeve him in this Contray I shall endevoʳ me to aide and Support him to attayn or gete the same / god willing Who have you in his blissed tuyssion written at Carelagh the xxviiiᵗ day of January

Dorso   youre loving cousyn.

To the right honnoʳable and my right good lord and Cousin Therl of Ormond.
                                                                    kylldar.

[1] A corrected draft on the back of the previous letter. Appendix XLVI.
[2] The letters in square brackets are missing.

APPENDIX XLIX

Gerald, eighth Earl of Kildare, to Thomas, Earl of Ormond. Maynooth, March 30, 1497/8

P.R.O. S.C.I. LI, 164

My Lord and Cousin In my right herty man*er* I recomaund me unto you And soo desire to here of yor welfare certifying you that suche bussines as I have unto you at this tyme I have instructed my full mynde therof to my trusty servauntes Thomas kente and to this berer To whom and aither of theim I pray you to yeve credence in all suche thing*es* as they shall enfourme you on my behalve And that ye wolde send me a direct aunswer upon the same in all hast And as for tyding*es* of this contray I certify you that OBrene which is nowe lately made is a mortalle enemye to all Englisshmen and most maliciously disposed of anny that ev*er* I herd speke of And intendith w^t the assistaunce of all Irisshmen to make warre upon youre parties of the Counties of kilkenny and Tipperare and also upon all the king*es* subgiett*es* here And nowe it is wele knowen that the cause of his aiding and assisting yor cousin s*ir* James was not for anny good wille ne affaccon he bare unto him but oony to destrue Englisshmen And for his resistance I have written unto the king*es* grace to send hidder an armye of $\overset{c}{\text{III}}$ archers and $\overset{xx}{\text{III}}$ gonners to bee wagid at the charge of me and other of my frend*es* in this contray Also I certify you that yor awen kynesmen in thes parties bee right eville disposed and ymagyn ev*er*iche others distruccon And I have suffred theim long trustint that s*ir* piers Butler wold woll remedye but he hath been disseased and may howe bee it or longe we shall see an ordre and dreccōn betwein theim by the grace of god who pr*es*erve you writin at maynoth the xxx^{li} day of Marche Also I pray you that I might be recomaunded unto my lady yor wiffe.

Youre loving cousin

G of k.

APPENDIX L

Henry VII's instructions to Norroy King of Arms, February 1497/8

B.M. Cotton, Vespasian, C xvi, fols. 118–119

Thies be the Instructions here folowyng yeven by the kyngis highnes to his trusty and Welbelovyd servaunt Norroy sent at this tyme by his highnes unto his broder the kyng of Scottis.

ffyrst his seid servaunt shall in the best maner that he can recommende the kyngis highnes unto his dere broder and Cousyn the kyng of Scottis thankyng hym for his kynde and lovyng lettres sent by his trusty and welbelovyd servaunt Lyons unto the kyngis grace. by the which lettres also his highnes understandith the goode mynde and zele that his seid Cousyn hath to the observyng and entreteynyng of suche amytees as be concludid bytwene hym and his seid Cousyn. And furthermore the kyngis highnes hath receyvyd by the hondes of the seid lyons letters patentis confirmatories of suche treties as have be concludid by theire Commissioners. In the which letters his seid Cousyn maketh a declaracion in the ffourthe article as apperith in the same. And forasmoche as the kyngis grace and his noble Councell thynkith that the declaracion of his seid Cousyn made uppon the ffourthe article[1] is not of that force and strength to bynde bothe prynces as were behowfull in that behalfe by cause his seid Cousyn in his seid letters of Conformacion by the way of an Inspeximus in hec verba of dyvers convencions made by the Commissioners of bothe prynces. And thoes convencions in the same letters patentes oonly confermeth and ynneweth[2] and so stondith the seid declaracions by force of thoes letters of Inspeximus in hec verba[3] —— and not of that effecte as were accordyng to be.

Itm in thies notre letters patentis which the kyngis grace hath nowe put to his seid Cousyn be left owte in the sixt article thies woordes Ad nocendum alteri etc. fforasmoche as bothe princes be bounde that they shall not geve Aide helpe nor socour to eny Enemyes or Rebellis of either other and by thoes woordes. Ad nocendum alteri. etc stondyng so still in the seid article. The prynce in whos lond or reame the seid Rebellis shulde happe to be myght have Colour to kepe them still and favour and ayde the same Rebellis seiyng. that he dothe hit not. Ad nocendum alteri. etc. ffor he woll so streitly kepe hym or them that they shall have no powar. Ad nocendum alteri. etc. And in so

---

[1] This article begins "conventum et conclusum est quod omnes et singuli malefactores", etc.; *Foedera*, XII, 674 b. and stands in the final treaty.

[2] "enneweth" = Middle English form of "reneweth".

[3] A fragmentary and illegible word.

kepyng the prynce so doyng shulde do contrar[y][1] to the residewe of the seid article. by the which he is [bo]unde within certeyn tyme to delyvere the seid Rebellis. And to thentent there shulde be no coloure of contradiccion in the seid article hit is thought necessary that thoes wordes. Ad nocendum alteri etc shulde be taken owte.

Itm in the same article be left out thies wordes Salvis conductibus etc ffor the principall cause moevyng his seid Cousyn to put in the se[id] wordes. Salvis conductibus etc was for a graunt of Save conductes made by [hym] to Perkyn and other his adherentes the kynges Rebelles And forasmuch as [at] this tyme the seid Perkyn is in the kynges kepyng and at the commaundem[ent] of his grace and shall never use the benefaicte of the seid Save conductes And also his adherentes the kinges Rebelles be departed out of his seid Cosyn is Realme. And if ther shuld under the colour of their seid Save conductes resorte and repaire unto the same Realme agayne and ther to have aide and secour. ther myght growe a gruge betwen the kynges grace and his seid Cousyn. And to thentent that betwen the kyng and his seid Cosyn ther shuld be no gruge nor colour of gruge it is thought expedient thoes wordes touchyng suche Save Conductes to be left out

The kynges grace in this behalve consideryng the good zele and tendre mynd that his seid Cousyn hath and allwey hath hade to the correction and punysshment of all murderers and roberies and also entendith not that by any darke or obscure wordes conteigned in any of the seid articles that any malefactor shuld have any audacite or boldnes to do eny Murder offence or trespace but that execucion shuld be don in every behalve [and] accordyng to iustice. thinketh and trusteth that his seid Cousyn w[uld] be contented w^t such lettres patentes reformatories as he doth send [by] his trusty and Welbeloved servaunt Norroy. And that his seid Cousyn woll deliver semblable lettres patentes sealed w^t his greate seale and subscribed with his owen hand Albeit the forseid reasons and consideracions notw'standyng the kynges grace putteth in the great wisdome discrecion and libertie of his seid Cousyn All thes premisses and as it shall pleas his seid Couson in every thyng in this behalve And wheder it shall pleas hym to accept the oon or the other lettres patentes. the kynges grace is contented and pleased as his seid Cousyn in this behalve shalbe best pleased and contented.

Itm if his seide Cousyn be contented and pleased w^t the kynges lettres patentes w^t suche reformacions as be before reherced then the kyng willeth and chargeth the seid Norroy to delyver to his seid Cousyn or oder his sufficient deputie in this behalf the seid lettres patentes refourmed in maner and fourme as is before reherced, and to resceyve of his seid Cousyn other lettres patentes sealed w^t his greate seale and subscribed w^t his owen hand of semblable strenght and effecte in every thyng as the kynges seid lettres patentes refourmed as is afore reherced bee.

[1] The letters in square brackets are missing.

And the seid Norroy shall endevour hym self in as good man*er*
and by as good reasons as he can / In nowise in worde or dede
offendyng ne displesyng his seid Cousyn to move and enduce hym
to be content w^t thies *lett*res patent*es* reformatories, the which the
kyng*es* gr*a*ce sendeth to his seid brod*er* and Cousyn at this tyme.
And if in no wise his seid Cousyn wolbe content to accepte the seid
*lett*res patent*es* Then the kyng*es* highnes willeth and chargith his seid
serva*u*nt Norroy to delyv*er* to his seid Cousyn or his sufficient deputie
his *lett*res patent*es* sealed w^t his greate seale and subscribed with his
owen hand which be of like tenn*our* and effecte in ev*er*y thyng as be
the *lett*res patent*es* sent to the kyng*es* highnesse from his seid Cousyn
by his trusty and welbeloved serva*u*nt lyon kyng of Armes.

H R

ADDENDUM. APPENDIX LI

Letter from Henry VII to Richard Fox, Bishop of Bath and Wells, Keeper of the Privy Seal. March 10, 1492/3

B.M. Cart. Cotton, IV, 19

H.R. By the king

Reverend fader in god right trusty and right welbeloved. We
grete ẏou wele. And for asmoch as we have appoincted o^r trusty and
welbeloved knight for o^r body sir Rogier Cotton to have W^t him at
this his voiage into our lande of Irlande five brode clothes of fẏne
Rede at VII nobl*es* or IIII mark*es* the clothe. ther to dispose and distribute them as we have comaunded him to doo We therfor Wol
and charge ẏou that under o^r prive seel being in yor warde ye doo
make o^r l$\overline{\text{re}}$s directed unto the Customers of our poor^t of Bristowe
comanding them by the same. that they in al goodly hast doo delivre
unto our said knight the said v clothes. And by our said l$\overline{\text{re}}$s. they
shalhave sufficient allowance of the same in their accompt. And
thies o^r l$\overline{\text{re}}$s shalbe yor sufficient warrant in that behalf yeven under
o^r signet at o^r manoir of shene the xth day of Marche

dorso. To the Right Reverend in god o^r right trusty and right
welbeloved the bisshop of Bath and Wells kep*er* of our prive seel.

INDEX

Aberdeen, Bishop of, *see* Elphinstone

Ailmer, Bartholomew, sheriff of Co. Kildare, 156, 162

Albany, Duke of, *see* Stewart

Amisfield, Laird of, 21

Angus, Earl of, *see* Douglas

Anliffy, *see* Liffey

Arbuthnot of Arbuthnot, 28 n. 2

Archebald, John, Marshal of the King's Courts in Ireland, 207

Ardmore, 111, 111 n. 4

Ardmulaghan, 172 n. 5

Argyll, Earl of, *see* Campbell

Armagh, Archbishop of, *see* Palatio

Armstrongs, the, 81 n. 2

Arnold, Richard, of Dublin, 219

Arteright, Anthony, 166, 193

Arthur, Prince of Wales, 34, 99

Arthureth, 15

Athboy, 89

Athlone, 125

Atholl, Earls of, *see* Stewart

Austyn, John, 168

Ayala, Don Pedro de, Spanish ambassador to Scotland, 110, 115, 116

Ayton Castle, 113

Peace of, 114–16, Appendix L

Bacon, Francis, Lord Verulam, 48, 52

Balfour, Sir James, 5

Ballaregan, 209

Ballymergy, Co. Dublin, 172 n. 5

Balrothery, Co. Dublin, 186

Baltiswell, Dr John, Clerk of the Council, 18, 19, 25

Bangor, Bishop of, *see* Deane

Barry, William, 11th Lord Barry of Buttevant, 94

Baskeny, Co. Meath, 172 n. 5, 188

Basnetts, 75, 88, 88 n. 1

Bathe, John, Chief Remembrancer of the Exchequer, Ireland, 173

Beaufort, Henry, Duke of Somerset, 82 n. 6

Beaufort, Lady Margaret, 46–8, 95

Beket, John, 208

Belgard, Co. Meath, 172 n. 5

Bell, Richard, Bishop of Carlisle, 10

"Bell-the-Cat", *see* Douglas

Bellingham, Sir Richard, 238

Bellingham, Robert, 238 n. 4

Bellingham, Roger, 238 n. 4

Bergavenny, Baron, *see* Neville

Bergen, Henry of, Bishop of Cambrai, 31

Bermingham, Richard, son of Patrick of Ballydongan, 172 n. 5, 188, 207

Bernewall, Edward, Chancellor of the Exchequer and Green Wax in Ireland, 187

Bernewell, Christopher, 208

Bernewell, Elis, 208

Berwick, contested between England and Scotland, 2–3, 9, 10–12, 105

Captains of, 33–4, 113, 238

defence of, 16, 25, 36

importance of, 35

Marshall of, 51

wooden bridge, 35

Bewcastle, Captain of, 101–2, 237 n. 3

Blackader, Robert, Archbishop of Glasgow, 1484–1508, 9, 17, 18, 28, 148

Blackcastle, Co. Meath, 150, 172 n. 5, 188

Blackheath, Battle of, 109, 110

Blackness, first Battle of, 19, 145

second Battle of, 20, 146

first Truce of, 17, 19, 145

second Truce of, 20, 21, 146

Blackness Castle, 17

Blagge, Hugh, Second Justice of the Court of Common Bench, Ireland, 173, 175

Blake, John, bailiff of Dublin, 55 n. 4

Blanchfield, 55

Blechingley, 50, 50 n. 13

Boece, Hector, 88–9

Boleyn, Thomas, 8th Earl of Ormond, 47, 112

Bosworth field, Scottish contingent at, 5–8, 63

Bothwell, Earl of, *see* Hepburn

Bothwell, Lord, *see* Ramsay, Sir John

245

For EU product safety concerns, contact us at Calle de José Abascal, 56–1°, 28003 Madrid, Spain or eugpsr@cambridge.org.

www.ingramcontent.com/pod-product-compliance
Ingram Content Group UK Ltd.
Pitfield, Milton Keynes, MK11 3LW, UK
UKHW010347140625
459647UK00010B/887